Predestination in Light of the Cross:
A Critical Exposition
of Luther's Theology

John B. King, Jr., M. Div., Ph. D.

Library of Congress Catalog Card Number:
ISBN 1-891375-19-9

Printed in the United States of America

Published by Chalcedon Foundation
P.O. Box 158
Vallecito, CA 95251

To R. J. Rushdoony,

for teaching me how to think.

I wish to thank my grandparents

John and Aletha King for raising me.

Without their sacrifice, support, and encouragement,

this work would not have been possible.

TABLE OF CONTENTS

Introduction

Dr. John King's study of the doctrine of predestination is very important for several reasons. *First*, as a Lutheran, he clarifies what Luther wrote and strikes at the erroneous views of Luther's position. *Second*, he gives us a fresh and clear view of the subject. King's background as a scientist, who teaches a branch of physics at a major university, gives him a precision in writing. *Third*, he approaches the subject from a fresh perspective and brings some light to the matter. *Fourth*, he enables us to understand better a key issue in the Reformation.

King writes with clarity and precision, and he gives us a sound understanding of the issues at stake. He does justice to both Luther and Calvin and leaves one grateful for his superior grasp of the subject. He makes us aware that the subject is not merely one of historical accuracy but present day action.

It should be noted that Dr. King has not only a university degree (and teaching experience) but also a seminary training and degree. He is theologically astute, and this little study is a contribution to church history and theology.

This is a work to be read and discussed.

Rousas John Rushdoony

Author's Foreword

The present manuscript grew from an attempt to teach the doctrine of "double predestination" to a group of Lutherans. Given this fact, the manner of presentation is necessarily affected by the characteristics of the target audience. In particular, the mode of presentation (but not the content) is calculated to resonate with the Lutheran approach to theology and to meet several of the standard objections which frequently arise. And while many of these objections are common to other denominations, some are peculiar to a Lutheran audience. In particular, Lutheran pastors frequently attempt to dismiss double predestination apart from a substantive consideration by pigeonholing it as a Reformed or "Calvinist" view. Accordingly, to secure an honest hearing for this doctrine, the mode of presentation has been crafted to neutralize this defensive maneuver. To appreciate this fact, it is necessary to consider some of the distinctives between Lutheran and Reformed (or "Calvinist") theology as well as some of the specific objections which Lutherans frequently bring forth.

With respect to theological distinctives, the words of Professor Richard E. Muller are most germane. As a Lutheran professor (Concordia Theological Seminary) educated at a Reformed seminary (Westminster Theological Seminary), Dr. Muller has been deeply immersed in both theological systems and so is particularly qualified to delineate the differences between Lutheran and Reformed theology. Dr. Muller writes:

Westminster in the 1960s espoused an authentic Calvinistic Reformed theology. It blended the British Puritan tradition with the Five Point Dutch T-U-L-I-P Calvinism and emphasized strongly the Sovereignty of God. In short, what it taught was consistent with how the Reformed have traditionally done theology — from the fixed point of the Sovereignty of God and the decrees of God, including the secret or hidden decrees. In contrast Lutherans do theology by focusing on the Crucified God, or the Cross of Christ and the revealed knowledge of God. (Muller, 79)

[T]here is a difference in the degree of coordination entertained between special revelation and natural revelation. The Reformed seem to be more at home with philosophy and the things of God provided through nature, such as law and reason. On the other hand the Lutheran emphasis on the proper distinction between Law and Gospel sets natural and special revelation farther apart. While neither tradition can be charged with the Barthian denial of natural revelation nor with a Thomistic flirtation with natural revelation, the Reformed seem to accommodate their theology more to the demands of the laws of reason and logic than do Lutherans. Lutherans are more comfortable with paradox. (Muller, 88)

From the two statements above, the major difference between the Lutheran and Reformed approaches to

iv

theology is clearly evident. In particular, Lutheran theology tends to be more Christological in its major orientation since it starts from the fixed point of the cross. Reformed theology, by contrast, begins from the fixed point of God's sovereignty and so is more theological in nature. Consequently, in approaching matters of doctrine and practice, Reformed theology will tend to be more ontological, philosophical, and theoretical whereas Lutheran theology will tend to be more existential, pastoral, and concrete. Thus, while sharing much of the same doctrinal content, the two systems have a vastly different ethos and "feel."

Given this fact, the mode of presentation in the following manuscript has been adjusted to prevent the discussion from "feeling" too Reformed. In particular, the cross is taken as a concrete datum upon which to illustrate the more abstract and paradoxical relation between predestination and human responsibility. Accordingly, while the following presentation maintains the philosophical rigor of Reformed theology, the theological construction begins from the fixed point of the cross. Given this fact, the following discussion should be more congenial to a Lutheran audience since it grapples with the problem of theological paradox while centering on the cross.

Moreover, beyond these general theological considerations, the mode of presentation is also calculated to meet a standard Lutheran objection. In this regard, it was mentioned above that Lutheran pastors frequently attempt to bypass a substantive discussion of double predestination by pigeonholing it as a "Calvinist" view. Obviously, such an approach is irrelevant on its face since the issue is to be decided Biblically and not by reference to theologians. Moreover, such an objection is easily neutralized since it is based on a tragic ignorance of the fact that double predestination originated with Luther, not Calvin. In this regard, Luther's views on the matter come into clearest focus in his classic treatise, *The Bondage of the Will*, which he wrote during Calvin's teenage years. Given that this work is a classic of the Protestant Reformation, it is incredible that so many Lutheran pastors are ignorant of Luther's views on the matter.[1] Yet, incredible as it is, it is precisely because of this ignorance that many of these pastors make Calvin the theological scapegoat in their pigeonholing of the doctrine. In particular, double predestination is often dismissed by stating that Calvin, due to his rigorous logic, took Luther's doctrine to unintended extremes and then imposed his dogmatic system upon the Biblical text. As mentioned above, however, this claim is demonstrably false since Calvin followed Luther almost to the letter in his view of double predestination with both men grounding their views in Scripture. In fact, the only difference between the two men at this point is that Calvin toned down Luther's sometimes fatalistic interpretations of the human will. In other words, contrary to popular caricatures, Calvin's view was actually the milder of the two! Given this fact, a direct appeal to Luther's writings should suffice to neutralize the pigeonholing tactic discussed above.

---

[1] In fact, given the importance of double predestination both to Luther and the Reformation generally, this ignorance reflects an inexcusable omission in the curriculum of Lutheran seminaries.

For this reason the material presented herein is supported by an abundance of Luther's pointed remarks in addition to scriptural proofs. In spite of the abundant use of Luther's views, however, it is not being suggested that one should embrace this doctrine merely on Luther's authority. On the contrary, Luther, like all men, was fallible and sinful. Given this fact, neither his opinions nor those of any other man form a suitable basis for doctrine. Rather, the abundant evidence of Luther's opinions is simply presented to prevent the knee jerk dismissal of double predestination as a Calvinist view. In other words, it is hoped that through the abundant use of Luther's writings, Lutherans will consider this doctrine apart from the Calvinist opprobrium and on the basis of its scriptural merit alone. Once a fair hearing for the doctrine has been obtained, the present writer feels optimistic about the results. The doctrines presented herein are demonstrably Biblical, and will thus carry the Spirit's witness.

Beyond this fact, it is also hoped that some of the antipathy for John Calvin will subside in Lutheran circles. For some reason, the Lutheran reaction is harsher against Calvinism than against any other theology (barring the cults, of course). As a consequence, while many Calvinists read Luther with profit, Calvin gets an icy reception from Lutheran divines. Whatever the ultimate origin of these feelings may be, one suspicions that their continuance is related to the mistaken notion that double predestination is the lurid outgrowth of Calvin's inflexible rationalism. If this assessment is true, the dissolving of this myth should open up a more congenial spirit among Lutherans toward the Genevan Reformer. After all, in formulating his views of predestination, Calvin was fully Lutheran. Moreover, if a friendlier attitude toward Calvin is taken, the result will be a windfall for Lutheran divines and laymen alike who have much to gain from his writings. Even if such people should never be convinced of the Biblical soundness of double predestination, there is still much in Calvin's writings that would commend itself as useful. In particular, Lutherans desperately need Calvin's insight into church polity and civil affairs. For all of these reasons, therefore, Luther's remarks have been amply quoted in the present work.

Moreover, beyond the abundant use of Luther's remarks, the following presentation reflects Luther's combination of caution and boldness in his approach to predestination. In this regard, Luther, like Calvin after him, sought to guard against two extremes. On the one hand, because predestination is a deep subject and shrouded in the mystery of God's being, Luther was wary of idle speculation and so sought to constrain discussion by the Biblical text. Here Luther saw clear limits to human inquiry:

> I say, as I said before, that we may not debate the secret will of Divine Majesty, and that the recklessness of man, who shows unabated perversity in leaving necessary matters for an attempted assault of that will, should be withheld and restrained from employing itself in searching out those secrets of Divine Majesty; for man cannot attain unto them, seeing that, as Paul tells us (cf. I Timothy 6:16), they dwell in inacces-

sible light. But let man occupy himself with God Incarnate, that is, with Jesus crucified, in whom, as Paul says (cf. Colossians 2:3), are all the treasures of wisdom and knowledge (though hidden); for by Him man has abundant instruction both in what he should and in what he should not know.

Here, God Incarnate says: "I would, and thou wouldst not." God Incarnate, I repeat, was sent for this purpose, to will, say, do, suffer, and offer to all men, all that is necessary for salvation; albeit He offends many who, being abandoned or hardened by God's secret will of Majesty, do not receive Him thus willing, speaking, doing and offering. As John says: "The light shineth in darkness, and the darkness comprehendeth it not" (John 1:5). And again: "He came unto His own, and His own received Him not" (v. 11). It belongs to the same God Incarnate to weep, lament, and groan over the perdition of the ungodly, though that will of Majesty purposely leaves and reprobates some to perish. Nor is it for us to ask why He does so, but to stand in awe of God, Who can do, and wills to do, such things. (Luther, *The Bondage of the Will*, 175, 176)

As can be seen from this citation, Luther advocated an awe filled submission to the Majesty of God as a restraint on the speculations of reason.

However, while Luther sought to restrain reason within the bounds of Scripture, he also sought to examine predestination up to the very limits of Biblical revelation since he believed that all of Scripture was profitable for man to know. Thus, the suggestion by Erasmus that such knowledge should be suppressed brought a well deserved rebuke from Luther:

> If, then, we are taught and believe that we ought to be ignorant of the necessary fore-knowledge of God and the necessity of events, Christian faith is utterly destroyed, and the promises of God and the whole gospel fall to the ground completely; for the Christian's chief and only comfort in every adversity lies in knowing that God does not lie, but brings things to pass immutably, and that His will cannot be resisted, altered or impeded.
>
> Observe now, my good Erasmus, where that cautious, peace loving theology of yours leads us! You call us back, and prohibit our endeavours to learn about God's foreknowledge and the necessity which lies on men and things, and advise us to leave behind, and avoid, and look down on such enquiries; and in so doing you teach us your own ill-advised principles — that we should seek after ignorance of God (which comes to us without our seeking, and indeed is born in us), and so should spurn faith, abandon God's promises, and discount all the consolations of the Spirit and convictions of our consciences. Epicurus himself would hardly give such advice! Moreover, not content with this, you call those who are concerned to acquire the knowledge in question godless,

idle and empty, and those who care nothing
for it you call godly, pious and sober. What
do you imply by these words, but that Christians are idle, empty, and godless fellows?
and that Christianity is a trivial, empty, stupid and downright godless thing? So here
again, in your desire to discourage us from
anything rash, you allow yourself to be carried to the contrary extreme (as fools do) and
teach the very quintessence of godless, suicidal
folly. Do you see, now, that at this point your
book is so godless, blasphemous and sacrile-
gious, that its like cannot be found anywhere?
(Luther, *The Bondage of the Will*, 84, 85)

As can be seen from the statement above, Luther felt
that predestination was a Biblically revealed, life giving doctrine which should therefore be examined and
proclaimed to the church. Accordingly, when Erasmus
sought to suppress this doctrine, the attempt earned
Luther's sharp rebuke as an impious and injurious
suggestion.[2] Thus, in addition to the prudent caution
witnessed above, Luther's approach to predestination
was also quite bold. After all, being loath to exceed
the bounds of Scripture, he was nevertheless most aggressive within these Biblical limits.

Accordingly, in response to Luther's example, both
of these strains have been honored in the present work.
As will be seen by reading the manuscript, the discussion is kept within the bounds of Biblical revelation.

---

[2] No doubt, Luther's fidelity to Scripture would bring a similar
blast against those who would suppress this doctrine today.

xi

Thus, the doctrine of predestination has here been grounded in Scripture and not the idle speculations of reason. However, while guarding against such speculation, the Biblical texts have been fully utilized, and no attempt has been made to suppress revealed knowledge. After all, as a revealed doctrine of Scripture, double predestination is essential to the awe filled worship of God and thus to the strength of His church.

Finally, having addressed the mode of presentation, it is necessary to briefly discuss the practical import of predestination and hence the motive underlying the present work. In this regard, it is frequently claimed by Lutherans that the practical import of predestination lies in the comfort of persecuted Christians. However, while such an application is certainly valid, the restriction of predestination to this use is deficient for two reasons. First, such a restriction reflects an anthropocentric (man centered) rather than a theocentric (God centered) perspective which views the doctrine in terms of human utility rather than divine glory. Second, this restriction is deficient even from an anthropocentric perspective since it reflects a passive rather than an aggressive posture. After all, with respect to human action, the purpose of predestination is not so much to comfort lambs in the slaughter as it is to embolden the church in its worldwide mission of evangelistic outreach and cultural warfare. Given these facts, the Lutheran attempt to make the comfort of martyrs the touchstone and litmus test for all discussions of predestination must be regarded as doubly deficient since it is both anthropocentric and passive. After all, in addition to minimizing God, it guts the social impact of the church.

However, when the doctrine of predestination is consistently expressed, such deficiencies can be corrected. After all, since double predestination has reference to eternal death as well as eternal life, it cannot be reduced to a doctrine of mere human comfort. Rather, by asserting God's control of all things good and bad, such a doctrine sets forth a pervasive divine control which forces theocentric thinking. Moreover, since God is then seen to control history itself, the church can operate in total confidence, knowing that its ultimate victory has been predestined by God and is therefore secure in advance. Thus, by forcing theocentric thinking, double predestination produces a resolute Christian boldness, thereby challenging both the anthropocentrism and the passivity of the Lutheran view. In other words, through its exaltation of divine sovereignty, double predestination enhances the vitality of the church.

Given these facts, it is seen that both the honor of God and the strength of His church require the vindication of double predestination. To this end, therefore, the goal of the present work will be to establish the doctrine from Scripture and illumine it with the help of Luther's writings. In so doing it is the intent of the author to demonstrate that the doctrine of double predestination reflects both a thorough going Christian orthodoxy and the heart of Luther's Reformation theology. Once these points have been established, any departure from this doctrine will be clearly seen as a divergence from Biblical fidelity, Christian dogmatics, and consistent Lutheranism.

John B. King Jr., M. Div., Ph. D.
Corvallis, Oregon
January 1, 2000

Statement
of the Problem

To begin a discussion of predestination, it is useful to commence with a succinct definition that captures the seemingly paradoxical relation between predestination and human responsibility. To this end the Westminster Confession of Faith may be profitably consulted. In so doing, however, it is in no way implied that anyone should assent to this doctrine on the mere basis of a Reformed confession. Rather, the Confession is cited here for pedagogical reasons only, since it summarizes the doctrine of predestination in a way that captures its intellectual tension. For the sake of pedagogy, therefore, and not for sectarian dogmatism, the doctrine will be set forth according to the Westminster Confession of Faith (London, 1648):

> God from all eternity did, by the most wise and holy counsel of his own will, freely and unchangeably ordain whatsoever comes to pass: yet so, as thereby neither is God the author of sin, nor is violence offered to the will of the creatures, nor is the liberty or contingency of second causes taken away, but rather established. (WCF, III:I)

As mentioned above, this definition reveals a profound intellectual tension. Taken at face value, it says that although God (as the ultimate cause) has foreordained everything that comes to pass in time, He is not guilty of sin. To the contrary, man (as the proximate cause) is responsible for the sin he commits since God's predestination does no violence to the will of the creature but rather establishes the liberty (freedom) and contingency (causal and chronological sequence) of secondary causes (historical causes) of which man's will is a part. So understood, the above statement sets forth a profound tension which centers on the relation between predestination and human responsibility and which comes to focus in a very simple question, namely:" How can such seeming opposites be simultaneously true?"

Postponing the answer for a moment, it should be mentioned that both entities, despite their seeming tension, are often present in one and the same passage of Scripture. As proof of this assertion, consider the following text:

> Men of Israel, listen to this: Jesus of Nazareth was a man accredited by God to you by miracles, wonders, and signs, which God did among you through him, as you yourselves know. This man was handed over to you by God's set purpose and foreknowledge; and you, with the help of wicked men, put him to death by nailing him to the cross. (Acts 2:22, 23)

In reference to this text, it is evident that predestination and human responsibility were operating simultaneously in the death of Christ. On the one hand, since Christ was handed over "by God's set purpose and foreknowledge," it is obvious that God predestined the event. On the other hand, it is also clear that this predestination did not conflict with human responsibility since Christ's murderers are referred to as "wicked men." Moreover, viewed from the divine perspective, the crucifixion must be regarded as the supreme example of divine goodness since "God so loved the world that He gave His only begotten Son" (John 3:16). Yet, viewed from the human perspective, this same crucifixion is the supreme example of human wickedness since these murderers killed the most precious Son of God.

So understood, the above passage clearly implies that predestination and human responsibility cohere in such a manner that God can work good through human evil in one and the same event. Given this fact, the question to be addressed in the following chapters concerns only the nature of this relationship, and not the relation itself. After all, since the coherence between predestination and human responsibility follows from the above passage, such harmony is scriptural and thus nonnegotiable. Moreover, since the integrity of each entity is there maintained, neither may be championed at the expense of the other in theological construction. Consequently, in seeking to resolve this theological tension, one may neither deny God's control nor reduce man to a puppet. Thus, it is within these constraints that the harmony between predestination and human responsibility is to be sought.

The Metaphysical Harmony of Predestination and Human Responsibility

2

To set forth the harmony between predestination and human responsibility, it is necessary to view these doctrines within a common metaphysical context. To this end, it will be shown below that the essential harmony between these doctrines derives from a two-layer theory of reality (metaphysics) which is unique to Christianity. Before proceeding with this exposition, however, it should be mentioned that due to the mystery surrounding God's being and ways, it is not possible for the human intellect to fully grasp this interrelation.[1] Accordingly, in setting forth this doctrinal coherence, an exhaustive explanation will not be attempted.

As noted above, the harmony between predestination and human responsibility springs from a two-layer metaphysics which is unique to Christianity.

---

[1] Because God's ways are higher and not lower than those of man, it may be said that God is suprarational (*i.e.*, infinitely rational and thus above man's finite reason) but not irrational. Accordingly, while man cannot completely harmonize predestination and human responsibility on the basis of his finite reason, he can show their logical consistency.

In this regard, layer one consists of the eternally existent and infinite being of God while layer two consists of the temporal and finite creation. Because of this distinction, the Infinite God is said to transcend the finite creation and, for this reason, God and the creation are represented by separate circles in Figure 1a. However, while God transcends His creation, He is not distant from it but rather is intimately present, creating, sustaining, and governing it.

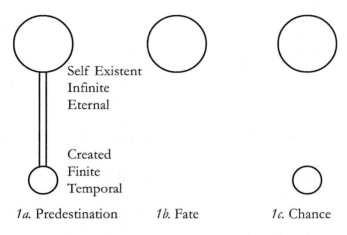

Self Existent
Infinite
Eternal

Created
Finite
Temporal

1a. Predestination   *1b.* Fate   *1c.* Chance

FIGURE 1: Schematic of Metaphysical Options

Accordingly, in addition to God's transcendence, there is also an immediate relation known as God's immanence which is represented by the connecting lines in Figure 1a. So understood, the chief feature of Christian metaphysics is a two-layer framework which provides for a God Who is simultaneously transcendent and immanent. As will be shown, it is precisely this combination of transcendence and immanence which establishes the coherence between predestination and human responsibility.

6

To see this point, recall that this unique combination of transcendence and immanence allows for a simultaneous distinction and connection between God and creation. In this regard, the distinction prevents God from being confused with the finite creation so that His essence is not reduced to the level of a finite material force. As a result, God remains infinitely personal and thus infused with ultimate purpose. However, while this distinction prevents a contaminating reduction of God's infinite and personal essence, the connection between God and creation ensures that the world is established by His transcendent personality and thus governed in accordance with His purpose. Accordingly, since the creation is exhaustively determined by an Infinite God at each and every point, man is dependent upon God for every facet of his finite existence and is therefore exhaustively predestined in his action. Moreover, since God's determination of man is exhaustively personal, it is precisely God's predestination which ensures the integrity of man's derivative personality and hence his human responsibility. However, while the connection between God and creation ensures that God is the ultimate cause of all human action, the distinction prevents the reduction of man to the level of a divine puppet and thereby preserves his distinct moral agency. Consequently, since human and divine actions therefore derive from distinct moral agents, the actions themselves remain distinct and therefore manifest distinct ethical qualities. Thus, since God's predestination establishes the human personality as a distinct moral agent, and thereby provides for the distinction between human and divine action, God is able to work good through human evil in such a way that divine goodness and human evil are simultaneously maintained. As a result, predestination and human responsibility necessarily cohere.

Within the two-layer metaphysics of Christianity, therefore, the coherence between predestination and human responsibility is rooted in a unique combination of transcendence and immanence which produces a scheme of dual causality and thus a unique relation between human and divine action. In terms of this scheme, every human action manifests a dual agency in which man is the proximate and secondary cause while God is the ultimate and primary cause. Consequently, despite the fact that man's proximate causation is totally determined by God's ultimate causation, human and divine actions remain distinct and therefore bear distinct ethical qualities. Accordingly, since God can work good through human evil, predestination and human responsibility cohere. Of course, the manner in which predestination and human responsibility cohere is a mystery, but the fact of their coherence is the clear revelation of Scripture and also follows from general theological and philosophical considerations as noted above. However, to grasp even the fact of this coherence, it is necessary to think in terms of two registers simultaneously. That is to say, one's thinking must be "both/and" and not "either/or."

In this regard, the chief problem that arises in considering these doctrines is that many people think in terms of unicausality (God or man) rather than dual causality (God and man). Given this fact, such people necessarily pit God's predestination against human responsibility rather than holding to both doctrines simultaneously. After all, once this false conceptual framework is adopted, one's thinking on the issue is governed by a false dilemma and thus driven toward two false alternatives. Consequently, one will either seek to preserve God's predestination at the expense of man's proximate causality and responsibility, or else to preserve man's responsibility at the expense of God's ultimate causation and predestination. Now if the former course is followed, the option of fate is chosen in which the distinction between human and divine action is collapsed as shown in Figure 1b. Under these conditions man loses his distinct personality and, therefore, reduces to the level of a divine puppet. On the other hand, if the latter course is followed, the option of chance is chosen in which the connection between human and divine action is removed as shown in Figure 1c. Under these conditions, man loses all connection to the Personal God and, therefore, reduces to an impersonal atom in a world devoid of connection and order. On either option, however, predestination and human responsibility are both destroyed making the attempt to preserve either doctrine at the expense of the other impossible. Accordingly, in preserving the integrity of these doctrines, it is never a choice between one or the other, but rather between both or none at all. To see the truth of this claim, the options of chance and fate must be separately examined to make their implications clear.

In examining these alternatives, it must first be noted that chance and fate form the philosophical building blocks of all non-Christian systems. Accordingly, since all such systems reduce to combinations of chance and fate, the analysis of these two alternatives is exhaustive of all non-Christian systems. Now the basis for this generalization lies in the fact that all systems, whether Christian or not, must account for unity and permanence on the one hand, and diversity and change on the other. However, since non-Christian systems have no Triune God in Whom unity (oneness) and diversity (threeness) are equally basic, unity and diversity become abstracted from one another in non-Christian systems. Accordingly, the unity becomes a fatalism devoid of all distinctions, even as the diversity becomes a chance collection devoid of all connection and order. Consequently, in their attempts to accommodate the static and dynamic aspects of reality, non-Christian systems frequently diverge between the extremes of fate and chance, and often incorporate these incompatible positions simultaneously. Given this fact, the analysis of chance and fate will suffice in principle to reveal the common antagonism of all non-Christian systems to predestination and human responsibility.

With respect to the former alternative, it may generally be said that a chance universe is characterized by a complete lack of connection and interrelation among its parts and is, therefore, devoid of any possible order. Consequently, in such a universe, a radical individuality prevails in which all quantities behave as brute atoms, moving in complete independence of one another. Thus, to the extent that God is even thought to exist, He becomes at

best another atom in a meaningless void, having no
relation or influence on any of the remaining parts.
Accordingly, the defining characteristic of a chance
universe is the lack of connection and, for this reason,
the option of chance has been diagramed as separate
circles in Figure 1c. So understood, the option of
chance is implicitly chosen by those seeking to guard
human responsibility by removing the connection between human and divine action.

That such a universe would destroy predestination and human responsibility may readily be seen.
First, because a chance universe would be random,
it would be directionless and thus devoid of purpose. Accordingly, in such a universe predestination
would be impossible since the events would occur
apart from any future aim (teleology). Moreover,
since man himself would become the product of an
impersonal chaos, the human personality would be
lost as man dissolved into the void. Finally, since
chance itself is the very negation of order, any basis for a binding moral law would also be destroyed.
Thus, in addition to destroying predestination, a
chance universe would also destroy human responsibility by obliterating the human personality and
the moral law. Given this fact, it can be seen that
the attempt to safeguard human responsibility by
denying predestination results in the destruction of
both quantities simultaneously.

In a system of fate, on the other hand, the results
are identical but for slightly different reasons. With
respect to this option, it may generally be said that a
fatalistic universe is characterized by a radical

connection and interrelation to the exclusion of all distinction or difference. Accordingly, in such a universe, a suffocating unity prevails which destroys the uniqueness of every part and locks the whole into a single system of rigid, impersonal law. Thus, to the extent that God is even thought to exist, He reduces to the level of a mindless force penetrating and quickening the whole. Accordingly, the defining characteristic of a fatalistic universe is a lack of distinction, and for this reason the option of fate has been diagramed by a single circle in Figure 1b. So understood, the option of fate is implicitly chosen by those who seek to safeguard predestination by collapsing the distinction between human and divine action.

That such a universe would destroy predestination and human responsibility may readily be seen. First, because a fatalistic universe would be driven by impersonal law rather than a conscious personality, the historical process would be unconscious, and thus devoid of purpose. Accordingly, even though a rigid determinism would prevail, predestination would still be impossible since the resulting determinism would lack an intelligent future aim (teleology). Moreover, since man himself would become the product of impersonal law, the human personality would also be lost as man reduced to a cog in an impersonal machine. Finally, since a personal "ought" could find no basis in a system of impersonal law, moral law, as a personal concept, would vanish. Thus, in addition to destroying predestination, a fatalistic universe would also destroy human responsibility by obliterating the human personality and the moral law. Given this fact, it can be seen that the attempt to safeguard predestination by denying human responsibility results in the destruction of both quantities simultaneously.[2]

On the basis of the preceding discussion, then, it has been shown that the opposition of predestination to human responsibility within a unicausal framework gives rise to the false alternatives of chance or fate, both of which destroy predestination and human responsibility. Thus, once the unicausal framework is adopted, the destruction of both quantities is guaranteed regardless of which alternative is chosen and which quantity one seeks to defend. In this regard, the reason for this common result is that despite the surface differences between chance and fate, a common impersonalism prevails in which the universe reduces to a product of matter and motion. Consequently, by adopting the unicausal framework up front, the discussion is constrained by two impersonal alternatives with the result that predestination and human responsibility are both destroyed on either option.

---

[2] Here, it should be noted that people often reject predestination because they confuse it with fate. As seen above, however, the resemblance between these views is superficial at best. After all, despite their common determinism, predestination is personal whereas fate is mechanistic. So understood, the mechanism of fate is destructive of both predestination and human responsibility whereas Biblical predestination sets forth a cosmic personalism in which human responsibility is grounded. However, while the two views are quite distinct, their confusion is most natural within a unicausal framework that pits God's ultimate causation against the proximate causation of man. In this regard, Luther's views sometimes bordered on fatalism due to his occasional denials of proximate causation. Accordingly, it was left to Calvin to tone down the occasional harshness of Luther's doctrine through the adoption of a dicausal framework.

Thus, to preserve predestination and human responsibility, it is necessary to reject the false antagonism of the unicausal framework and embrace the dicausal framework of Christian metaphysics. Within this framework, as shown in Figure 1a, the unique combination of transcendence and immanence allows for a simultaneous connection and distinction between the Infinite God and the finite universe. In this regard, the distinction prevents God from being confused with the finite creation so that His essence is not reduced to the level of an impersonal chance or fate. As a result, the Infinite God remains irreducibly personal and thus infused with an ultimate purpose. However, while this distinction prevents the personality of God from being compromised, the connection between God and creation ensures that the world is established by His infinite personality and thus governed in accordance with His purpose. Moreover, since man and the universe are exhaustively determined by a Personal God, the connection also ensures the integrity of the human personality and a system of moral order, the very criteria of human responsibility. However, while this connection ensures that God is the ultimate cause of all human action, the distinction between God and creation prevents the respective acts of God and man from being ethically confused. Consequently, just as the crucifixion of Christ was simultaneously the most gracious act of God and the most wicked act of man, so the character of human evil is not altered by God's benevolent determination of it. Thus, counter to one's natural intuition, human responsibility is established precisely because of, and not in spite of God's predestination.[3] Luther writes:

> Since God moves and works all in all, He moves and works of necessity even in Satan and the ungodly. But He works according to what they are, and what He finds them to be: which means, since they are evil and perverted themselves, that when they are

---

[3] Having set forth the coherence between predestination and human responsibility, it is most convenient to consider a classic objection to the Christian view of God, namely problem of evil. In this regard, atheist objectors, assuming that a good and powerful God would eliminate every trace of evil, use the existence of evil as evidence that God cannot be both good and all powerful. Unfortunately, the Christian response to this attack is often neutralized by framing the issue in terms of a unicausal framework as choice between God causing or merely permitting evil. However, since God must therefore be evil or weak, this choice is substantively identical to the original dilemma posed by the atheist. Thus, the adoption of a unicausal framework necessarily plays into the atheist's hands. Accordingly, to properly respond to the atheist, it is necessary to embrace a dicausal framework in which God's goodness and power can be simultaneously maintained. Thus, instead of saying that God merely permits evil, one must affirm God to be the ultimate cause of *human* evil. Similarly, rather than saying that God causes evil, one must affirm man's proximate causation as the source of evil. After all, while the ultimate cause totally conditions the proximate cause, the two remain distinct and unconfused. Consequently, in response to the atheist, one should say that because God is the ultimate, but not the proximate cause of *human* evil, He brings it about infallibly, yet in such away that He works good while man does evil. (Note: the problem of evil is substantively identical to the problem of human responsibility. However, while the former concerns the relation of evil to a predestinating God, the latter concerns its relation to a predestined man.)

impelled to action by this movement of Divine omnipotence they do only that which is evil and perverted. It is like a man riding a horse with only three, or two, good feet; his riding corresponds with what the horse is, which means that the horse goes badly. But what can the rider do? He is riding this horse in company with sound horses; this one goes badly, though the rest go well; and so it is bound to be, unless the horse is healed.

Here you see that when God works in and by evil men, evil deeds result; yet God, though He does evil by means of evil men, cannot act evilly Himself, for He is good, and cannot do evil; but He uses evil instruments, which cannot escape the impulse and movement of His power. The fault which accounts for evil being done when God moves to action lies in these instruments, which God does not allow to be idle. In the same way a carpenter would cut badly with a saw-toothed axe. Hence it is that the ungodly man cannot but err and sin always, because under the impulse of Divine power he is not allowed to be idle, but wills, desires and acts according to his nature.

This is sure and certain, if we believe that God is omnipotent; as it is also certain that the ungodly man is a creature of God, but one which, being perverted and left to itself without the Spirit of God, cannot will or do good. God's omnipotence makes it impossible

16

for the ungodly man to escape the action upon him of the movement of God; of necessity he is subject to it, and obeys it; but his corruption, his turning of himself from God, makes it impossible for him to be moved and made to act well. God cannot suspend His omnipotence on account of man's perversion, and the ungodly man cannot alter his perversion. As a result he sins and errs incessantly and inevitably until he is set right by the Spirit of God. (Luther, *Bondage of the Will*, 204, 205)

The Decretive and Preceptive Wills of God

In the previous chapter, the coherence between predestination and human responsibility was established by demonstrating the essential harmony between divine and human causation. In the present chapter, this coherence will be further explicated by resolving an apparent conflict relating to the will of God. In this regard, the conflict arises because human responsibility requires what predestination seems to deny, namely the possibility of breaking God's will. Given this fact, the coherence of predestination and human responsibility would seem to be logically impossible since it would require the possibility of simultaneously breaking and following of God's will in one and the same act. Consequently, for predestination and human responsibility to cohere in a logical manner, it must be shown that the sense in which God's will can be broken differs from the sense in which it is necessarily followed. To this end, it will prove useful to distinguish between the decretive and preceptive wills of God. To justify and explain this distinction, a previous passage concerning the death of Christ will here be reviewed.

Men of Israel, listen to this: Jesus of Nazareth was a man accredited by God to you by

19

> miracles, wonders, and signs, which God did
> among you through him, as you yourselves
> know. This man was handed over to you
> by God's set purpose and foreknowledge;
> and you, with the help of wicked men, put
> him to death by nailing him to the cross.
> (Acts 2:22, 23)

On the basis of this passage, it is readily apparent that two distinct wills of God were operating in the death of Christ. On the one hand, since God foreordained Christ's death according to His "set purpose and foreknowledge," it is evident that God willed the event in terms of His eternal decree. On the other hand, since Christ's murderers are referred to as "wicked men," it is also evident that God willed against Christ's death in terms of His moral law or precept. Thus, there is clear scriptural support for the concurrent operation of God's decretive and preceptive wills. In terms of this distinction, God's decretive will has reference to historical eventuation (*i.e.*, what God *will* do.) while His preceptive will has reference to moral obligation (*i.e.*, what man *should* do.). Consequently, since the decretive and preceptive wills therefore involve distinct senses (indicative *vs.* imperative) and envision distinct moral agents (God *vs.* man), there is no logical contradiction in the simultaneous keeping and breaking of these respective wills. Thus, predestination and human responsibility logically cohere since it is possible for man to break God's preceptive will even as God's decretive will necessitates his actions. To see this coherence in a direct and positive manner, however, it will be necessary to examine the structure of moral law.

In this regard, observe that moral law is composed of two basic parts, precept (stipulation) and penalty (sanction). Moreover, these two parts are held together in the form of a conditional statement that suspends a penalty or sanction (reward or punishment) upon preceptive obedience or disobedience. Thus, a parent says to a child, "If you clean your room, you may have dessert, but if you don't, you'll go without." From this example, moral law is seen to operate in the following manner: preceptive obedience or disobedience produces a state of innocence or guilt, which state renders one liable to the appropriate sanction (*i.e.*, reward or punishment). So understood, the law is simply a conditional statement which suspends reward and punishment upon the respective conditions of preceptive obedience or disobedience. With this understanding, then, it is necessary to determine how this conditional structure allows the decretive and preceptive wills of God to harmonize, thereby reconciling

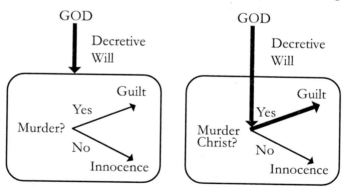

Figure 2a.
Decretive Will Establishes
Preceptive Will Generally

Figure 2b.
Decretive Will Works Through
Preceptive Will Specifically

FIGURE 2: Schematic Illustrating the Coherence between God's Decretive and Preceptive Wills

predestination and human responsibility. Here again, it will be instructive to consider the death of Christ.

In this regard, observe from Figure 2a. that it was precisely by God's predestination (decretive will) that the conditions of His law (preceptive will) were generally established prior to Christ's death. Moreover, as shown in Figure 2b., God worked through these very conditions in His specific decree of Christ's death. Consequently, since God's decretive will established the very conditions of His preceptive will and worked through them, the two wills harmonized completely. Thus, when Christ died in accordance with God's decretive will, His murderers incurred guilt for violating God's preceptive will with the result that a complete coherence between predestination and human responsibility was established.

In this regard, the reason for this coherence is two fold. First, as shown in the last chapter, God is the ultimate personal cause who establishes and works through man's distinct personality. Thus, it is precisely God's predestination that establishes man as a distinct moral agent. Moreover, on the basis of His predestination or decretive will, God establishes His preceptive will and works through the conditions thereof. Consequently, since God's predestination establishes both the human personality and the moral law to which it is held, it is precisely because of God's predestination that man can violate God's law in a personally accountable fashion. Thus, far from eliminating human responsibility, predestination establishes human responsibility by securing the integrity of the human personality and a binding moral law.

When this result is traced to its theoretical foundations, it is found that the two layer metaphysics of Christian theology allows for a simultaneous transcendence and immanence which enables God to govern creation exhaustively while remaining distinct from it. Consequently, since there is a simultaneous distinction and interconnection between God and His creation at every point, there is a relation and a distinction between ultimate and proximate causation, on the one hand, and between God's decretive and preceptive wills, on the other. Accordingly, just as God's ultimate causation establishes and works through the human personality, so His decretive will establishes and works through His precepts. Yet, because of the divine transcendence, God remains distinct from both the human personality and His moral law. Consequently, while man's actions are ultimately caused by a personal God, human and divine actions remain metaphysically distinct and, therefore, may not be ethically confused in an attempt to shift blame from man to God. Moreover, while God's law (preceptive will) is produced in accordance with His holy decree (decretive will), the two remain metaphysically distinct and, therefore, may not be ethically confused by using God's law (preceptive will) to judge His actions (decretive will). Accordingly, since God remains distinct from the creation He exhaustively governs, God's predestination establishes human responsibility without making God the author of sin. To see these points more clearly, consider the following example:

Person A kills person B as a result of God's predestination. In killing person B, person A incurs guilt for his action since God's predestination establishes A's distinct personality and the moral law to which A is held. From the divine perspective, however, God is not guilty of evil since the law does not apply to Him, and since He is working good through the process. That the law does not apply to God follows from His prerogatives as the Creator and Owner of the earth. As such, He has the absolute right to take person B's life at any time and to use person A in the process. As to God's working good, the death of Christ attests the fact that God works good through human evil. Clearly, there is much mystery here, yet no contradiction. After all, by securing man's distinct personality and the moral law to which he is held, God's predestination establishes the very conditions of human responsibility.

For Luther's views on the relation between the decretive and preceptive wills of God, see the discussion in Chapter 11.

Free Will vs.
Free Agency

4

In Chapters 2 and 3, the coherence between predestination and human responsibility was established by demonstrating the essential harmony
between divine and human causation and between
God's decretive and preceptive wills. In the present chapter, this coherence will be further explicated by resolving
an apparent conflict related to the issue of human freedom. In this regard, the conflict arises because
predestination seems to deny the very freedom required
for personal responsibility. Thus, the coherence between
predestination and human responsibility would seem to
be logically impossible since such coherence would require human action to be simultaneously determined (*i.e.*,
not free) and free. Consequently, for predestination and
human responsibility to cohere in a logical manner, it
must be shown that the sense in which one is determined
differs from the sense in which one is free. To this end, it
will prove useful to distinguish between free will and
free agency. Once these terms have been clearly distin-
guished, it will be shown that by negating free will and
not free agency, predestination determines human behavior without violating man's responsible freedom of
choice. To justify this distinction, a previous passage concerning the death of Christ will here be reviewed:

> Men of Israel, listen to this: Jesus of Nazareth
> was a man accredited by God to you by
> miracles, wonders, and signs, which God did
> among you through him, as you yourselves
> know. This man was handed over to you
> by God's set purpose and foreknowledge;
> and you, with the help of wicked men, put
> him to death by nailing him to the cross.
> (Acts 2:22, 23)

On the basis of the above passage, it is readily apparent that Christ's murderers were both determined (not free) and free. On the one hand, since God foreordained Christ's death according to His "set purpose and foreknowledge," it is evident that their murderous actions were necessitated and thus inevitably bound to occur. On the other hand, since Christ's murderers are here referred to as "wicked men," it is also evident that their actions were freely chosen in order to merit such condemnation. So understood, the above passage would seem to support the concurrent operation of God's exhaustive determination together with true human freedom. However, since God's determination would also seem to deny human freedom, the above concurrence would seem to require the simultaneous denial and affirmation of human freedom. Accordingly, to avoid an internal contradiction in the passage above, it is necessary that the sense in which freedom is denied be distinct from the sense in which it is simultaneously maintained. Thus, to satisfy the constraint of the above passage, it is necessary to distinguish two senses of human freedom, namely free agency and free will.

In regard to this distinction, free agency refers to a lack of external compulsion and therefore implies an external freedom to choose between options. Free will, by contrast, refers to an internal equilibrium of the will and thus a consequent lack of bias toward any particular option.[1] So understood, free agency is absolutely essential to human responsibility since the power of choice is essential to any moral agent. After all, one could not be held liable for murder if someone else put a gun into his hand and mechanically forced him to squeeze the trigger. Free will, by contrast, would destroy human responsibility since an internal equilibrium of the will would eliminate any driving motive as the basis for human action. With respect to human responsibility, then, the implications of free agency and free will are diametrically opposed. Yet, while the importance of free agency is clear, the effects of free will are far from obvious. To illumine these effects, therefore, the balance of the present chapter will be devoted to clarifying the effect of free will on human responsibility. To this end, the ethical connection between motive and action must first be established as essential to human responsibility. Then, having demonstrated this point, it will be shown that the metaphysics of free will severs this ethical connection.

With respect to ethical predication, human actions are evaluated on the basis of their impelling motives, the means employed, and the ends obtained. In terms of these criteria, an action is judged to be good when it is driven by pure motives through the use of lawful

---

[1] Incidentally, since the will is the very faculty of choice, one never chooses against his will.

means toward the accomplishment of beneficent ends. Accordingly, in all ethical judgments there is a necessary connection between the subjective (motives) and objective (means and ends) aspects of human action which makes motive essential to moral value and hence to human responsibility. After all, apart from this subjective element, one could not be a proper ethical subject (*i.e.*, a moral agent) and thus could not be held accountable for his actions.[2] However, since the motive for any action arises from a systematic bias of the will, the motive vanishes apart from a driving bent toward good or evil which defines the ethical character of the person. Consequently, since human responsibility depends upon a credible motive for human action, it necessarily hinges upon the ethical and metaphysical conditioning factors which provide this driving bent to the human will. Accordingly, to determine the relationship between human responsibility and free will, it is necessary to examine the implications of these underlying factors.

With regard to the ethical factors, it may readily be shown that the moral value of any action requires the stable character of a determined will. For instance, God and the glorified saints are said to be perfectly good precisely because they cannot (*i.e.*, are not free to) do evil. Moreover, Satan and the damned are regarded as perfectly evil precisely because they cannot do good. Thus, it is not because their respective wills are free

---

[2] Thus, despite the often deadly effects of such natural phenomena as electric currents, earthquakes, and tidal waves, such phenomena cannot be regarded as evil because they are impersonal and therefore lack the capacity for motive.

28

to vacillate between good and evil that the actions of God, Satan, and their perfected followers carry moral value. Rather, their acts carry moral value precisely because they derive from the set ethical character of perfectly determined wills which are consistently and irreversibly bent toward good or evil, respectively. After all, since motive is the spring of personal action and thus essential to moral value, the moral value of any action is ultimately determined by the character of the will as expressed in the driving motive and therefore vanishes apart from the systematic bias of the will needed to sustain the particular motive.[3] Thus, in contrast to popular wisdom, the moral value of an action arises from the set character of a determined will and not the vacillating character of a free one.

Given this fact, human responsibility for evil ultimately derives from the inborn depravity which enslaves the human will to its evil bent and thereby produces the consistent ethical character from which man's motives and actions spring. In other words, man sins because he is a sinner, not the reverse. But if man sins as a result of his sinful character, then his respon-

---

[3] While civil magistrates are incapable of assessing hidden motives and so must punish crime on the basis of objective criteria (means and ends) alone, God is able to look directly upon the heart and so is capable of a subjective analysis. Accordingly, from a divine perspective, an evil motive renders an action evil even when the action itself is objectively good. Similarly, the sinfulness of an objectively evil action is lessened (though not eliminated) when it is committed through ignorance in accordance with pure motives. Consequently, from the ultimate perspective of divine justice, the character of an action is to a large degree determined by the character of its driving motive.

sibility for evil ultimately derives from a determined will, not a free one. Accordingly, free will is diametrically opposed to human responsibility since it would destroy the set ethical character upon which motive and human responsibility depend. To see this point more clearly, consider some of the absurdities that free will would entail.

In this regard, recall that a free will would be characterized by an internal equilibrium with respect to every behavioral option and would therefore be devoid of any moral bent. Accordingly, a free will would be morally neutral and would, therefore, move by random fluctuation (or else be paralyzed by indecision). After all, for a will to be governed by any law or pattern whatsoever, even the internal law of its own nature, would negate its cherished freedom.[4] Thus, a truly free will would be driven by chance alone and would therefore manifest itself in queer statements such as the following: "Boy, it sure is a nice day. I think I'll go help my mother in the garden. No, on second thought I'll kill her!"[5] However, under such conditions of randomness, there could be no orientation to the will and hence no moral value to its choices. After all, since a free will would lack a moral bent, it would operate apart from a driving motive and thus destroy the moral value of human action. Accordingly, by severing the connection between motive and ac-

---

[4] In this regard, it should be recalled that God's will is not totally free since it is determined internally by the holy requirements of His nature.

[5] Of course, no one actually thinks this way, except psychopathic murders and existentialist philosophers obsessed with free will.

tion, a free will would destroy human responsibility.[6] Consequently, while free agency (the lack of external compulsion) is essential to human responsibility, free will (the lack of internal drive) is antithetical to it.

Given this fact, the coherence between predestination and human responsibility requires that predestination simultaneously negate free will and establish free agency. That God's predestination satisfies these criteria can be seen from a consideration of God's transcendence and immanence. First, because God is immanent, there is a connection between God and man which ensures that the human personality is established by God's defining control and thus prevented from dissolving into the chance universe which free will assumes. Accordingly, the human capacity for motive is established precisely because God's predestination denies free will. Yet, because God is also transcendent, there is a distinction between God and man which preserves man's distinct moral agency and thereby prevents it from collapsing into a world of fatalistic compulsion. Accordingly, while God's predestination negates free will, it establishes free agency since it preserves man's distinct moral agency and therefore places him under no external compulsion. Thus, while every aspect of man's existence is fixed

---

[6] Since a free will would require a random universe for its field of operation, there would be no external order of any kind, moral law included. Thus, there could be no basis in justice to punish crimes since there would be no just desert. Moreover, since a random universe would also destroy cause and effect, even the deterrent value of punishment would be lost. So understood, free will would reduce human interaction to a meaningless hell.

by God's eternal decree, man's creaturely freedom is not thereby violated. After all, by establishing the human will as a distinct secondary cause, God is able to impel man internally in such a way that he fulfills God's plan most freely. In other words, God's predestination determines man constitutionally so that he is internally driven, yet externally free.

Consequently, predestination is seen to establish human responsibility by simultaneously affirming free agency and denying free will. Because man has free agency, he has the freedom of choice which is essential to his responsibility. Yet, because free will is denied, man does not lose his personal responsibility to a universe of chance. So understood, there is a complete coherence between predestination and human responsibility. After all, since free will and free agency are distinct entities, the determinism of predestination does not contradict the particular freedom which human responsibility requires:

> For I showed above that free-will belongs to none but God only. You are no doubt right in assigning to man a will of some sort, but to credit him with a will that is free in the things of God is too much. For all who hear mention of "free-will" take it to mean, in its proper sense, a will that can and does do, God-ward, all that it pleases, restrained by no law and no command; for you would not call a slave, who acts at the beck of his lord, free. But in that case how much less are we right to call men or angels free; for they live under the complete mastery of God (not to

mention sin and death), and cannot continue by their own strength for a moment. Here then, right at the outset, the definition of the term and the definition of the thing are at odds, for the term connotes one thing and what is really in mind is another. It would be more correct to call it "veritible-will" or "mutable-will." (Luther, *The Bondage of the Will*, 137)

I said "of necessity"; I did not say "of compulsion"; I meant, by a necessity, not of compulsion, but of what they call immutability. That is to say:a man without the Spirit of God does not do evil against his will, under pressure, as though he were taken by the scruff of the neck and dragged into it, like a thief or foot pad being dragged off against his will to punishment; but he does it spontaneously and voluntarily. And this willingness or volition is something which he cannot in his own strength eliminate, restrain or alter. He goes on willing and desiring to do evil; and if external pressure forces him to act otherwise, nevertheless his will within remains averse to so doing and chafes under such constraint and opposition. But it would not thus chafe were it being changed, and were it yielding to constraint willingly. This is what we mean by necessity of immutability: that the will cannot change itself, nor give itself another bent, but, rather, is the more provoked to crave the more it is opposed, as its chafing proves;

for this would not occur, were it free or had "free-will." Ask experience how impervious to dissuasion are those whose hearts are set on anything! If they abandon their quest of it, they only do so under pressure, or because of some counter-attraction, never freely — whereas, when their hearts are not thus engaged, they spare their labour, and let events take their course. (Luther, *The Bondage of the Will*, 102, 103)

Had there been in Pharaoh any power to turn, or freedom of will that might have gone either way, God could not with such certainty have foretold his hardening. But as it is, He who neither deceives nor is deceived guarantees it: which means that it is completely certain, and necessary, that Pharaoh's hardening will come to pass. And it would not be so, were not that hardening wholly beyond the strength of man, and in the power of God alone, in the manner that I spoke of above: that is, God was certain that He would not suspend the ordinary operation of omnipotence in Pharaoh, or on Pharaoh's account — indeed, He could not omit it; and He was equally certain that the will of Pharaoh, being naturally evil and perverse, could not consent to the word and work of God which opposed it: hence, while by the omnipotence of God the energy of willing was preserved to Pharaoh within, and the word and work that opposed him was set before him without, nothing could happen in Pharaoh but the offending and hardening of his heart. If God had suspended the action of His omnipotence in Pharaoh when He set before him the word of Moses which opposed him, and if the will of Pharaoh might be supposed to have acted alone by its own power, then there could perhaps have been a place for debating which way it had power to turn. But as it is, since he is impelled and made to act by his own willing, no violence is done to his will; for it is not under unwilling constraint, but by an operation of God consonant with its nature it is impelled to will naturally, according to what it is (that is, evil). Therefore, it could not but turn upon one word, and thus become hardened. Thus we see that this passage makes most forcibly against "free-will," on this account God, who promises, cannot lie; and, if He cannot lie, then Pharaoh cannot but be hardened. (Luther, *The Bondage of the Will*, 211, 212)

See how successfully the Diatribe retains freedom alongside necessity when it says: "not all necessity excludes 'free-will.' thus, God the father begets a Son of necessity; yet He begets Him willingly and freely, for He is not forced to do so." Are we now discussing compulsion and force? Have I not put on record in many books that I am talking about necessity of immutability? I know that the Father begets willingly, and that Judas betrayed Christ willingly. My point is that this act of will in Judas was certainly and infallibly bound to take place, if God fore-knew it. That is to say (if my meaning is not yet grasped), I distinguish two necessities: one I call necessity of force, referring to action; the other I call necessity of infallibility, referring to time. Let him who hears me understand that I am speaking of the latter, not the former: that is, I am not discussing whether Judas became a traitor willingly or unwillingly, but whether it was infallibly bound to come to pass that Judas should willingly betray Christ at a time predetermined by God. (Luther, *The Bondage of the Will*, 220)

Predestination and
the Doctrine of God

5

In Chapters 2, 3, and 4 the coherence between predestination and human responsibility was set forth. In that discussion, it was shown that predestination establishes human responsibility through the provision of man's distinct moral agency, and a binding moral law. Thus, counter to one's natural intuition, human responsibility is established precisely because of, and not in spite of God's predestination. Having shown the coherence between predestination and human responsibility, therefore, a major stumbling block has been removed from the subsequent discussion since it is precisely this concern for human dignity and responsibility that causes many to reject predestination. Consequently, having removed this major objection, the positive evidence for predestination may now be more profitably set forth. To this end, it will be the burden of the next two chapters to show that predestination is demanded by the respective natures of God and man.

With respect to the divine nature, predestination is demanded by God's infinitude. After all, since God is an infinite being, an infinite magnitude characterizes all of His properties, including His knowledge and power. Accordingly, with respect to knowledge and power, God is both omniscient (all knowing) and omnipotent (all powerful). Moreover, because God's properties are infinite, they exhaustively interpenetrate one another with the result that they are coextensive or coterminus (literally having the same boundaries). Thus, as part of His infinitude, God is seen to have an indivisible, non-composite nature and is therefore said to be simple. Given this divine simplicity, therefore, God's knowledge and power are necessarily coterminus with God's being and hence with one another. Accordingly, being omniscient, God is exhaustively conscious of His being and actions, and being omnipotent, He is in control of His being and knowledge. Consequently, since God therefore infallibly knows and controls His own being and actions, and since all external reality (*i.e.*, the creation) is solely dependent upon Him, there is nothing within God or about Him which escapes His exhaustive knowledge or control. Thus, God's actions are purposeful, and His purposes are actual. What God foreknows He necessarily foreordains and vice versa.

To see this point, consider the unique relation in which God stands to His creation. In this regard, observe first of all that the finite creation was brought forth from nothing by an eternal God Who existed apart from creation. Furthermore, since God and His creation represent the totality of existence, there is no outside factor to limit God in His creating and governing activity. Consequently, since God and His creation account for all reality, since God existed eternally apart from the creation, and since the latter was brought into existence solely by the power of God, it follows that God is the sole ground and determinant of all existence, of Himself first of all, and of His creation by extension. Thus, while God is radically independent of His creation, His creation is 100% dependent upon His creating and sustaining power. Accordingly, to the extent that God can first control Himself, He must exhaustively determine the existence of the created order.

However, because God is simple and infinite, His being, knowledge, and power are mutually exhaustive. Thus, God controls Himself completely, since He has no hidden depths to elude His knowledge, nor any involuntary movements which resist His power. And since God controls Himself first of all, it follows that He exhaustively determines and infallibly executes the blueprint in terms of which He brings His creation forth. After all, since the creation derives from God's activity and has not one iota of independence from Him, God's exhaustive self control ensures that the creation will have precisely that existence, and only that existence, which God assigns it. Thus, because God is omniscient and omnipotent, because God therefore controls His own being, and because He is the sole definer and determinant of the universe, every element of the creation conforms to a comprehensive, eternal plan which unfolds infallibly, inevitably, and irresistibly. In other words, because God is a simple, infinite being, and the sole ground of all reality, His creating and sustaining activity imply an absolute predestination of the created order. Accordingly, with respect to creation God's actions are purposeful, and His purposes are actual. What God foreknows, He necessarily foreordains, and vice versa. Consider Luther's view of the matter:

It is, then, fundamentally necessary and wholesome for Christians to know that God foreknows nothing contingently, but that He foresees, purposes, and does all things according to His own immutable, eternal and infallible will. This bombshell knocks "free-will" flat, and utterly shatters it; so that those who want to assert it must either deny my bombshell, or pretend not to notice it, or find some other way of dodging it. Before I establish this point by my own arguments and Scriptural authority, I shall first state it with the aid or your words.

Surely, it was you, my good Erasmus, who a moment ago asserted that God is by nature just, and kindness itself? If this is true, does it not follow that He is immutably just and kind? that, as His nature remains unchanged to all eternity, so do His justice and kindness? And what is said of His justice and kindness must be said also of His knowledge, His wisdom, His goodness, His will, and the other Divine attributes. But if it is religious, godly and wholesome, to affirm these things of God, as you do, what has come over you, that now you should contradict yourself by affirming that it is irreligious, idle and vain to say that God foreknows by necessity? You insist that we should learn the immutability of God's will, while forbidding us to know the immutability of His foreknowledge! Do you suppose that He does not will what He foreknows, or that He

40

does not foreknow what He wills? If He wills what He foreknows, His will is eternal and changeless, because His nature is so. From which it follows, by resistless logic, that all we do, however it may appear to us to be done mutably and contingently, is in reality done necessarily and immutably in respect of God's will. For the will of God is effective and cannot be impeded, since power belongs to God's nature; and His wisdom is such that He cannot be deceived. Since, then His will is not impeded, what is done cannot but be done where, when, how, as far as, and by whom, He foresees and wills. (Luther, *Bondage of the Will*, 80, 81)

But if the foreknowledge and omnipotence of God are conceded, it naturally follows by irrefutable logic that we were not made by ourselves, nor live by ourselves, nor do anything by ourselves, but by His omnipotence. Seeing that He foreknew that we should be what we are, and now makes us such, and moves and governs us as such, how, pray, can it be pretended that it is open to us to become something other than that which He foreknew and is now bringing about? So the foreknowledge and omnipotence of God are diametrically opposed to our 'free-will'. Either God makes mistakes in His foreknowledge, and errors in His action (which is impossible), or else we act, and are caused to act, according to His foreknowledge and action. And by the omnipotence of God I mean, not the power

41

by which He omits to do many things that He could do, but the active power by which He mightily works all in all. It is in this sense that Scripture calls Him omnipotent. This omnipotence and foreknowledge of God, I repeat, utterly destroy the doctrine of "free-will." (Luther, *The Bondage of the Will*, 216, 217)

On your view, God will elect nobody, and no place for election will be left; all that is left is freedom of will to heed or defy the long-suffering and wrath of God. But if God is thus robbed of His power and wisdom in election, what will He be but just that idol, Chance, under whose sway all things happen at random? Eventually, we shall come to this:that men may be saved and damned without God's knowledge! For He will not have marked out by sure election those that should be saved and those that should be damned; He will merely have set before all men His general long-suffering, which forbears and hardens, together with His chastening and punishing mercy, and left it to them to choose whether they would be saved or damned, while He Himself, perchance, goes off, as Homer says, to an Ethiopian banquet! (Luther, *The Bondage of the Will*, 199, 200)

Doubtless it gives the greatest possible offense to common sense or natural reason, that God, Who is proclaimed as being full of mercy and goodness, and so on, should of His own mere will abandon, harden and damn men, as though He delighted in the sins and great eternal torments of such poor wretches. It seems an iniquitous, cruel, intolerable thought to think of God; and it is this that has been a stumbling block to so many great men down the ages. And who would not stumble at it? I have stumbled at it myself more than once, down to the deepest pit of despair, so that I wished I had never been made a man. (That was before I knew how health-giving that despair was, and how close to grace.) That is why so much toil and trouble has been devoted to clearing the goodness of God, and throwing the blame on man's will.... None the less, the arrow of conviction has remained, fastened deep in the hearts of learned and unlearned alike, whenever they have made a serious approach to the matter, so that they are aware that, if the foreknowledge and omnipotence of God are admitted, then we must be under necessity. (Luther, *The Bondage of the Will*, 217, 218)

Predestination and the Doctrine of Man

6

I n the previous chapter, predestination was advanced on the basis of the doctrine of God. There it was shown that the very nature of God demands predestination as a consistent expression of the divine being. In the present chapter, predestination will be derived from the doctrine of man, and here it will be the burden of the discussion to show that predestination is demanded by man's nature, state, and character. In regard to these categories, man's nature refers to his metaphysical status as a creature of God; his state refers to his judicial status as guilty or innocent before God, and his character refers to his ethical status as a depraved sinner or a sanctified saint. In terms of these distinctions, the metaphysical attributes of man's being are comprehended under his nature while the effects of sin are comprehended under the latter two categories, respectively. So understood, it will be convenient to begin the discussion with a consideration of man's nature since the metaphysical considerations of human nature are more basic to a discussion of predestination than are the effects of sin. After all, while the effects of sin are occasioned by the fall and are therefore unessential to the created order, the metaphysical considerations are basic to creation itself and therefore applicable even apart from sin. Accordingly, by addressing the metaphysical considerations first, predestination will emerge as an inescapable reality transcending all historical contingencies.

In regard to metaphysics, it is apparent from man's creaturely nature that he has a space-time origin and so cannot be the ground of his own existence. Rather, as a derivative being, man is part of the finite creation and is therefore 100% dependent upon divine conditioning. Consequently, when man comes into existence, he does so in terms of an eternal, divine blueprint which exhaustively determines every aspect his being, including his will. Accordingly, free will vanishes on metaphysical grounds since man cannot evade this divine conditioning without negating the very ground of his contingent being.[1] Thus, the metaphysical considerations basic to human nature imply predestination even apart from sin.

-----

[1] Note that not even God is free of conditioning since he is internally conditioned by the requirements of His own nature. Thus, there is a proper sense in which even God is restricted since He must act in accordance with His own nature and so, for instance, cannot sin. However, since God is the ground of His own existence, He is conditioned internally by Himself alone and not by external reality. Accordingly, God is said to be *a se*, a Latin term which literally means, "of Himself." Consequently, in comparison with man who is conditioned externally both by God and the world about him, God's freedom consists in the fact that He is internally determined by Himself alone and not by anything beyond Him. Thus, while God is a determined being, He is totally *self* determined and therefore totally free.

Given this fact, it follows that predestination extends to prefall history, thereby determining the fall itself. After all, as God's creature, Adam was directly dependent upon God even prior to the fall, and was therefore exhaustively conditioned in every facet of his existence. Moreover, through the provision of his distinct personality and the moral Law to which he was held, it was precisely this predestination of God which established Adam's moral responsibility in the first place (see Chapters 2, 3, and 4). Consequently, by securing Adam's personal responsibility and by determining his actual behavior, God's predestination must be seen as determining both the possibility and actuality of the fall, and hence the resulting depravity of mankind. Thus, by establishing predestination apart from sin, the metaphysical considerations advanced above extend predestination to prefall history, making the fall itself contingent upon predestination.

However, when predestination is argued on the basis of sin alone, the above priority is unwittingly reversed with the result that predestination is made contingent upon the fall. Accordingly, since it then becomes impossible to extend predestination to prefall history, a theological loophole is opened whereby the fall and its subsequent effects are attributed to free will. Needless to say, by making predestination contingent upon a free will event, the doctrine is thereby decimated at every succeeding point in history. After all, since the fall is pivotal and thus determinative of all subsequent events, the ultimate course of history would then be contingent upon free will, not predestination. However, by extending predestination to prefall history, the metaphysical considerations advanced above effectively close this loophole, thereby guarding the doctrine against theological erosion. Having closed this loophole, therefore, the relation between sin and predestination may now be more profitably examined.

As mentioned previously, the effects of sin relate to the state and character of man. Accordingly, in setting forth the relation between sin and predestination, it is necessary to consider the implications of man's state and character. In this regard, it may generally be said that due to the fall, every man (except Christ) is born into a state of guilt and with a moral character that is totally depraved. As a result of his state, fallen man is guilty before God and thus liable to God's wrath and punishment. Moreover, as a result of his ethical character, he is totally depraved and thus incapable of doing good. So understood, original sin involves a twofold effect relating to the guilt and pollution of sin.[2] In support of this dual effect, the following passages may be cited:

> Therefore, just as sin entered the world through one man, and death through sin, and in this way death came to all men, because all sinned — for before the law was given, sin was in the world. But sin is not taken into account when there is no law. Nevertheless,

---

[2] In justification, the external problem of guilt is solved as Christ's merit and substitutionary punishment provide for a new judicial standing of innocence with God. In sanctification, on the other hand, the internal problem of pollution is progressively reversed as the Holy Spirit writes God's Law upon the human heart (Jeremiah 31:31-34).

death reigned from the time of Adam to the time of Moses, even over those who did not sin by breaking a command, as did Adam, who was a pattern of the one to come.

But the gift is not like the trespass. For if the many died by the trespass of the one man, how much more did God's grace and the gift that came by the grace of the one man, Jesus Christ, overflow to the many! Again, the gift of God is not like the result of the one man's sin: The judgment followed one sin and brought condemnation, but the gift followed many trespasses and brought justification. For if, by the trespass of the one man, death reigned through that one man, how much more will those who receive God's abundant provision of grace and of the gift of righteousness reign in life through the one man, Jesus Christ.

Consequently, just as the result of one trespass was condemnation for all men, so also the result of one act of righteousness was justification that brings life for all men. For just as through the disobedience of the one man the many were made sinners, so also through the obedience of the one man the many will be made righteous.

The law was added so that the trespass might increase. But where sin increased, grace increased all the more, so that, just as sin reigned in death, so also grace might reign through righteousness to bring eternal life through Jesus Christ our Lord. (Romans 5:12-21)

Surely, I was sinful at birth, sinful from the time my mother conceived me. (Psalm 51:5)

The mind of sinful man is death, but the mind controlled by the Spirit is life and peace; the sinful mind is hostile to God. It does not submit to God's law, nor can it do so. Those controlled by the sinful nature cannot please God. (Romans 8:6-8)

The man without the Spirit does not accept the things that come from the Spirit of God, for they are foolishness to him, and he cannot understand them, because they are spiritually discerned. (I Corinthians 2:14)

There is no one righteous, not even one; there is no one who understands, no one who seeks God. All have turned away, they have together become worthless; there is no one who does good, not even one. Their throats are open graves; their tongues practice deceit. The poison of vipers is on their lips. Their mouths are full of cursing and bitterness. Their feet are swift to shed blood; ruin and misery mark their ways, and the way of peace they do not know. There is no fear of God before their eyes. (Romans 3:10-18)

On the basis of these passages, the guilt and pollution of original sin are clearly evident. From the first passage, it is seen that every man is born into a state of guilt as a result of Adam's one sin. Moreover, the remaining texts show man to be born into a condition of total depravity which is both extensively and intensively total. That is to say, it encompasses the breadth of humanity and permeates the depth of every man's being. So understood, the sweep of original sin is seen to be total in each of its effects. First, because of imputed guilt, every man is born liable to God's wrath and thus subject to His temporal and eternal punishment. Moreover, as a result of inherited depravity, every man is born spiritually dead, and thus hostile to the living God. In its total impact, then, original sin produces a dual effect which renders every man guilty and corrupt. Therefore, having established the nature and universality of these effects, it remains to determine their implications for predestination.

In this regard, it must first be observed that since all men are guilty before God and thus liable to His eternal wrath, the guilt of original sin eliminates the objection that predestination is unfair. After all, since God would be justified in damning all men, it is not unfair for God to save some in distinction from others. On the contrary, given the implications of man's guilt, God must be regarded as most gracious in saving any at all. After all, since the guilt of sin eliminates any claim to divine goodness, such goodness must come to man, if at all, by means of grace. And since grace is gift and not reward, it is free by its very nature and thus may not be constrained by considerations of merit or fairness. Consequently, since all claims to

51

God's goodness have been forfeited by universal guilt, and since God's goodness must therefore come by way of gift, such goodness cannot be demanded on the basis of merit or fairness. In other words, because the guilt arising from original sin is universal, all men have forfeited their claims to God's goodness and thus have no grounds upon which to object to a limited extension of divine favor. Thus, God is free to extend His goodness universally, partially, or not at all since the guilt of original sin eliminates every objection to the discriminating benevolence of predestination.

However, while the guilt of original sin eliminates every objection to predestination, the pollution of sin demands predestination as the very condition of salvation. After all, since man is born into a condition of spiritual death, his depraved character renders him incapable of moving toward God apart from divine grace. Thus, just as a dead man could not avail himself of a life giving potion until his doctor first poured it into his mouth, so the natural man cannot avail himself of the Gospel until he is first regenerated by the Spirit of God. Accordingly, since God's saving activity must causally precede the human response, one must be born again in order to come to Christ, not the reverse. Moreover, because the depraved sinner is incapable of even the least cooperation with God's grace, man's salvation must occur by virtue of a single divine action (monergism = a working alone) rather than a cooperation of human and divine action (synergism = a working with). Thus, in addition to the causal priority of God's grace, its monergism is implied as well. However, if God's saving action is prior to the human response, and if man's regeneration is 100% due to divine action, then God, and God alone, makes the difference between the saved and the lost, a fact which necessarily implies predestination. In other words, because man is spiritually dead, his salvation is 100% due to God's activity and therefore hinges upon God's desire to save him. Consequently, whereas the guilt of original sin eliminates every objection to predestination, the pollution of sin demands predestination as the very condition of salvation. In regard to these implications, Luther will be quoted voluminously below since it was precisely this insight on the part of Luther that launched the Protestant Reformation:

> Again: since by the single offense of the one man, Adam, we all lie under sin and condemnation, how can we set our hand to anything that is not sinful and damnable? When he says "all," he excepts none; not the power of "free-will," nor any worker, whether he works and endeavors or not; he is of necessity included with the rest among the "all." Neither should we sin or be condemned by reason of the single offense of Adam, if that offense were not our own; who could be condemned for another's offense, especially in the sight of God? But his offense becomes ours; not by imitation, nor by any act on our part (for then it would not be the single offense of Adam, since we should have committed it, not he), but it becomes ours by birth. (We must, however, discuss this elsewhere.) Original sin itself, then, does not allow "free-will" any power at all except to sin and incur condemnation. (Luther, *The Bondage of the Will*, 297, 298)

It remains absurd to reason's judgment that God, Who is just and good, should require of "free-will" impossibilities; and that though "free-will" cannot will good and serves sin of necessity He should lay sin to its charge; and that, by not giving the Spirit, He should act so severely and mercilessly as to harden or allow to be hardened. Reason will insist that these are not the acts of a good and merciful God. They are too far beyond her grasp; and she cannot bring herself to believe that the God Who acts and judges thus is good; she wants to shut out faith, and to see, and feel, and understand, how it is that He is good and not cruel. She would certainly understand, were it said of God that He hardens none and damns none, but has mercy on all and saves all, so that hell is destroyed, and the fear of death may be put away, and no future punishment need be dreaded! It is along this line that reason storms and contends, in order to clear God of blame, and to vindicate His justice and goodness! But faith and the Spirit judge otherwise, believing that God is good even though he should destroy all men. And what do we gain by wearying ourselves with these speculations, so as to throw back upon "free-will" the blame for man's hardening? Let all the "free-will" in the world do all it can with all its strength; it will never give rise to a single instance of ability to avoid being hardened if God does not give the Spirit, or of meriting mercy if it is left to its own strength. What difference does it make whether it is "hardened" or "deserves

hardening," if hardening necessarily super-
venes as long as there remains in it that
impotence which, as the Diatribe itself informs
us, disables "free-will" from willing good.
(Luther, *The Bondage of the Will*, 201, 202)

Suppose we imagine that God ought to be a
God who regards merit in those that are to be
damned. Must we not equally maintain and
allow that He should also regard merit in those
that are to be saved? If we want to follow Reason, it is as unjust to reward the undeserving
as to punish the undeserving, so let us con-
clude that God ought to justify on the grounds
of merit preceeding; or else we shall be de-
claring Him to be unjust. One who delights in
evil and wicked men, and who invites and
crowns their impiety with rewards! But then
woe to us poor wretches with such a God! For
who shall be saved?

Behold, therefore, the wickedness of the human heart! When God saves the undeserving
without merit, yes, and justifies the ungodly,
with all their great demerit, man's heart does
not accuse God of iniquity, nor demand to
know why He wills to do so, although by its
own reckoning such action is most unprin-
cipled: but because what God does is in its own
interest, and welcome, it considers it just and
good. But when He damns the undeserving,
because this is against its interest, it finds the
action iniquitous and intolerable; and here man's
heart protests, and grumbles, blasphemes....

But if a God who crowns the undeserving pleases you, you ought not be displeased when He damns the undeserving! If He is just in the one case, He cannot but be just in the other, in the one case, He pours out grace and mercy on the unworthy; in the other, He pours out wrath and severity upon the undeserving; in both He transgresses the bounds of equity in man's sight, yet is just and true in His own sight. How it is just for Him to crown the unworthy is incomprehensible now; but we shall see it when we reach the place where He will be no more an object of faith, but we shall with open face behold Him. So, too, it is at present incomprehensible how it is just for Him to damn the undeserving; yet faith will continue to believe that it is so, till the Son of Man shall be revealed. (Luther, *The Bondage of the Will*, 233-235)[3]

---

[3] In this quote, Luther's conception does not properly reflect the asymmetry of merit and reward in the doctrine of predestination. While it is true, as Luther notes, that the elect do not deserve to be saved, Luther is wrong in saying that the reprobate do not deserve to be damned. In this regard, Luther's error probably reflects a strain of fatalism in His thinking which made his view of predestination unduly harsh. However, if one properly distinguishes between ultimate and proximate causation, as Luther elsewhere does, then man's distinct personality together with his moral responsibility is seen to be established by God's predestination, not destroyed by it. Thus, the reprobate are not damned apart from human demerit, but precisely because they are guilty before God. Here, however, Luther seems to take a more fatalistic and Islamic view where man is cast into hell on the sole basis of divine whim and therefore apart from guilt. Given this fact, Calvin must be regarded as softening Luther's views since he eliminated this fatalistic strain from Reformed theology.

Firstly, I would remark that the first words you quote refer to the time before the fall of man, when what God had made was very good. But the immediate sequel, in the third chapter, tells how man became evil, and was abandoned by God and left to himself. Of that one man, thus corrupt, all men were born ungodly, Pharaoh included; as Paul says: "We were all by nature the children of wrath, even as others" (Ephesians 2:3). So God created Pharaoh ungodly, that is, of an ungodly and corrupt seed; as is says in the Proverbs of Solomon: "The Lord hath made all things for Himself, yea, even the ungodly for the day of evil" (Proverbs 16:4). It does not follow that, because God made the ungodly, he is therefore not ungodly! How can he fail to be ungodly, coming of an ungodly seed? It is as Psalm 50 says: "Behold I was conceived in sin" (Psalm 51:5); and as Job says: "Who can make a clean thing (when it is conceived) out of an unclean (seed)?" (Job 14:4). Though God does not make sin, yet He does not cease to form and multiply our nature, from which the Spirit has been withdrawn and which sin has impaired. He is like a carpenter who makes statues out of warped wood. As is the nature, so are men made; for God creates and forms them out of that nature. (Luther, *The Bondage of the Will*, 202, 203)

As for the other paradox, "all we do is done, not by free-will, but of mere necessity" — let us take a brief look at it, for we must not let such a mischievous remark go unchallenged. My comment is simply this: if it be proved that our salvation is not of our own strength or counsel, but depends on the working of God alone (which is something I hope to demonstrate later in the main discussion), does it not clearly follow that when God is not present to work in us, all is evil, and of necessity we act in a way that contributes nothing towards our salvation? For if it is not we, but God alone, who works salvation in us, it follows that, willy-nilly, nothing we do has any saving significance prior to His working in us. (Luther, *The Bondage of the Will*, 102)

And where then is our belief that Satan is the prince of this world, and reigns, as Christ and Paul tell us, in the wills and minds of men, who are his prisoners, and serve him? Will this roaring lion, this restless, implacable enemy of the grace of God and the salvation of men, suffer man, who is his slave and part of his kingdom, to make endeavors towards good at any time, or by any movement, whereby he might escape Satan's tyranny? Will he not rather spur and urge man on to will and to do with all his power that which is contrary to grace? Why, the righteous, whose acts are wrought by the Spirit of God, find it hard to resist him and to will and do good, so furiously does he rage against them! You, who imagine that the human will is something placed in an intermediate position of "freedom" and left to itself, find it easy to imagine that there is at the same time an endeavoring of the will in either direction; for you imagine that both God and the devil are far away, mere spectators, as it were, of this mutable free-will; you do not believe that they are the prompters and drivers of an enslaved will, and each raging relentless war against the other! If this alone is believed, then my case stands strong enough, and "free-will" lies prostrate: as I showed above. Either the kingdom of Satan in man is unreal, in which case Christ will be a liar; or else, if his kingdom is as Christ describes it, "free-will" will be merely a beast of burden, Satan's prisoner, which cannot be freed unless the devil is first cast out by the finger of God. (Luther, *The Bondage of the Will*, 262)

Though the great theologians who guard "free will" may not know, or pretend not to know, that Scripture proclaims Christ categorically and antithetically, all Christians know it, and commonly confess it. They know that there are in the world two kingdoms at war with each other. In the one, Satan reigns (which is why Christ calls him "the prince of this world" [John 12:31], and Paul "the god of this world" [II Corinthians 4:4]). He, so Paul again tells us, holds captive at his will all that are not wrested from him by the Spirit of Christ; nor does he allow them to be plucked away by any other power but the

Spirit of God, as Christ tells us in the parable of the strong man armed keeping his palace in peace. In the other kingdom, Christ reigns. His kingdom continually resists and wars against that of Satan; and we are translated into His kingdom, not by our own power, but by the grace of God, which delivers us from this present evil world and tears us away from the power of darkness. The knowledge and confession of these two kingdoms, ever warring against each other with all their might and power, would suffice by itself to confute the doctrine of "free-will," seeing that we are compelled to serve in Satan's kingdom if we are not plucked from it by Divine power. The common man, I repeat, knows this, and confesses it plainly enough by his proverbs, prayers, efforts and entire life. (Luther, *The Bondage of the Will*, 312)

What I say on this point is as follows: Man, before he is created to be man, does and endeavors nothing towards his being made a creature, and when he is made and created he does and endeavours nothing towards his continuance as a creature; both his creation and his continuance come to pass by the sole will of the omnipotent power and goodness of God, Who creates and preserves us without ourselves. Yet God does not work in us without us: for He created and preserves us for this very purpose, that He might work in us and we might cooperate with Him, whether that occurs outside His kingdom, by His general omnipotence, or within His kingdom, by the special power of His Spirit. So, too, I say that man, before he is renewed into the new creation of the Spirit's kingdom, does and endeavors nothing to prepare himself for that new creation and kingdom, and when he is recreated he does and endeavors nothing towards his perseverance in that kingdom; but the Spirit alone works both blessings in us, regenerating us, and preserving us when regenerate, without ourselves; as James says: "Of His own will begat He us with the word of His power, that we should be the first fruits of His creation" (James 1:18). (James is speaking of the renewed creation.) But He does not work in us without us for He recreates and preserves us for this very purpose, that He might work in us and we might co-operate with Him. Thus he preaches, shows mercy to the poor, and comforts the afflicted by means of us. But what is hereby attributed to "free-will"? What, indeed, is left it but — nothing! In truth, nothing! (Luther, *The Bondage of the Will*, 268)

I shall here end this book, ready though I am to pursue the matter further, if need be; but I think that abundant satisfaction has here been afforded for the godly man who is willing to yield to truth without stubborn resistance. For if we believe it to be true that God foreknows and foreordains all things;

61

that He cannot be deceived or obstructed in His foreknowledge and predestination; and that nothing happens but at His will (which reason itself is compelled to grant): then, on reason's own testimony, there can be no "free-will" in man, or angel, or in any creature.

So, if we believe that Satan is the prince of this world, ever ensnaring and opposing the kingdom of Christ with all his strength, and that he does not let his prisoners go unless he is driven out by the power of the Divine Spirit, it is again apparent that there can be no "free-will."

So, if we believe that original sin has ruined us to such an extent that even in the godly, who are led by the Spirit, it causes abundance of trouble by striving against good, it is clear that in a man who lacks the Spirit nothing is left that can turn itself to good, but only to evil.

Again, if the Jews, who followed after righteousness with all their powers, fell into unrighteousness instead, while the Gentiles, who followed after unrighteousness, attained to an un-hoped-for righteousness by God's free gift, it is equally apparent from their very works and experience that man without grace can will nothing but evil. (Luther, *The Bondage of the Will*, 317, 318)

The Biblical Case for
Election and Predestination

7

I n the preceding chapters, the doctrine of predestination has been advanced on the basis of general theological considerations, such as the doctrine of God or the nature of man. In this regard, such an approach was determined by the need to advance the doctrine in a way that simultaneously established a conceptual framework for the discussion. Having established this conceptual framework, however, it is now necessary to consider the witness of specific Biblical texts dealing directly with the doctrine of predestination. Accordingly, the next two chapters will consist largely of brief commentaries on individual texts. In this regard, the present chapter will focus on texts dealing with the positive side of predestination, namely predestination to eternal life, whereas the following chapter will examine the predestination to eternal death. Prior to this discussion, however, it will be necessary to briefly consider the doctrine itself in order to define some basic terms. To this end, a doctrinal statement taken from the Westminster Larger Catechism will prove most useful for the following discussion. In using such a statement, however, it is not being claimed that anyone should embrace predestination on the basis of a Reformed confession.

Rather, the statement is here quoted for pedagogical purposes only:

> God, by an eternal and immutable decree, out of his mere love, for the praise of his glorious grace, to be manifested in due time, hath elected some angels to glory; and in Christ hath chosen some men to eternal life, and the means thereof: and also, according to his sovereign power, and the unsearchable counsel of his own will, (whereby he extendeth or withholdeth favour as he pleaseth,) hath passed by and foreordained the rest to dishonour and wrath, to be for their sin inflicted, to the praise of the glory of his justice. (WLC, Q. 13)

On the basis of this statement, two related aspects of God's activity clearly emerge, namely God's choosing and His destinating. Accordingly, God is seen to act both in His discriminating choice and in His destination of those so chosen. With regard to God's choosing, "election" refers to God's choice of certain individuals unto eternal life while "reprobation" refers to His bypassing of the remainder. Moreover, since these distinct choices have divergent ends in view, the elect are said to be predestined unto eternal life while the reprobate are said to be predestined unto eternal death. So stated, the doctrine is referred to as "double predestination" (*i.e.*, a predestination unto both life and death) in distinction from the Lutheran view which affirms only "single predestination" (*i.e.*, a predestination to life alone). With this understanding, then, the burden of this chapter and the next will be to show that double predestination is abundantly attested in Scripture. To this end, the present chapter will focus on the election to glory while the following chapter will examine the predestination unto death. Moreover, in each case, the discussion will center on the examination of individual texts as noted above.

In considering the positive aspects of predestination, perhaps the classic text is Romans 8:28-30:

> And we know that in all things God works for the good of those who love him and who have been called according to his purpose. For those God foreknew, he also predestined to be conformed to the likeness of his Son, that he might be the firstborn among many brothers. And those he predestined, he also called; those he called, he also justified; those he justified, he also glorified. (Romans 8:28-30)

In setting forth the import of this passage, it is necessary to notice two things. First, the predestination of the elect has their final glorification in view which is here defined as conformity to the image of Christ. Second, since those who are foreknown and predestined are also called, justified, and glorified, each of the divine operations envisions the same group of people, no more and no less. Consequently, since all of those who have been predestined must therefore also be glorified, a doctrine of final perseverance also follows from the passage. After all, since God's predestination necessarily reaches its aim, the elect cannot be lost and must therefore persevere in their faith unto final glorification.

Yet, while the force of the passage seems clear, some seek to negate these conclusions through their misinterpretation of the foreknowledge mentioned in this passage. In this regard, such people claim that since the passage clearly roots God's predestination in foreknowledge, God merely foreknows but does not foreordain the end result. In response to this evasion, it must first be said that even such quibbling fails to achieve the intended result. After all, since God's foreknowledge is eternal and infallible, His creation of humanity subject to certain foreknowledge is equivalent to predestination. But beyond this point is the fact that opponents of predestination misinterpret the term "foreknowledge" in the context of the above passage. In particular, they give the term a passive and cognitive sense when a more active and relational sense is demanded by the passage. Consequently, to refute such false interpretation, the correct meaning of "foreknowledge" must be advanced, and to this end two steps will be required. First, it must be shown on the basis of Scriptural parallels that the term "foreknowledge" can be taken in a more active and relational sense. Then, once this point has been established, it must be shown that this active sense is demanded by the context of the passage in question.

With regard to the first point, abundant scriptural parallels demonstrate that "knowledge" can be taken in a more active and relational sense. Thus, Scripture says that Adam "knew" Eve and she became pregnant (Genesis 4:1). Clearly, a relational sense of knowledge is here implied since one does not become pregnant by mere cognition. Furthermore, at the last judgment Christ says to the reprobate, "I never 'knew'

66

you. Away from me, you evildoers!" (Matthew 7:22)
Here again, a relational sense of knowledge is clearly
intended since Christ could not judge such people apart
from cognitive knowledge. Thus, it seems that "knowledge" can be taken in a more active and relational
sense, and this conclusion is supported by the semantic range of the Greek and Hebrew words for
knowledge. The only remaining question, therefore,
is whether this more active sense is demanded by the
context of the above passage.

In answering this question, it may be said that the
flow of the passage demands the more active sense of
"foreknowledge" and therefore militates against the
more passive and cognitive sense of the term. After
all, within the context of the passage itself, Paul's appeal to God's foreknowledge is used to buttress his
claim that God works all things to the good of those
who are called according to His purpose. Such reasoning, however, would be idiotic if "foreknowledge"
were used in a merely cognitive sense since Paul would
then base God's saving activity in an ultimate passivity and thus fail to establish his point. After all, since
an effect is dependent upon a proper cause, an active
foreknowledge is needed to produce the effect of God's
benevolent purpose. Moreover, this conclusion is
strengthened from a consideration of the other terms
to which "foreknowledge" is linked in the passage. In
particular, since God's predestination, calling, justification, and glorification are seen to be rooted in His
foreknowledge, the active-relational meaning of the
former quantities must also attach to the foreknowledge from which they derive. After all, God's strong
and purposeful activity cannot be rooted in a passive

source. Thus, it may be concluded that the more active and relational meaning of "foreknowledge" is demanded by the above passage so that the sense of the term would be one of eternally fore loving or intimately foreknowing the elect. Consequently, as the eternal basis of God's relationship with the elect, the foreknowledge in the above passage is not a quantity that passively notes the differences among men but more basically is the very cause and ground of those differences in the first place. Given this fact, the passage gives excellent proof of God's active election and predestination and thus of the necessary perseverance of God's elect.[1]

This conclusion is strengthened by the fact that the meaning advanced for the above passage is consistent with the Paul's usage elsewhere. Consider the following:

> Praise be to the God and Father of our Lord Jesus Christ, who has blessed us in the heavenly realms with every spiritual blessing in Christ. For he chose us in him before the creation of the world to be holy and blameless in his sight. In love he predestined us to be adopted as his sons through Jesus Christ, in accordance with his pleasure and will.... In him we were also chosen, having been predestined according to the plan of him who works out everything in conformity with the purpose of his will. (Ephesians 1:3-5, 11)

---

[1] For additional insight into the meaning of this passage, see Luther's commentary below.

> For we are God's workmanship, created
> in Christ Jesus to do good works, which
> God prepared in advance for us to do.
> (Ephesians 2:10)

The force of these passages is largely self explanatory and confirms the interpretation of Romans 8:28-30 above. In this regard, notice especially that the emphasis is placed upon the eternal activity of God who predestines according to His fixed plan and who is expressedly said to work out everything in conformity with the purpose of His will. Note further that predestination by the Father is predestination in and through Christ and is particularly said to be in accordance with the Father's love. In this regard, the predestination by love in Ephesians 1:4 (*i.e.*, "In love he predestined us....") forms a most illumining parallel to the predestination by foreknowledge in Romans 8:29 (*i.e.*, "For those God foreknew, he also predestined....") since "love" and "foreknowledge" are seen to be interchangeable in similar contexts. Accordingly, since interchangeability in similar contexts implies a semantic equivalence, the juxtaposition of these two passages lends support to the conclusion mentioned above that "to foreknow" means "to fore love" in Romans 8:29. However, whether or not one accepts this linguistic argument, the passages from Ephesians nevertheless remain clear in their own import and thus add to the cumulative evidence in favor of predestination.

Additional evidence may be gathered from the opening lines of Peter's first epistle:

Peter, an apostle of Jesus Christ,

To God's elect, strangers in the world, scattered throughout Pontus, Galatia, Cappadocia, Asia and Bithynia, who have been chosen according to the foreknowledge of God the Father, through the sanctifying work of the Spirit, for obedience to Jesus Christ and sprinkling by his blood:

Grace and Peace be yours in abundance.

Praise be to the God and Father of our Lord Jesus Christ! In his great mercy he has given us new birth into a living hope through the resurrection of Jesus Christ from the dead, and into an inheritance that can never perish, spoil or fade — kept in heaven for you, who through faith are shielded by God's power until the coming of salvation that is ready to be revealed in the last time. (1 Peter 1:1-5)

In this passage Peter speaks of being chosen according to the foreknowledge of God the Father and of being shielded by God's power through faith unto a coming salvation. Thus, the doctrine of predestination together with the related doctrine of perseverance would seem to be straightforwardly affirmed. Once again, however, the determining question is whether "foreknowledge" assumes an active or a passive sense in the passage. After all, since divine foreknowledge forms the basis of all subsequent action in the passage, the predestinarian witness of the passage hinges upon an active interpretation of "foreknowledge." Consequently, to establish the pre-

70

destinarian implications of the passage, it is necessary to demonstrate the occurrence of this active sense.

In this regard, it is most significant that the passage sets forth a Trinitarian pattern relating the foreknowledge of the Father to the sprinkling of the Son and the sanctifying activity of the Spirit as integral components of man's salvation.[2] In so doing, the passage thrice affirms God's work in salvation while man's contribution, conspicuous by its triple absence, is thrice denied. Thus, on a holistic level, the significance of the Trinitarian pattern is to show that salvation results from God's work alone (monergism) and is therefore devoid of any contribution on the part of man. Needless to say, such driving emphasis on the salvific action of God necessarily demands an active sense for the foreknowledge upon which the salvation is based.

But beyond this holistic consideration, the details of the passage support this same conclusion. In the first place, since the work of the Son (sprinkling) and the Spirit (sanctifying) are both active, the Father's foreknowledge must be taken in an active sense in order to maintain the Trinitarian symmetry in the passage. Moreover, since the passage roots the historical operations of the Son and the Spirit in the eternal election and foreknowledge of the Father, the Father's foreknowledge forms the basis for the work of the Son and the Spirit. Consequently, an active sense is again demanded for "foreknowledge" since a cause must be sufficient to its effects. After all, it makes no

---

[2] Theolgians refer to this divine "division of labor" as the Trinitarian economy.

sense to base the work of the Son and the Spirit upon a merely passive knowledge of their future operations. Finally, an active sense of "foreknowledge" is demanded even by the Father's work alone since it makes no sense to base the Father's active choice (election) on a merely passive foreknowledge. Once again, the cause must be sufficient to its effect. From this discussion, then, it may be concluded that the details of the above passage, no less than its major thrust, demand an active sense for "foreknowledge." Given this fact, this passage adds to the cumulative scriptural evidence in favor of divine predestination and the resulting perseverance of God's elect.

To add to this evidence, three parallel passages will now be examined from the Gospel of John which bring out the prominence of this theme in his theology. To begin this discussion consider the first of these passages:

> Then Jesus declared, "I am the bread of life. He who comes to me will never go hungry, and he who believes in me will never be thirsty. But as I told you, you have seen me and still you do not believe. All that the Father gives me will come to me, and whoever comes to me I will never drive away. For I have come down from heaven not to do my will but to do the will of him who sent me. And this is the will of him who sent me, that I shall lose none of all that he has given me, but raise them up at the last day. For my Father's will is that everyone who looks up to the Son and believes in him shall have eternal life, and I will raise him up at the last day."

> At this the Jews began to grumble about him because he said," I am the bread that came down from heaven." They said, "Is this not Jesus, the son of Joseph, whose father and mother we know? How can he now say, 'I came down from heaven?'"
>
> "Stop grumbling among yourselves," Jesus answered. "No one can come to me unless the Father who sent me draws him and I will raise him up at the last day...." (John 6:35-43)

In this passage Jesus says that no one can come to Him unless drawn by the Father, and that He will raise up those so drawn on the last day. He further says that all that the Father has given Him will come to him, and that it is the Father's will that He should lose none of those whom the Father has given Him. Thus, the passage would seem to have two implications. First, no one can come to Christ unless he is first chosen and drawn by the Father, and second, those so drawn are irresistibly drawn since they cannot fall away. In the first instance, then, the passage witnesses to the predestination and security of the elect. Yet, the negative aspect of predestination is also evident from the context of the passage since Jesus is asserting this election and security against those who do not believe despite seeing the Son Himself. After all, since Jesus states that those chosen and drawn by the Father necessarily come to faith in the Son and remain in Him, Jesus is necessarily asserting to the unbelievers that their unbelief results from the fact that they have not been chosen and drawn by the Father. Accordingly, a divine discrimination is evident in the passage since Jesus is clearly implying that this latter group is reprobate.

Consider another passage:

> Jesus answered, "I did tell you but you did not believe. The miracles I do in my Father's name speak for me, but you do not believe because you are not my sheep. My sheep listen to my voice; I know them, and they follow me. I give them eternal life, and they shall never perish; no one can snatch them out of my hand. My Father, who has given them to me is greater than all; no one can snatch them out of my Father's hand. I and the Father are one." (John 10:25-30)

Here, Jesus says that His Father has given His sheep to Him, that He gives His sheep eternal life, and that His sheep are eternally secure since no one can snatch them out of His Father's hand. In short, Christ says that His sheep are given to Him by the Father and protected by the Father from falling away. Once again, therefore, Christ's words attest the predestination and security of the elect since no one comes to Christ apart from the Father's work, and no one so moved can fall away. Yet, as in the previous passage, the negative aspect of predestination is again apparent from the context since Christ is asserting this election and security against those who resist His message. Thus, in stark contrast to Christ's sheep who are drawn and protected by the Father, Jesus tells the unbelievers that they do not believe, even in the face of His unambiguous miracles, because they are not His sheep. In the context of the passage, therefore, Jesus' positive emphasis on the election and security of His sheep is being asserted negatively against the people to whom He is speaking. In fact, Jesus plainly tells them that they are not His sheep. Given this fact, a divine discrimination is again manifest.

Consider a final passage:

> After Jesus said this, he looked toward heaven and prayed:
>
> "Father, the time has come. Glorify your Son, that your Son may glorify you. For you granted him authority over all people that he might give eternal life to all those you have given him....
>
> I have revealed you to those whom you gave me out of the world. They were yours; you gave them to me and they have obeyed your word. Now they know that everything you have given me comes from you. For I gave them the words you gave me and they accepted them. They knew with certainty that I came from you, and they believed that you sent me. I pray for them. I am not praying for the world, but for those you have given me, for they are yours.... Holy Father, protect them by the power of your name — the name you gave me — so that they may be one as we are one. While I was with them, I protected them and kept them safe by that name you gave me. None has been lost except the one doomed to destruction. (John 17:1-12)

In this passage, the doctrine of election is clearly present since Jesus here prays for the protection of a select group (*i.e.*, "those you have given me"). Moreover, since Christ's prayer to the Father is necessarily effective, a doctrine of perseverance is also implied. Furthermore, since these people are repeatedly referred to as those whom the Father has given to Christ, they must form a discreet and stable set in order to be thus transferable. Accordingly, the elect are seen to be eternally secure since both their election and their protection ultimately derive from the Father. Yet, once again, a discrimination in divine election is also indicated since Christ prays for His elect in distinction from the world, and this discrimination is reinforced by the fact that Judas is described as having been doomed to destruction. After all, in saying that "none has been lost except the one doomed to destruction," Christ is necessarily implying that Judas is eternally reprobate, not elect.[3] Thus, while the passage shows the elect to be chosen by God and to persevere necessarily, it also shows the reprobate to be eternally bypassed and thus doomed to perish. Given this fact, a divine discrimination again stands forth.

Having examined several passages, therefore, the doctrine of election and predestination has been shown to be basic to the theology of Paul, Peter, and John. Moreover, in each case a necessarily related doctrine of perseverance is clearly present. Beyond these references, however, examples could be drawn from

---

[3] In support of this interpretation is the fact that Judas is referred to as a devil in John 6:70.

Matthew, Mark, Luke (who also wrote Acts), James, and Jude. In short, direct evidence of this doctrine can be seen in all the writers of the New Testament, except the author of Hebrews. And even in Hebrews the doctrine is implied through God's providential ordering of redemptive-history. But the doctrine goes deeper still since the entire Old Testament is based on the idea of God's covenantal discrimination. After all, in God's saving purpose, Israel was a nation specially chosen for God's salvation in distinction from all the other nations of the world. Consequently, since a discriminating election (with direct or implicit reprobation) therefore emerges as a "deep theological structure" of the entire Bible, attempts to avoid the predestinarian implications of Scripture are futile. In regard to these implications, Luther's comments on Romans 8:28-30 are here cited for perspective:

> This passage is the foundation on which rests everything that the Apostle says to the end of the chapter; for he means to show that to the elect who are loved of God and who love God, the Holy Spirit makes all things work for good even though they are evil. He here takes up the doctrine of predestination or election. This doctrine is not so incomprehensible as many think, but it is rather full of sweet comfort for the elect and for all who have the Holy Spirit. But it is most bitter and hard for the wisdom of the flesh. There is no other reason why the many tribulations and evils cannot separate the saints from the love of God than that they are the called "according to his purpose." Hence God makes

all things work together for good to them, and to them only. If there would not be this divine purpose, but our salvation would rest upon our will or work, it would be based upon chance. How easily in that case could one single evil hinder or destroy it! But the Apostle says: "Who shall lay anything to the charge of God's elect?" "Who is he that condemneth?" "Who shall separate us from the love of Christ?" (8:33, 34, 35), he shows that the elect are not saved by chance, but by God's purpose and will. Indeed for this reason, God allows the elect to encounter so many evil things as are here named, namely, to point out that they are saved not by their merit, but by His election, His unchangeable and firm purpose. They are saved despite their many rapacious and fierce foes and the vain efforts.

What then is there to our own righteousness? to our good works? to the freedom of the will? to chance in the things that occur? That (the denial of these things) is what we must preach, for that means to preach rightly. That means to destroy the wisdom of the flesh. So far the Apostle has destroyed merely the hands, feet, and tongue of the wisdom of the flesh: now he wipes it out utterly. Now he makes us see that it amounts to nothing, and that our salvation altogether lies in His hands. God absolutely recognizes no chance: it is only men who speak of chance. Not a single leaf falls from the tree without the will of the Father. All things are essentially in His hands, and so are also our times.

There are yet three thoughts that should be considered in connection with the subject (of divine predestination). First, there are proofs of God's unchangeable election, gathered from the words of Scripture and His works. The Apostle says: "Who are called according to his purpose." "Purpose" here stands for God's predestination, or His free election, or His (eternal) counsel (regarding the salvation of individual persons)....

The second thought is that all objections to predestination precede from the wisdom of the flesh. Hence, whoever does not deny himself and does not learn to keep his thoughts in subjection to the divine will, never will find an answer to his questions. And that rightly so, for the foolish wisdom of the flesh exalts itself above God and judges His will, just as though this were of little importance. It should rather let itself be judged by God....

The third thought is that this doctrine is indeed most bitter to the wisdom of the flesh, which revolts against it and even becomes guilty of blasphemy on this point. But it is fully defeated when we learn to know that our salvation rests in no wise upon ourselves and our conduct, but is founded solely upon what is outside us, namely, on God's election.

Those who have the wisdom of the Spirit become ineffably happy through the doctrine, as the Apostle himself illustrates this.... Everywhere in Scripture those are praised and encouraged who listen to God's Word with trembling. As they despair of themselves, the Word of God performs its work in them. If we anxiously tremble at God's Word and are terrified by it, this is indeed a good sign.

If one fears that he is not elected or is otherwise troubled about his election, he should be thankful that he has such fear; for then he should surely know that God cannot lie when in Psalm 51:17 He says: "The sacrifices of God are a broken spirit: a broken and contrite heart, O God, thou wilt not despise." Thus he should cheerfully cast himself on the faithfulness of God who gives this promise, and turn away from the foreknowledge of the threatening God. Then he will be saved as one that is elected. It is not the characteristic of reprobates to tremble at the secret counsel of God; but that is the characteristic of the elect. The reprobates despise it, or at least pay no attention to it, or else they declare in the arrogance of their despair: "Well, if I am damned, all right, then I am damned." (Luther, *Commentary on Romans*, 128-132)

The Biblical Case
for Reprobation

8

I n the previous chapter, passages dealing with election and predestination were examined to demonstrate that the doctrine of election is directly attested by Scripture. However, since this discussion largely treated predestination in its positive dimension (namely, the predestination unto life), the issue of reprobation must now be considered. Here, as before, the discussion will largely center on the exposition of selected texts. However, before beginning this examination, it is necessary to explain both the necessity and the major purpose of this chapter.

With respect to purpose, the present chapter might seem superfluous. After all, having already established the positive aspects of predestination, reprobation would seem to follow by a logical necessity. Yet, direct Scriptural evidence is also needed since it is precisely at this point that the Lutheran party demurs against a perceived Calvinistic rationalism. In particular, while agreeing that Scripture attests the election to life, the Lutheran Church argues that the Biblical evidence opposes the doctrine of reprobation. Accordingly, the Lutherans accuse the Calvinists of imposing a logical system upon the Biblical text (eisegesis) rather than reading this doctrine out of the Scriptures themselves (exegesis).[1] Thus, the Lutheran Church affirms only a single predestination (*i.e.*, a predestination unto life alone) in contrast to the double predestination (*i.e.*, a predestination unto both life and death) of the Reformed Church. Given the state of this controversy, then, it would seem that direct Biblical evidence is necessary to decide the issue. Accordingly, to defend

---

[1] In making this charge, however, many Lutheran pastors reveal a studied (and frequently smug) ignorance that it was Luther, and not Calvin, who first came forth with double predestination in the Reformation. Indeed, in 1525 when Calvin was a mere 16 years old, Luther wrote his classic work, *The Bondage of the Will*, in which he systematically defended this doctrine and set it forth as the very hinge of Reformation theology. And far from taking Luther's doctrine to logical and unintended extremes, it was Calvin who originally toned it down by removing the fatalistic elements in Luther's thought. But the doctrine of Luther and Calvin was not new. At this point they were simply following the venerable Augustine who, in turn, got the doctrine from Christ and his Apostles.

Given these facts, it is both ignorant and mean spirited for modern Lutherans to make Calvin the whipping boy in discussions of predestination. Moreover, given the importance of Luther's views to the Reformation generally, it is absolutely stupefying that many Lutheran pastors go through seminary without ever once having read Luther's classic work, *The Bondage of the Will*. While this work is insufficient apart from Scripture to attest the soundness of double predestination, it nevertheless provides the historical evidence of Luther's seminal work on this topic. Thus, while not compelling a Lutheran to agree with Calvin, it should at least compel him to treat Calvin with greater charity.

double predestination against Lutheran charges of rationalism, it will be the burden of the present chapter to show that the doctrine of reprobation is directly attested by Scripture. To this end, the approach here, as in the preceding chapter, will consist of commentary on selected texts.

To begin this discussion, consider the following text from the Gospel of Matthew:

> The disciples came to him and asked, "Why do you speak to the people in parables?"

> He replied, "The knowledge of the secrets of the kingdom of heaven has been given to you, but not to them. Whoever has will be given more, and he will have an abundance. Whoever does not have, even what he has will be taken from him. This is why I speak to them in parables:

> "Though seeing, they do not see; though hearing, they do not hear or understand."

> In them is fulfilled the prophecy of Isaiah:

> You will be ever hearing
> but never understanding;
> you will be ever seeing
> but never perceiving.
> For this people's heart
> has become calloused;
> they hardly hear with their ears,
> and they have closed their eyes.

> Otherwise they might
> see with their eyes,
> hear with their ears,
> understand with their
> hearts and turn,
> and I would heal them."

> But blessed are your eyes because they see,
> and your ears because they hear.
> (Matthew 13:10-16)

With respect to the previous passage, the message of reprobation is clear and follows from several interlocking pieces of evidence. To begin with, Christ explicitly speaks of a discrimination between two groups of people in terms of the distribution of saving knowledge. In particular, while the one group has been given the knowledge of the kingdom of heaven, such knowledge has been deliberately withheld from the second group. Moreover, Christ represents His parabolic speech as the very means by which this discrimination is to be affected since it is designed both to reveal and to conceal the saving truth. Then, in confirmation of this fact, Christ interprets His actions as the fulfillment of Isaiah 6, thereby showing His actions to spring from the deeper ground of God's eternal counsel. Finally, even beyond these acts of divine concealment, the language of the prophecy clearly shows the people to be hardened by sin and therefore incapable of heeding even the clear revelation of God. Consequently, since the people are blind to the truth, and since Christ will not open their eyes, a message of reprobation is clear from the passage. After all, since

He refuses to correct their damning blindness, it is evident that the people perish by divine intent.[2]

Consider a similar passage:

> Then Jesus began to denounce the cities in which most of his miracles had been performed, because they did not repent...." And you, Capernaum, will you be lifted up to the skies? No, you will go down to the depths. If the miracles that were performed in you had been performed in Sodom, it would have

---

[2] I reply: They were thus blind for the praise and the glory of 'free-will', so that this highly-vaunted 'power by which a man can apply himself to things that concern eternal salvation' might be shown up for what it is-namely, a power which neither sees what it sees, nor hears what it hears, much less understands those things, or seeks after them. To it apply the words which Christ and the evangelists so often quote from Isaiah: 'Hearing ye shall hear and shall not understand, and seeing ye shall see and shall not perceive' (6:9). What is this but to say that free-will' (or, the human heart) is so bound by the power of Satan that, unless it be wondrously quickened by the Spirit of God, it cannot of itself see or hear things which strike upon ear and eye so manifestly that they could almost be touched by hand? So great is the misery and blindness of mankind! Thus, too, the very evangelists, when they wondered how it could be that the Jews were not won by the works and words of Christ, incontrovertible and undeniable as they were, answered themselves from that self-same passage of Scripture, which teaches that man, left to himself, seeing sees not and hearing hears not. What is more fantastic? 'The light shineth in darkness, and the darkness comprehendeth it not' (John 1:5). Who would believe it? Who ever heard of such a thing? — that light should shine in darkness, yet the darkness remain darkness, and not receive illumination (Luther, *The Bondage of the Will*, 132).

remained to this day. But I tell you that it will be more bearable for Sodom on the day of judgment than for you."

At that time Jesus said, "I praise you, Father, Lord of heaven and earth, because you have hidden these things from the wise and learned, and revealed them to little children. Yes, Father, for this was your good pleasure." (Matthew 11:20-26)

In the passage above, a number of factors combine to provide a strong witness to reprobation. First, since it is immediately after denouncing Capernaum that God is said to conceal the truth, it is obvious that the residents of Capernaum are perishing by divine intent. Moreover, in saying that God reveals the truth to the simple and not the wise, Jesus directly attributes salvation and damnation to a divine discrimination. Furthermore, since one would normally expect the wise, and not the simple, to have the greater comprehension of the truth, the reversal of these expectations here underscores the fact that saving knowledge is not grasped by human ability but rather is given by God alone to those whom He so chooses. Finally, the fact that the citizens of Capernaum did not repent in the face of Jesus' evident miracles brings their reprobation into bold relief since it clarifies both the nature of their problem and thus the manner in which God's "revelation" is said to be hidden from them. After all, since God's external revelation was abundantly clear, it is obvious that their problem was a lack of internal revelation (*i.e.*, illumination or regeneration) resulting in the continuing hardness of their unregenerate hearts. Accordingly, when Christ thanks the Father for hiding and revealing the truth, He is not referring to external revelation but rather is thanking the Father for regenerating the simple and bypassing the wise. Given this fact, the witness of the above passage to reprobation could not be more clear.[3]

Another passage giving direct evidence of reprobation comes from I Peter:

> Now to you who believe, this stone is precious. But to those who do not believe,
>
>> "The stone the builders rejected
>> has become the capstone."
>
> and,
>
>> "A stone that causes men to stumble
>> and a rock that makes them fall."
>
> They stumble because they disobey the message — which is also what they were destined for.

---

[3] For the sake of completeness, it should be added that while these people were not subjects of God's election (decretive will), they were nevertheless under obligation (preceptive will) to receive God's external revelation. Thus, Jesus denounced the citizens for their obstinance even though they were not eternally elect. After all, while they were not internally capacitated to receive God's revelation, such revelation was nevertheless a gracious act on God's part, the rejection of which rendered them culpable. Thus, God's external revelation was not without its effect. While it was not sufficient to save them apart from His gracious election, it was clearly sufficient to increase their guilt.

But you are a chosen people, a royal priesthood, a holy nation, a people belonging to
God that you may declare the praises of him
who called you out of darkness into his wonderful light. Once you were not a people, but
now you are a people of God; once you had
not received mercy, but now you have received mercy. (I Peter 2:7-10)

In this passage the note of reprobation is most clear
since Peter directly refers to unbelievers as being "destined" to stumble at the message of Christ. Moreover,
this conclusion is strengthened by the fact that the
Greek verb τιθημι which is here translated as "destined" ordinarily means to place, put, or set.
Consequently, since the semantic range of this verb is
entirely active, it must refer to a destinating activity
of God and not to some passive foreknowledge of
events. Thus, barring a metaphorical interpretation of
the verb, the direct language of the passage would
seem to attest the doctrine of reprobation. To resolve
the issue definitely, however, it is necessary to turn to
the context of the passage.

With regard to context, it should be noted that the
entire passage is governed by an overriding contrast
which juxtaposes the divergent destinies of two
groups. In particular, while the one group is chosen in
God's mercy to be His people, the other is destined to
stumble at the message of Christ. Now the significance of this fact is that a specific contrast requires
and therefore implies a generic similarity among the
contrasting elements. For instance, when it is said that
black and white are opposites, it is in the very nature

of such a contrast to imply that both are colors. Given these observations, the above contrast between the specific destinies of two groups underscores the more generic and basic truth that both groups are destined. In other words, the predestination unto death in the present passage is underscored by an equal and opposite predestination unto life. Thus, when Peter speaks of the one group as being "destined" to stumble at the message of Christ, the context of the passage confirms that his direct language is to be taken at face value with the verb τιθημι translated in its natural sense and not obscured by some metaphorical twisting of its meaning. In short, the combination of the specific verb used by Peter together with the overriding contrast of the passage itself render its witness to reprobation unassailable.

Additional evidence for Peter's view may be obtained from several parallel passages dealing with the reprobation of false teachers:

> In their greed these teachers will exploit you with stories they have made up. Their condemnation has long been hanging over them, and their destruction has not been sleeping. (II Peter 2:3)

> But these men blaspheme in matters they do not understand. They are like brute beasts, creatures of instinct, born only to be caught and destroyed, and like beasts they too will perish. (II Peter 2:12)

> These men are springs without water and mists driven by a storm. Blackest darkness is reserved for them. (II Peter 2:17)

On the basis of these passages, the previous assessment of Peter's view is confirmed. After all, in saying that the false teachers have been born unto a reserved destruction, Peter straightforwardly affirms the doctrine of reprobation Given this fact, the above passages provide solid Biblical evidence for reprobation which is both clear and unassailable. Once again, therefore, the doctrine of reprobation is seen to be scripturally attested and not drawn from a mere doctrinal inference.

A similar theme is also evident in the Johanine writings. In this regard, two brief passages from Revelation are most significant:

> All inhabitants of the earth will worship the beast — all whose names have not been written from the creation of the world in the book of life belonging to the lamb that was slain. (Revelation 13:8)

> The inhabitants of the earth whose names have not been written in the book of life from the creation of the world will be astonished when they see the beast, because he once was, now is not, yet will come. (Revelation 17:8)

On the basis of the above passages, a doctrine of reprobation is clearly implied from the divine operations surrounding the book of life. After all, while it is obvious from the very name of this book that those recorded in it will live, it is directly stated by the passages themselves that those omitted from it will perish. Moreover, since such recording is said to precede the foundation of the earth, it is clear that God Himself does the recording and omitting. Thus, the destiny of each individual would seem to hinge upon the divine recording or omission of his name since all the recorded ones live and all the omitted ones die. So understood, the above passages set forth an exhaustive correlation between God's activity and human destiny. The only remaining problem, therefore, is the proper delineation of cause and effect.

However, when the broader Biblical data are examined, there is every reason to believe that God's action is the here cause and not the effect of human destiny. That is to say, the presence or absence of names in God's book is the very cause of human destiny and not merely the result of God foreknowing the destiny of particular individuals. To see this point, note first of all that it is the elect whose names are recorded in the book of life and the reprobate whose names are omitted. Consequently, since Jesus elsewhere says that the elect cannot be deceived (Matthew 24:24), it is clear that the elect are protected by God due to the eternal recording of their names. In other words, it is the eternal recording of their names in the book of life that causes their perseverance, and not their foreknown perseverance which causes their names to be so recorded. However, if the elect are protected by the eternal recording of their names, then the reprobate are at the least denied such protection by their eternal omission, and since such protection is essential for their salvation, the reprobate necessarily fall.[4]

---

[4] In this regard, it must be said that the omission of the reprobate from the book of life is the negative ground of their perishing. The positive ground, by contrast, is their personal guilt before God from both original and actual sin.

Consequently, since the reprobate fall by virtue of a divine omission, it follows that the reprobate perish by divine intent. Given this fact, a doctrine of reprobation is clearly implied.

On the basis of the preceding development, it should be clear that reprobation is directly attested by Scripture itself and not merely a doctrinal inference. If any doubt remains, however, such doubt should be obliterated by the following passage. Of all the passages dealing with reprobation, Romans 9:10-24 is the classic text since its implications in this regard are clear and strong. Accordingly, this text together with Luther's comments upon it has been saved for a *grand finali*:

> Not only that, but Rebekah's children had one and the same father, our father Isaac. Yet, before the twins were born or had done anything good or bad — in order that God's purpose according to election might stand: not by works but by him who calls — she was told, "The older will serve the younger." Just as it is written: "Jacob I loved, but Esau I hated."

> What then shall we say? Is God unjust? Not at all! For he says to Moses,

> "I will have mercy on whom I have mercy,
>   and I will have compassion
>   on whom I have compassion."

> It does not, therefore, depend on man's desire or effort, but on God's mercy. For the

Scripture says to Pharaoh: "I raised you up for this very purpose, that I might display my power in you and that my name might be proclaimed in all the earth." Therefore, God has mercy on whom he wants to have mercy, and he hardens whom he wants to harden.

One of you will say to me: "Then why does God still blame us? For who resists his will?" But who are you, O man, to talk back to God: "Shall what is formed say to him who formed it, 'Why did you make me like this'?" Does not the potter have the right to make out of the same lump of clay some pottery for noble purposes and some for common use?

What if God, choosing to show his wrath and make his power known, bore with great patience the objects of his wrath — prepared for destruction? What if he did this to make the riches of his glory known to the objects of his mercy, whom he prepared in advance for glory — even us, whom he also called, not only from the Jews but also from the Gentiles?

As should be evident from the above passage, its witness to reprobation is clear and strong, stemming as it does from converging lines of direct and indirect evidence. With respect to the direct evidence, four of Paul's pointed remarks independently attest this doctrine. To begin with, Paul attributes the divergent destinies of Jacob and Esau to the discriminating love and hatred of God, thereby extending predestination to the reprobate as well as the elect. Then, to reinforce this point, Paul asserts the foreordination of Pharaoh's destruction by describing him as a foil for the revelation of God's power. Moreover, to set forth the equal ultimacy of election and reprobation, Paul next compares God's action in salvation to that of a potter making noble and common vessels out of the same lump of clay. Finally, expounding God's discrimination in the plainest language, Paul refers to the elect as objects of mercy prepared in advance for glory and to the reprobate as objects of wrath prepared for destruction. Thus, through several direct statements, Paul unflinchingly asserts the foreordained destruction of the reprobate. However, beyond this direct evidence, it is the anticipated objections of Paul's opponents that clinches the case for reprobation: "Then why does God still blame us? For who resists his will?" After all, since this is the common objection to reprobation, its presence in Paul's argument provides the strongest evidence that Paul is speaking of reprobation in the first place and that the above inferences have therefore been correctly drawn from the passage. Consequently, since this interpretative benchmark confirms the inferences drawn above, the cumulative evidence adduced in favor of reprobation is seen to be strong and unimpeachable.

As a result of the foregoing discussion, the doctrine of reprobation is seen to rest upon strong scriptural evidence and therefore cannot be dismissed as a doctrinal imposition. Moreover, as will be seen from Luther's discussion below, the doctrine cannot be passed off as a "Calvinist" view either. Having examined the scriptural evidence, therefore, it remains to consider some of Luther's comments on Romans 9.

In this regard, Luther's treatment of Pharaoh will be omitted below since it more closely fits the subject matter of Chapter 4 where it has already been employed:

> As for the passage of Malachi which Paul appends, "Jacob have I loved, but Esau have I hated" (1:2-3), the Diatribe contrives three distinct methods of wresting it. The first is this: "If you press the literal sense, God does not love as we love, nor does He hate anyone, for passions of this kind do not overtake God."
>
> What do I hear? Do we now inquire how God loves and hates and not rather why He loves and hates? The question is, through what merit on our part does He love and hate? We know well enough that God does not love and hate as we do for we love and hate inconstantly, but He loves and hates according to His eternal and immutable nature. Thus it is that unexpected incidents and passions do not overtake God. And it is just this that compels the conclusion that there is no such thing as "free-will": namely, the fact that the love and hate of God towards men is immutable and eternal, existing, not merely before there was any merit or work of "free-will," but before the world was made; and that all things take place in us of necessity, according as He has from eternity loved or not loved. So not only the fact of God's love, but even the manner of His loving, imposes necessity on us. You see how much its evasions profit the Diatribe; the more it strives to get away from the truth, the more

95

it everywhere crashes into it — so unsuc-
cessfully does it struggle against it!

...Now, God either loves or hates what He
wills. Tell me, then, by what desert is Jacob
loved and Esau hated before they were born
and began to work? Paul therefore stands
vindicated as quoting Malachi most aptly to
support the statement of Moses — that is,
that God called Jacob before he was born, because He loved him, and that He was not loved
by Jacob first, nor influenced by any desert on
Jacob's part. Thus the case of Jacob and Esau
shows what power our "free-will" has!

...Paul proves from Malachi that this affliction
was laid on Esau without reference to desert,
by reason of God's hatred alone, and thence
concludes that "free-will" is nonexistent.

...Paul teaches that faith and unbelief come to
us by no work of our own, but through the love
and hatred of God. (Luther, *The Bondage of
the Will*, 225-229)

Now I return to Paul. If in Romans 9 he does
not explain this point, and clearly state that
we are under necessity by virtue of the foreknowledge and will of God, why need he
have introduced the analogy of the potter,
who makes of the self same clay one vessel
to honour and another to dishonour; and yet
the thing formed does not say to him that
formed it: "Why hast thou made me thus?"

(cf. 9:20-21). He is speaking of men, comparing them to clay and God to a potter. The comparison is surely pointless — inappropriate, indeed, and futile — if he does not think that our freedom is nil. Yes, and in that case Paul's whole argument in defense of grace is futile. (Luther, *The Bondage of the Will*, 218,219)

In a word, if your evasion stands, Paul's entire argument falls to the ground. It is pointless for him to introduce persons grumbling against the Divine potter, if it appears that the fault is not in the potter, but in the vessels; for who would grumble if he were to hear of the damnation of one that merited damnation? (Luther,*The Bondage of the Will*, 232)

What was your inquiry about the will of God? Was it not, whether it imposes necessity on our will? Paul is replying that it is so: "He has mercy on whom he will have mercy, and whom he will he hardeneth. It is not of him that willeth, nor of him that runneth, but of God that showeth mercy" (vv. 15, 16, 18). Not content with having given this explanation, he goes on to introduce those who in the name of "free-will" grumble against it, and rattle on to the effect that there is then no merit, and we are damned through no fault of our own, and the like; and he silences their grumbling and displeasure, saying: "Thou sayest to me then, Why doth He yet find fault? for who shall resist His will?" (v. 19). Do you see to whom he addresses himself? To those who, when they hear that the will of God brings necessity upon us, blasphemously complain and say: "Why doth He yet find fault?" That is, "Why does God thus press, urge, exact and so find fault? Why does He accuse? Why does He reprove? As though we men could do what He requires, if we would! He has no just cause for His complaint; let Him rather accuse His own will; there let Him find fault, and press His demands! "For who shall resist His will?" Who can obtain mercy when that is not His will? Who can be softened, if He wills to harden? It is not in our power to change His will, much less to resist it when it wills our hardening; by that will we are compelled to be hardened, willy-nilly!"

If Paul had not explained this point, and definitely assured us that necessity is imposed upon us by the foreknowledge of God, what need was there to introduce these objectors, who complain that His will cannot be resisted? Who would object or take offense, if he did not think that this necessity had been enunciated?...

The apostle, therefore, is bridling the ungodly who take offense at his plain speaking, telling them they should realize that the Divine will is fulfilled by what to us is necessity, and that it is definitely established that no freedom or "free-will" is left them, but all things depend on the will of God alone. And he bridles them by commanding them to be silent, and to revere the majesty of God's power and will, against which we have no rights, but which has full rights against us to do what It pleases. No injustice is done to us, for God owes us nothing, He has received nothing from us, and He has promised us nothing but what He pleased and willed.

...Is this not an audacious way of searching, to try and harmonize the wholly free foreknowledge of God with our own freedom, and to be ready to deny the foreknowledge of God if it does not allow us freedom and if it imposes necessity upon us, to say with the blasphemous complainers: "Why doth He yet find fault? For who shall resist His will? Where is the God Whose nature is kindness itself? Where is He that willeth not the death of the sinner? Has He created us merely to delight Himself in men's torments?" — and the like: which sentiments the damned in hell will be howling out to all eternity. (Luther, *The Bondage of the Will*, 214-216)

Doubtless it gives the greatest possible offense to common sense or natural reason, that God, Who is proclaimed as being full of mercy and goodness, and so on, should of His own mere will abandon, harden and damn men, as though He delighted in the sins and great eternal torments of such poor

99

wretches. It seems an iniquitous, cruel, intolerable thought to think of God; and it is this that has been a stumbling block to so many great men down the ages. And who would not stumble at it? I have stumbled at it myself more than once, down to the deepest pit of despair, so that I wished I had never been made a man. (That was before I knew how health-giving that despair was, and how close to grace.) That is why so much toil and trouble has been devoted to clearing the goodness of God, and throwing the blame on man's will.... None the less, the arrow of conviction has remained, fastened deep in the hearts of learned and unlearned alike, whenever they have made a serious approach to the matter, so that they are aware that, if the foreknowledge and omnipotence of God are admitted, then we must be under necessity. (Luther, *The Bondage of the Will*, 217, 218)

Thus God conceals His eternal mercy and loving kindness beneath eternal wrath, His righteousness beneath unrighteousness. Now, the highest degree of faith is to believe that He is merciful, though He saves so few and damns so many; to believe that He is just, though of His own will He makes us perforce proper subjects for damnation, and seems (in Erasmus' words) "to delight in the torments of poor wretches and to be a fitter object for hate than for love." If I could by any means understand how this same

100

God, who makes such a show of wrath and unrighteousness, can yet be merciful and just, there would be no need for faith. But as it is, the impossibility of understanding makes room for the exercise of faith when these things are preached and published; just as, when God kills, faith in life is exercised in death. (Luther, *The Bondage of the Will*, 101)[5]

---

[5] In many of the quotes above, Luther states that the reprobate are damned apart from demerit just as the elect are saved apart from merit. In this regard, Luther's doctrine is unduly harsh and arbitrary because he seems to imply that God damns those who are not truly guilty. The reason for this harshness is that Luther does not consistently distinguish between ultimate and proximate causation and therefore fails to see that predestination establishes human responsibility. Consequently, while properly noting that the elect are undeservedly saved, Luther often fails to note that the reprobate are deservedly damned. Thus, due to his fatalistic tendencies, Luther fails to account for a certain asymmetry in the relationship of merit to reward (see the next chapter) and thus fails to properly maintain the fairness of the doctrine.

The Asymmetry of Election and Reprobation

9

Having examined the Biblical evidence for election and reprobation, God's predestination has been shown to extend to the reprobate as well as the elect. Thus, the doctrine of "double predestination" would seem to be scripturally attested. In spite of this abundant scriptural evidence, however, opponents continue to assail the doctrine on the basis of other Biblical texts which are alleged to deny predestination. To secure the Biblical argument for predestination, therefore, it will be necessary in several following chapters to examine these so called "problem texts."

Before proceeding along these lines, however, it will be necessary in the present chapter to attack the common psychological ground of these various objections. In this regard, it should be observed that the primary motivation for bringing the various objections forward is the perception that predestination is unfair. In response to this underlying motivation, it will be argued herein that predestination is most fair due to the fact that election and reprobation manifest asymmetric relationships of merit to reward and involve asymmetric modes of divine action. Accordingly, before considering the so called "problem texts," the ethical implications of these asymmetries will here be examined in order to demonstrate the fairness of predestination and thereby destroy the various objections at their common psychological root. To begin this discussion, the implications of the merit-reward asymmetry will first be considered.

With respect to the merit-reward relationship, the asymmetry of predestination results from the fact that the elect are saved in spite of guilt while the reprobate are damned because of it. In other words, the normal relation between demerit and punishment is graciously suspended for the elect and justly maintained for the reprobate. Thus, while the elect are graciously saved, the reprobate are justly damned. So understood, the doctrine of predestination is most fair since no one is damned apart from personal guilt. Of course, if a perfect symmetry prevailed, the doctrine would be most unfair since the reprobate would then be as undeservedly damned as the elect are undeservedly saved. However, due to the merit-reward asymmetry, justice (fairness) and grace are each maintained since God damns the deserving and saves the undeserving. Thus, God's action is like that of a wealthy benefactor who ransoms certain criminals from prison (*i.e.*, pays the just price for their release) while leaving the rest to suffer for their crimes. While such action is clearly gracious, it is not unfair since no one suffers apart from personal guilt. In a similar manner, God's predestination is also fair because the merit-reward asymmetry allows for the simultaneous combination of justice and grace.[1]

Beyond the merit-reward relationship, however, election and reprobation also manifest a modal asymmetry with respect to the manner of divine action as noted above. In particular, while God leaves the reprobate to themselves and governs them according to His general providence, He actively intervenes in the lives of His elect to change their ultimate destiny.

---

[1] In this regard, Luther's doctrine of predestination was unduly harsh since it did not consistently recognize the proper asymmetry in the merit-reward relationship. Thus, in some of the quotes above, Luther's thought degenerates into a fatalism where human responsibility vanishes so that people are both saved and damned without regard to merit. In other words, Luther sometimes implies a complete symmetry between election and reprobation so that the reprobate are damned apart from guilt, even as the elect are saved apart from merit. In this regard, Luther's failure to recognize the proper asymmetry and thus attribute damnation to human guilt most likely resulted from his failure to maintain the distinction between God's ultimate and man's proximate causation and thereby see how God's predestination establishes human responsibility. In other words, Luther attempted to account for predestination within a unicausal (God or man) rather than a dicausal (God and man) framework and was therefore forced to employ an "either/or" rather than a "both/and" approach to the doctrine. As a consequence of his unicausal framework, therefore, Luther was forced to deny man's proximate causation in order to maintain God's predestination. Thus, there was a fatalistic strain in Luther's thought which caused him to neglect human responsibility and therefore to miss the asymmetric merit-reward relationship between election and reprobation. As a result, Luther's views were unduly harsh. Fortunately, however, this fatalistic strain was by no means consistent, since he elsewhere recognized the validity of human choice and human guilt.

Accordingly, the modal asymmetry consists in the fact that while God does positive good to His elect, He does no harm to the reprobate. To see this point consider the following analogy. Imagine man to be like a lead ball, falling under the weight of His sin just as a ball falls by virtue of its physical weight. Suppose further that there are two such balls falling into a fiery furnace when God suddenly changes one of the balls into a Helium balloon which then floats to safety even as the other ball continues into the fire. Now in both cases, God's predestination is equally absolute, but it operates according to different modes. In this regard, the second ball corresponds to the reprobate who are governed by God's general providence. Accordingly, just as God creates and sustains both the nature (weight) and environment (gravity) of the ball, so God predestines sinful man through His general providence by working in harmony with the human nature and the human environment which He has created. And just as God did not add weight to the falling ball, so God does not intervene to infuse additional evil into the reprobate. In contrast to this case, however, the first ball corresponds to the elect who are saved by a direct intervention of God's saving grace. Accordingly, just as God directly intervened to transform the ball and change its course, so God intervenes to transform His elect and change their direction. And just as God intervened to change the very nature of the first ball, so God intervenes to infuse goodness into His elect.[2]

---

[2] While the above analogy accurately illustrates the modal asymmetry of election and reprobation, a vital distinction must be maintained between the salvation of the elect and the transformation of the ball in the example above. In this regard, it must be maintained that the transformation of the ball mirrors only the sanctification of the elect whose behavior is radically changed as a result of the goodness [continued]

that God infuses into them. However, since man is saved as a result of imputed and not infused grace, the above analogy could suggest heretical conclusions if pressed beyond its intended limits. After all, if a man were saved by virtue of an infused goodness, man would then attempt to merit his salvation by works, albeit by the works of a graciously changed nature. But such a works salvation would be impossible for two reasons. First, man's sanctification is not perfect in this life and therefore cannot measure up to God's perfect standard. Second, even if man's sanctification were perfect, it would do nothing to alleviate the guilt of previous or original sin. Consequently, since man is guilty, he cannot be saved by virtue of an infused goodness.

Accordingly, in salvation the Holy Spirit brings man into a vital union with Christ which addresses both the guilt and the pollution of sin. With respect to guilt, the positive merits of Christ's holy life and his sacrificial death are imputed to the believer (reckoned to his account) to remove his guilt and thus his liability to punishment. Consequently, the legal status of the believer is changed from guilty to innocent. This change in the believer's legal status is referred to as justification and is a legal (forensic) effect external to the believer. With respect to pollution, the dominion of sin is broken as the Holy Spirit infuses Christ's holy character into the believer. Thus, the character of the believer is changed from evil to good with the result that the pollution of sin is gradually reversed (though never eliminated in life). This change in the believer's ethical status is called sanctification and is a character effect internal to the believer.

Justification and sanctification are therefore twin effects of the believer's union with Christ which answer to the guilt and pollution of sin. On the one hand, therefore, justification and sanctification may not be separated from one another in the life of the believer since both flow from a vital union with Christ. Thus, justification never occurs apart from sanctification. On the other hand, justification and sanctification cannot be theologically confused since it is the former alone which removes the guilt of sin. Consequently, while sanctification cannot be abstractly separated from justification, it is not the cause of justification either. In other words, (to use an electrical analogy) because justification and sanctification are inseparable parallel effects, and not series effects, salvation can neither be separated from personal holiness, nor based upon personal holiness. Consequently, unlike the lead ball in the above analogy which is saved by virtue of its transformation to Helium, man is not saved on the basis of an infused righteousness. To make such a jump would strain the above analogy beyond its intended limits.

Thus, beyond the merit-reward asymmetry considered previously, election and reprobation are seen to manifest a modal asymmetry with respect to the manner of divine action. In particular, while God governs the reprobate in strict accordance with their nature, God directly intervenes to change the nature and destiny of His elect. Thus, the asymmetry consists in the fact that while God infuses good into His elect, He most emphatically does not infuse evil into the reprobate. So understood, the doctrine of predestination is most fair since God does good for His elect without harming the reprobate. Of course, if God acted symmetrically in election and reprobation, predestination would be unfair, for God would then infuse evil into the reprobate, even as He imparted goodness to His elect. Accordingly, God would then be unfair and arbitrary in blaming the reprobate for an evil which He Himself put into them. However, due to the modal asymmetry noted above, a complete fairness is maintained since God helps the elect without harming the reprobate. Consequently, while both groups are infallibly predestined in every detail of their existence, there is a modal distinction whereby God intervenes to change the nature and destiny of the elect without intervening to change the reprobate. Rather, since God works in accordance with the nature of this latter group, they freely do God's bidding apart from any violence being done to their wills. Accordingly, the doctrine of predestination is most fair because its modal asymmetry allows for the simultaneous combination of grace and justice.

On the basis of the previous discussion, predestination has been shown to manifest a twofold asymmetry.

With respect to merit and reward, the elect are seen to be saved in spite of sin while the reprobate are damned because of it. Moreover, with respect to the mode of divine action, God intervenes to change the nature and destiny of the elect while working in strict accordance with the nature of the reprobate (*i.e.*, not intervening to harm them). In both respects, therefore, the elect are graciously aided while the reprobate are justly left to their chosen course. So understood, election is seen to form the positive ground of salvation, since it is the very basis of God's gracious intervention. By contrast, reprobation forms only the negative ground of one's perishing since it implies no more than a lack of saving intervention with respect to one's freely chosen course. Accordingly, the reprobate can no more grumble against the justice of God's operations than a man jumping from a tall building could blame God for not catching him. Given this fact, the doctrine of predestination is seen to be most fair, and this essential fairness, when properly grasped, eliminates the psychological and motivational ground for the various objections against it.

With respect to the mode of divine operations, Luther's comments are particularly sound:

> Let none think, when God is said to harden or work evil in us (for hardening is working evil) that he does it by, as it were, creating fresh evil in us, as you might imagine an ill-disposed innkeeper, a bad man himself, pouring and mixing poison into a vessel that was not bad, while the vessel itself does nothing, but is merely the recipient, or passive

vehicle, of the mixer's own ill-will. When men hear us say that God works both good and evil in us, and that we are subject to God's working by mere passive necessity, they seem to imagine a man who is in himself good, and not evil, having an evil work wrought in him by God: for they do not sufficiently bear in mind how incessantly active God is in all his creatures, allowing none of them to keep holiday. He who would understand these matters, however, should think thus: God works evil in us (that is, by means of us) not through God's own fault, but by reason of our own defect. We being evil by nature, and God being good, when He impels us to act by His own acting upon us according to the nature of His omnipotence, good though He is in Himself, He cannot but do evil by our evil instrumentally; although, according to His wisdom, He makes good use of this evil for His own glory and for our salvation.

Thus God, finding Satan's will evil, not creating it so (it became so by Satan's sinning and God's withdrawing), carries it along by His own operation and moves it where He wills: although Satan's will does not cease to be evil in virtue of this movement of God....

Thus God hardens Pharaoh: He presents to the ungodly, evil will of Pharaoh His own word and work, which Pharaoh's will hates, by reason of its own inbred fault and natural

110

corruption. God does not alter that will within by His Spirit, but goes on presenting and bringing pressure to bear; and Pharaoh, having in mind his own strength, wealth and power, trusts to them by this same fault of his nature. So it comes to pass that, being inflated and uplifted by the idea of his own greatness, and growing vaingloriously scornful of lowly Moses and of the unostentatious word of God, he becomes hardened; and then grows more and more irked and annoyed, the more Moses presses and threatens him. His evil will would not have been moved or hardened of itself, but as the omnipotent Agent makes it act (as He does the rest of His creatures) by means of His own inescapable movement, it needs must actively will something. As soon as God presents to it from without something that naturally irritates and offends it, Pharaoh cannot escape being hardened, even as he cannot escape the acting of Divine omnipotence and the perversion and villainy of his own will. So God's hardening of Pharaoh is wrought thus: God presents from without to his villainous heart that which by nature he hates; at the same time, He continues by omnipotent action to move within him the evil will which He finds there. Pharaoh, by reason of the villainy of his will, cannot but hate what opposes him, and trust to his own strength; and he grows so obstinate that he will not listen nor reflect, but is swept along in the grip of Satan like a raging madman. (Luther, *The Bondage of the Will*, 206, 207)

111

Objections to Reprobation; the Universal Benevolence of God[1]

10

In the previous chapter, the fairness of predestination was advanced on the basis of a twofold asymmetry between election and reprobation. In this regard, it was shown that while God graciously and positively intervenes to save His elect, He bypasses the reprobate to the just condemnation of their sins. Consequently, since the reprobate are guilty before God, and since God's bypassing action does them no positive harm, predestination was seen to be most fair. As a result, the psychological ground for objecting to predestination vanishes since it is precisely an alleged unfairness that provides the motivation for objecting against it.

Accordingly, having generally answered the objecting mind set, it remains to consider some of the specific

---

[1] In seeking to harmonize the doctrine of reprobation with those texts expressing a universal benevolence of God, the method employed in the present chapter differs from Luther's approach. With regard to this class of texts, Luther argued along the lines presented in the following chapter by distinguishing between the decretive and preceptive wills of God. Thus, the present chapter represents a divergence from a strict exposition of Luther's theology.

exegetical arguments advanced against predestination. To this end, the next four chapters will examine different classes of Biblical texts which are commonly brought forth. In considering these texts, it will be shown that the objections arising from them result from a deficient understanding of the texts themselves, and that their proper interpretation well accords with the doctrine of predestination. Thus, it will be the aim of the following discussion to show that the so called "problem texts" are actually no problem at all.

In considering the various classes of texts advanced by the opponents of predestination, perhaps the most common concern is the universal benevolence of God. Of these, the following passages are frequently cited:

> For God has bound all men over to disobedience so that He may have mercy on them all. (Romans 11:32)

> This is good, and pleases God our Savior, who wants all men to be saved and to come to a knowledge of the truth. (I Timothy 2:3,4)

> The Lord is not slow in keeping his promise, as some understand slowness. He is patient with you, not wanting anyone to perish, but everyone to come to repentance. (II Peter 3:9)[2]

---

[2] Note that in this last passage an antipredestinarian bias has influenced the NIV translation, since the Greek words τινας and παντας are plural and should therefore be translated simply and indefinitely as ":any" and "all," not as "anyone" and "everyone."

114

At first glance the above texts seem to imply a desire on God's part to save every individual, and since such a desire would surely militate against a doctrine of reprobation, it is most natural that opponents of pre-destination would appeal to such texts. However, to the extent that this surface interpretation is false, such objections necessarily fall to the ground. Accordingly, to evaluate soundness of these objections, it is necessary to determine the proper interpretation of the texts in question. In particular, it is necessary to determine whether or not the above texts imply a desire on God's part to save every individual.

To make this determination, the three texts cited above must first be juxtaposed with parallel passages by the same authors carrying a seemingly opposite sense:

> Not only that, but Rebekah's children had one and the same father, our father Isaac. Yet, before the twins were born or had done any-thing good or bad — in order that God's purpose according to election might stand: not by works but by him who calls — she was told, "The older will serve the younger." Just as it is written: "Jacob I loved, but Esau I hated."

> What then shall we say? Is God unjust? Not at all! For he says to Moses,

> "I will have mercy
> on whom I have mercy,
> and I will have compassion
> on whom I have compassion."

It does not, therefore, depend on man's desire or effort, but on God's mercy. For the Scripture says to Pharaoh: "I raised you up for this very purpose, that I might display my power in you and that my name might be proclaimed in all the earth." Therefore, God has mercy on whom he wants to have mercy, and he hardens whom he wants to harden.

One of you will say to me: "Then why does God still blame us? For who resists his will?" But who are you, O man, to talk back to God: "Shall what is formed say to him who formed it, 'Why did you make me like this'?" Does not the potter have the right to make out of the same lump of clay some pottery for noble purposes and some for common use?

What if God, choosing to show his wrath and make his power known, bore with great patience the objects of his wrath — prepared for destruction? What if he did this to make the riches of his glory known to the objects of his mercy, whom he prepared in advance of glory — even us, whom he also called, not only from the Jews but also from the Gentiles (Romans 9:10-25)?

Now to you who believe, this stone is precious. But to those who do not believe,

> "The stone the builders rejected
> has become the capstone."

116

and,

"A stone that causes men to stumble
and a rock that makes them fall."

They stumble because they disobey the message — which is also what they were destined for.

But you are a chosen people, a royal priesthood, a holy nation, a people belonging to God that you may declare the praises of him who called you out of darkness into his wonderful light. Once you were not a people, but now you are a people of God; once you had not received mercy, but now you have received mercy. (I Peter 2:7-10)

In their greed these teachers will exploit you with stories they have made up. Their condemnation has long been hanging over them, and their destruction has not been sleeping. (II Peter 2:3)

But these men blaspheme in matters they do not understand. They are like brute beasts, creatures of instinct, born only to be caught and destroyed, and like beasts they too will perish. (II Peter 2:12)

These men are springs without water and mists driven by a storm. Blackest darkness is reserved for them. (II Peter 2:17)

As should be evident by inspection and as shown also in Chapter 8, the above passages provide an unimpeachable witness to the doctrine of reprobation. Given this fact, a profound tension arises when these passages are juxtaposed with those in the first set above. After all, when the two sets are compared, diverse statements by the same authors seem to contradict one another with the first set denying and the second set affirming reprobation.

However, since the Bible is God's inerrant and infallible word, it cannot contradict itself and must therefore manifest a harmony of meaning among its various passages. Consequently, the perceived tension between the two sets of passages must be apparent only and must therefore arise from a false interpretation. Moreover, since the second set of passages has previously been shown to set forth an unimpeachable witness to reprobation, the interpretative error must therefore center on the first set of passages. Given this fact, the passages in the first set above must be regarded as obscure since their true sense differs from that which is immediately apparent. However, since Scripture must be internally consistent with itself, it is a principle of Biblical interpretation that Scripture be used to interpret Scripture and, therefore, that the meaning of obscure passages be obtained in light of those more clear. Accordingly, since the second of passages provides a clear and unimpeachable witness to reprobation, it is necessary to interpret the obscure passages of the first set in a manner consistent with these latter passages.

Now in seeking to interpret the first set of passages, the word "all" is of central importance. Since the passages uniformly indicate that God would have "all" to be saved, it is necessary to determine whether this "all" may be interpreted in such a way as not to include every individual. To this end, two stages will be necessary. First, to establish the possibility of such usage, it must be shown by solid Biblical example that the word "all" can be used in such a noninclusive sense. Then, having established the possibility of such usage, its actual occurrence in the above passages must be demonstrated by showing this usage to function harmoniously within their particular contexts. Once these steps have been accomplished, both the possibility and the actuality of this noninclusive sense will have been demonstrated for the passages in the first set above. Accordingly, since they will then be seen to imply a noninclusive benevolence, their compatibility with reprobation will be clear. However, before demonstrating this major point, the possibility of this noninclusive usage must first be established. To this end, the following texts have been listed below:

> And so John came, baptizing in the desert region and preaching a baptism of repentance for the forgiveness of sins. The whole Judean countryside and all the people of Jerusalem went out to him. Confessing their sins they were baptized by him in the Jordan River. (Mark 1:4,5)

> There came a man who was sent from God; his name was John. He came as a witness to testify concerning that light, so that through him all men might believe. He himself was

119

not the light; he came only as a witness to the light. The true light that gives light to every man was coming into the world. (John 1:6-9)

You will be betrayed even by parents, brothers, relatives and friends, and they will put some of you to death. All men will hate you because of me. (Luke 21:16,17)

Then they called them in again and commanded them not to speak or teach at all in the name of Jesus. But Peter and John replied, "Judge for yourselves whether it is right in God's sight to obey you rather than God. For we cannot help speaking about what we have seen and heard." After further threats they let them go. They could not decide how to punish them, because all the people were praising God for what had happened. For the man who was miraculously healed was over forty years old. (Acts 4:18-22)

But Christ has indeed been raised from the dead, the first fruits of those who have fallen asleep. For since death came through a man, the resurrection of the dead comes also through a man. For as in Adam all die, so in Christ all will be made alive. But each in his own turn: Christ, the first fruits; then, when he comes, those who belong to him. (I Corinthians 15:20-23)

As can be seen from these examples, Scripture frequently uses the word "all" in a noninclusive sense.

For instance, the "all" of Mark 1:4,5 does not imply that every inhabitant of Jerusalem went out to John the Baptist confessing his sins, since it is obvious that the Pharisees did not. In this passage, Scripture uses the word "all" in a figurative sense that indicates a great number, but which does not include every individual. Similar conclusions follow from a consideration of the remaining passages as well. Thus, when John 1:6-9 speaks of an intent that "all" men might believe through John the Baptist, the "all" is obviously limited in scope, since John's ministry was limited to Israel. Once again, therefore, the "all" does not include every individual in a universal sense. Similarly, Luke 21:16,17 does not imply that "all" men individually considered will hate God's people, since it is obvious that all true believers and even many unbelievers do not. Likewise, when Acts 4:18-22 says that "all" the people of Jerusalem were praising God for the miracle wrought through Peter and John, it is obvious that the scribes and Pharisees antagonistic to Peter and John are not included by this "all." Finally, I Corinthians 15: 20-23 does not imply that " all" men inclusively considered will be made alive in Christ, since the context expressedly limits the number of those quickened to those who belong to Christ. Consequently, as these examples clearly demonstrate, Scripture frequently uses the word "all" in a sense that does not include every individual. Thus, it is at least possible that a noninclusive "all" is operative in the first set of passages above.

However, as seen from the examples above, there are many ways in which the word "all" may be used noninclusively. Yet, despite this clear variety, generally only one particular sense will harmonize with any given context. Accordingly, to establish a noninclusive "all" for the passages in the first set above, it is necessary to put forth the specific noninclusive sense that functions harmoniously within their particular contexts. To this end, the following discussion will attempt to establish an ethnic sense for the word "all" since such usage is both noninclusive and specifically germane to the contexts of Romans 11:23; I Timothy 2:3,4; and II Peter 3:9. On such an interpretation, the language expressing a divine desire to save "all" men will be ethnically and not individually construed. That is to say, such language will be taken as a desire to save all peoples, Gentiles as well as Jews, and not every person. Once again, however, before demonstrating the occurrence of this usage in any particular passage, it will be necessary to establish the possibility of this usage itself. To this end, consider the following texts:

> But I, when I am lifted up from the earth, will draw all men to myself. (John 12:32)

> In the last days, God says, I will pour out my Spirit on all people. Your sons and daughters will prophesy, your young men will see visions, your old men will dream dreams. (Acts 2:17)

With respect to the first passage above, it is obvious that the "all" cannot be taken in an individual sense for then the statement that Jesus "will draw all men" to Himself would imply the salvation of the entire race. Rather, when Jesus speaks of drawing "all" men to Himself, His words must be taken in an ethnic sense since such usage is supported by the context. In this regard, it is most significant that Jesus' speech is occasioned by a group of Gentiles (specifically Greeks) who have sought Him out. Furthermore, this Gentile action of seeking the Messiah must be viewed against the prophetic background in which a prominent theme was the eventual extension of salvation to the Gentiles. Thus, given the Gentile ethnicity of Jesus' specific audience and this general prophetic background, it is most natural to take Jesus' words in an ethnic sense as indicating the dawn of a new age in which salvation would be extended to all peoples. Consequently, while it is impossible to take Jesus' words in an individual sense, the ethnic sense is seen to tightly fit the context. Thus, in John 12:32 the "all" has an ethnic import.

In a similar fashion, Peter's statement must likewise be taken in an ethnic sense. After all, if Peter's language were taken in an individual sense, the pouring out of God's Spirit on "all" flesh would imply the Spirit baptism of the entire race. However, while such a consideration prevents the "all" from having an individual import, an ethnic sense is both possible and supported by the context. In this regard, it is most significant that Peter's language is occasioned by the miracle of Pentecost in which diverse foreign languages are being spoken to an ethnically varied audience. The immediate context is therefore ethnically charged. Moreover, as with Jesus' speech above, Peter's language must be viewed against a prophetic background in which Israel's prophets repeatedly spoke of an eventual extension of salvation to the Gentiles. Indeed, this prophetic background is particularly evident since Peter is here applying a prophesy of Joel to the Pentecostal event. Consequently, given the diverse ethnicity of Peter's audience and this prophetic background, it is most natural to take Peter's words in an ethnic sense as indicating the dawn of a new age in which salvation extends to all peoples. Moreover, since Pentecost marks the birth of the church and thus of Christian missions, the foundational significance of Pentecost to the missionary movement in the book of Acts confirms the ethnic interpretation given above. After all, as the basis of an overall missionary thrust where the Gospel is taken from Jerusalem to the nations, the tongues of Pentecost are seen to have an ethnic significance of epochal proportions as a sign of the Spirit's empowerment for foreign missions. Consequently, while it is impossible to take Peter's words in an individual sense, an ethnic sense well fits the context. Thus, as with Jesus' speech above, the "all" is seen to have an ethnic, and not an individual sense.

On the basis of the preceding discussion, Scripture has been shown to use the word "all" in ways that do not include every individual. Moreover, in passages dealing with the salvation of "all" people, Scripture has been shown to use the word "all" in an ethnic and not an individual sense. In other words, such language describes a divine intent to extend salvation to "all" peoples and not to every individual. Accordingly, since an ethnic "all" does not implicate every individual, the universal texts mentioned above (Romans 11:32; I Timothy 2:3,4; and II Peter 3:9) may be interpreted in complete harmony with the reprobation texts (Romans 9:10-25; I Peter 2:7-10; and II Peter 2:3,12,17) in the second set.

That such an option is at least possible has been demonstrated by the preceding development. However, having established the possibility of such an option, it is next necessary to demonstrate from the context of each particular passage that such an interpretation is actually the case. Accordingly, the following analysis will be devoted to an examination of Romans 11:32, I Timothy 2:3-4, and II Peter 3:9 within their various levels of context. Once an ethnic "all" has been shown to fit these contexts, the ethnic interpretation of these texts will have been established, allowing them to be interpreted in complete harmony with the doctrine of reprobation.

In examining these various passages, it is first necessary to consider the context of the New Testament itself since this is a broad level of context common to all three passages. In this regard, a particular stress of the New Testament is the contrast between the universalism of the new age and the Jewish exclusivism of the old. Consequently, to the extent that this new universalism is seen to be ethnic, an ethnic interpretation of Romans 11:32; I Timothy 2:3,4; and II Peter 3:9 will be rendered more probable due to its resonance with this overarching theme. To this end, it is necessary to consider the evidence for the ethnic character of this new universalism. In this regard, the words of Loraine Boettner are most significant (Boettner, 290, 291).

> In some instances the word "all" is used in order to teach that the gospel is for the Gentiles as well as for the Jews. Through the many centuries of their past history the Jews had, with few exceptions, been the exclusive recipients of God's saving grace. They had greatly abused their privileges as the

chosen people. They supposed that this same distinction would be kept up in the Messianic era, and they were always inclined to appropriate the Messiah exclusively to themselves. So rigid was the Pharisaic exclusivism that the Gentiles were called strangers, dogs, common, unclean; and it was not lawful for a Jew to keep company with or have any dealings with a Gentile (John 4:9; Acts 10:28; 11:3).

The salvation of the Gentiles was a mystery which had not been made known in other ages (Ephesians 3:4-6; Colossians 1:27). It was for that reason that Peter was taken to task by the Church at Jerusalem after he had preached the Gospel to Cornelius, and we can almost hear the gasp of wonder in the exclamation of the leaders when after Peter's defense they said, "Then to the Gentiles also hath God granted repentance unto life," Acts 11:18. To understand what a revolutionary idea this was, read Acts 10:1-11:18. Consequently this was a truth which it was then peculiarly necessary to enforce, and it was brought out in the fullest and strongest terms. Paul was to be a witness "unto all men," that is, to Jews and Gentiles alike, of what he had seen and heard, Acts 22:15. As used in this sense the word "all" has no reference to individuals, but means mankind in general.

As may be gathered from Boettner's discussion, the word "all" is frequently used to contrast the universalism of the new age with the Jewish exclusivism of the old. Accordingly, since the exclusivism of the old age is ethnic in character, the new and contrasting universalism must be ethnic as well. To see this point, observe that a specific contrast by its very nature requires and therefore implies a generic similarity. For instance, the specific contrast between black and white depends for its very existence upon their generic similarity as colors. In a similar fashion, the Jewish exclusivism and Christian universalism must share a generic similarity in order to maintain a specific contrast. Consequently, since the Jewish exclusivism is obviously ethnic in scope, the contrasting Christian universalism must be ethnic as well. Thus, within the broad context of the New Testament where the glories of the new age are being contrasted with the comparative shadows of the old, language indicating God's desire to save "all" men should be interpreted in an ethnic and not an individual sense. In other words, such language implies a desire to extend salvation to all peoples, Gentiles as well as Jews, and not to every person.

To see the plausibility of this assertion, imagine Luther or Calvin arguing with a modern day white supremacist and responding to his bigotry with the statement that God loves "all" men and wants "all" to be saved. Now since it would be known that Luther and Calvin upheld the doctrine of reprobation, it would be clear that they were not using "all" in an individual sense. Moreover, since they would be setting God's universalism over against the racial exclusivism of the white supremacist, the specific nature of the contrast would demand an ethnic (racial) universalism. Within such a context, then, the use of the words "all men" to denote men of every race would be most natural and unstrained. In a similar fashion since it is known from

Scripture that Paul and Peter uphold the doctrine of reprobation (Romans 9:10-25; I Peter 2:7-10; and II Peter 2:3,12,17) and since they are frequently responding to a narrow, Jewish exclusivism, it is most natural to interpret their universal passages (Romans 11:32; I Timothy 2:3,4, and II Peter 3:9) in an ethnic sense.[3]

---

[3] This ethnic usage coheres with the life situation of first century Christianity in which a prominent feature of the opposition to Christianity was Jewish exclusivism. In this regard, many of the first century Jews failed to acknowledge the Gospel freedom and universalism anticipated by their own prophets and instead placed their confidence in the narrowly Jewish institutions of their nation and Temple which had symbolized the presence of God among them. At Christ's death, however, something radical happened; the curtain of the Temple was torn in two. Previously, only the high priest could go behind this curtain to enter the Holy of Holies, and this he could do only once per year. The tearing of this curtain at Christ's death therefore symbolized a radical and discontinuous change in redemptive-history. Thus, in contrast to the previous age of Jewish exclusivism, entrance to the presence of God, as symbolized by the Holy of Holies, was suddenly universalized. Furthermore, this revolution initiated at Calvary was completed at Pentecost where God's Spirit descended upon the people. The significance of this descent is that it mirrors the Spirit's descent (in the form of the Glory Cloud) on the tabernacle in the Old Testament (Exodus 40). The implication, of course, is that the New Testament church is the Temple of God the Holy Spirit, or even more profoundly, the church is the new Holy of Holies. This universalization of access to God was denied, however, by Jewish adherents who continued to cling to the old exclusivism as symbolized by their Temple and nation. Thus, the environment of the early church was characterized by an intense theological (and sometimes physical) warfare between competing and antagonistic truth claims. In terms of this battle, the apostles sought to advance an ethnic universalism against a Jewish exclusivism as a distinguishing feature of the new age. Thus, their ethnic use the word "all" makes perfectly good sense given the life situation of the early church.

To establish this conclusion, however, an ethnic interpretation must be shown compatible with the respective contexts of these passages. Thus, having examined the broad context of the New Testament, attention must now shift to an analysis of the specific passages themselves.

Of the three passages mentioned above, Romans 11:32 will first be considered. In this regard, it will be shown below that this verse assumes an ethnic sense and is therefore consistent with the doctrine of reprobation. However, since Romans 11:32 forms the culmination of Paul's argument in Romans 11:1-32, it will be necessary to view this verse within the context of the argument itself to set forth its ethnic sense. To this end, Paul's entire argument has been reproduced below with the contested verse italicized for clarity:

> I ask then: Did God reject his people? By no means! I am an Israelite myself, a descendant of Abraham, from the tribe of Benjamin. God did not reject his people, whom he foreknew. Don't you know what the Scripture says in the passage about Elijah — how he appealed to God against Israel: "Lord, they are trying to kill me"? And what was God's answer to him? "I have reserved for myself seven thousand who have not bowed the knee to Baal." So too, at the present time there is a remnant chosen by grace. And if by grace, then it is no longer by works; if it were, grace would no longer be grace.

What then? What Israel sought so earnestly it did not obtain, but the elect did. The others were hardened, as it is written:

"God gave them a spirit of stupor,
eyes so that they could not see
and ears so that they could not hear,
to this very day."

And David says:

"May their table become a snare and a trap,
a stumbling block and a retribution for them.
May their eyes be darkened so they cannot see,
and their backs be bent forever."

Again I ask: Did they stumble so as to fall beyond recovery? Not at all! Rather, because of their transgression, salvation has come to the Gentiles to make Israel envious. But if their transgression means riches for the world, and their loss means riches for the Gentiles, how much greater riches will their fullness bring!

I am talking to you Gentiles. Inasmuch as I am the apostle to the Gentiles, I make much of my ministry in the hope that I may somehow arouse my own people to envy and save some of them. For if their rejection is the reconciliation of the world, what will their acceptance be but life from the dead? If the part of the dough offered as first fruits is holy, then the whole batch is holy; if the root is holy, so are the branches.

If some of the branches have been broken off, and you, though a wild olive shoot, have been grafted in among the others and now share in the nourishing sap from the olive root, do not boast over those branches. If you do, consider this: You do not support the root, but the root supports you. You will say then, "Branches were broken off so that I could be grafted in." Granted. But they were broken off because of unbelief, and you stand by faith. Do not be arrogant, but be afraid. For if God did not spare the natural branches, he will not spare you either.

Consider therefore the kindness and sternness of God: sternness to those who fell, but kindness to you, provided that you continue in his kindness. Otherwise, you also will be cut off. And if they do not persist in unbelief, they will be grafted in, for God is able to graft them in again. After all, if you were cut out of an olive tree that is wild by nature, and contrary to nature were grafted into a cultivated olive tree, how much more readily will these, the natural branches, be grafted into their own olive tree!

I do not want you to be ignorant of this mystery, brothers, so that you may not be conceited: Israel has experienced a hardening in part until the full number of the Gentiles has come in. And so all Israel will be saved, as it is written:

"The deliverer will come from Zion;
he will turn godlessness away from Jacob.
And this is my covenant with them
when I take away their sins."

As far as the gospel is concerned, they are
enemies on your account; but as far as election is concerned, they are loved on account
of the patriarchs, for God's gifts and his call
are irrevocable. Just as you who were at one
time disobedient to God have now received
mercy as a result of their disobedience, so
they too have now become disobedient in
order that they too may now receive mercy
as a result of God's mercy to you. *For God
has bound all men over to disobedience so
that he may have mercy on them all.*
(Romans 11:1-32)

As should be apparent from the above passage, Paul
is trying to explain the seemingly anomalous fact that
while the Gospel is the fulfillment of Jewish prophecy, the Gentiles are more receptive to it. To this end,
Paul enters upon an extended discussion concerning
the relative position, timing, and fortunes of Jews and
Gentiles within redemptive-history. Accordingly,
Paul's entire discussion assumes an ethnic character
since he is here seeking to explain an ethnic phenom-
enon. Given this fact, the presence of Romans 11:32
within this context provides *prima facie* evidence that
the "all" in Romans 11:32 is to be ethnically interpreted. Thus, arguing solely from the character of
Paul's argument, the nature of his universalism is seen
to be ethnic.

Beyond this general consideration, however, the details of Paul's argument advance the same conclusion. In this regard, observe, first of all, that the initial portion of Paul's argument (Romans 11:1-10) makes room for an ethnic universalism by ruling out an individual interpretation. To see this point recall that Paul is here comparing the apostasy of his own day to that of Elijah's time when Israel turned from God to Baal. Thus, in deliberate correspondence to Elijah's day, Paul refers to the faithful Jews as "a remnant chosen by grace" and as an elect people "whom God foreknew." Moreover, to accentuate the difference between this chosen remnant and the apostate majority, Paul says that the bulk of Israel was hardened in seeking the very salvation which the elect attained by grace. Accordingly, since this salvation is freely given to the elect and denied to the remainder, Paul's language indicates that salvation is due to a saving grace intended for the elect alone. Consequently, since Paul's own language confines God's saving grace to an elect remnant, it follows that God does not want everyone to be saved. Given this fact, the "all" in Romans 11:32 cannot be individually interpreted.

However, while an individual interpretation is thereby ruled out, positive evidence from the second half of Paul's argument (Romans 11:11-32) indicates that the "all" of Romans 11:32 is to be ethnically construed. In this regard, observe that Paul here invokes the analogy of the olive tree to explain the relative fortunes of the Jews and Gentiles within God's plan of salvation. In particular, Paul refers to Israel as natural olive branches broken off for disobedience and to the Gentiles as the formerly disobedient, wild branches grafted in by grace. Moreover, throughout the discussion, Paul indicates that this ingrafting of the Gentiles will make Israel envious and thereby cause them to return to God. Then, in verses 30-32, Paul summarizes and concludes his argument by saying:

> 30 Just as you who were at one time disobedient to God have now received mercy as a result of their disobedience, 31 so they too have now become disobedient in order that they too may now receive mercy as a result of God's mercy to you. 32 For God has bound all men over to disobedience so that he may have mercy on them all. (Romans 11:30-32)

Now since verses 30 and 31 recapitulate the preceding argument, it is evident that the "you" and "they" of these verses refer to the Gentiles and the Jews, respectively. Moreover, due to the flow and the structure of the verses above, it is also evident that this "you" and "they" combine to form the "all" of verse 32. Thus, when Paul says that "God has bound all men over to disobedience so that he may have mercy on them all," it is evident that Paul's language is to be ethnically construed since the very context defines this "all" as the sum of the Gentiles and the Jews. So understood, Paul's language refers to humanity is its ethnic fullness and therefore does not implicate every individual. Consequently, while the first part of Paul's argument rules out an individual interpretation, the second part shows an ethnic interpretation to be most sound. Thus, Romans 11:32 is completely harmonious with the doctrine of reprobation since Paul's language does not imply a divine desire to save every individual.

In a similar fashion, I Timothy 2:3,4 may also be shown to manifest an ethnic universalism and thus to cohere with the doctrine of reprobation. To demonstrate this point, it will be necessary to consider both the historical and the literary context of I Timothy 2:3,4. With respect to the historical context, it will be shown below that Paul is contending with a Jewish exclusivism in I Timothy and that his universal statements are therefore to be taken in an ethnic sense. Then, after addressing the historical context, the specific literary context will be examined to show that this ethnic universalism is also demanded by the details of Paul's argument in I Timothy 2:1-7. Thus, by moving from the general to the specific, an ethnic interpretation of I Timothy 2:3,4 will be advanced on the basis of its historical and literary coherence.

With respect to the historical context, several passages concerning Paul's opponents are most significant to the historical background of I Timothy:

> As I urged you when I went into Macedonia, stay there in Ephesus so that you may command certain men not to teach false doctrines any longer nor to devote themselves to myths and endless genealogies. These promote controversies rather than God's work — which is by faith. The goal of this command is love, which comes from a pure heart and a good conscience and a sincere faith. Some have wandered away from these and turned to meaningless talk. They want to be teachers of the law, but they do not know what they are talking about or what they so confidently affirm. (I Timothy 1: 3-7)

The Spirit clearly says that in later times some will abandon the faith and follow deceiving spirits and things taught by demons. Such teachings come through hypocritical liars, whose consciences have been seared as with a hot iron. They forbid people to marry and order them to abstain from certain foods which God created to be received with thanksgiving by those who believe and who know the truth. For everything God created is good, and nothing is to be rejected if it is received with thanksgiving, because it is consecrated by the word of God and prayer. (I Timothy 4:1-5)

If anyone teaches false doctrines and does not agree to the sound instruction of our Lord Jesus Christ and to godly teaching, he is conceited and understands nothing. He has an unhealthy interest in controversies and quarrels about words that result in envy, strife, malicious talk, evil suspicions and constant friction between men of corrupt mind, who have been robbed of the truth and who think that godliness is a means to financial gain. (I Timothy 6:3-5)

From these passages, the purpose of the epistle clearly emerges. Essentially Paul has left Timothy behind in Ephesus to establish order in the face of some disruptive heretics and is writing the epistle to further this end. Evidently, these heretics are driven by monetary greed and are spreading a heresy which may be described as a Jewish-Gnostic hybrid. In this regard, the

Jewish emphasis is evident from their obsession with genealogies and the law while the Gnostic strain is seen in their demands to abstain from marriage. (The dietary restrictions, by contrast, can support either a Jewish or a Gnostic identity, depending upon whether a ceremonial or an ascetic abstinence is being enjoined.) Moreover, since the heretics desire to be teachers of the law, it is likely that they are elders of the Ephesian churches, a fact which would also explain their effectiveness in stirring up controversy. Thus, based on the texts above, it would seem that Paul is writing I Timothy in response to a group of greedy, heretical elders who are disrupting the good order of the Ephesian churches through the propagation of a Jewish-Gnostic heresy. Consequently, since Paul is writing I Timothy to re-establish the order which these heretics have undermined, I Timothy is permeated by a polemical thrust which is therefore programmatic to the exposition of its contents. In other words, I Timothy cannot be viewed primarily as a manual of church order dispassionately addressed to Timothy, but rather as a highly reasoned polemic directed through Timothy to the Ephesian churches and against the heretical elders. Thus, Paul's instructions concerning liturgical prayer (I Timothy 2) and church polity (I Timothy 3) must not be viewed in a merely didactic fashion as a simple transfer of information, but rather must be seen as an aspect of theological warfare.

Given this fact, Paul's instructions concerning universal prayer in I Timothy 2:1-7 must be viewed against the backdrop of the heresy he is opposing.

Now since this heresy is characterized by a strongly Jewish emphasis, its obsession with genealogies and the law is likely symptomatic of a more general and deep seated resistance to the new covenant, which would also entail a Jewish exclusivism. Consequently, when Paul in I Timothy 2:1-7 enjoins liturgical prayer for "all" men, it is likely that he is attacking a Jewish exclusivism and is thus urging a Christian universalism in response. However, since a specific contrast requires and therefore implies a generic similarity, it follows that Paul's universalism must be ethnic in scope to provide the proper contrast for the ethnic exclusivism he is opposing. Given this fact, considerations of the historical context favor an ethnic universalism as the proper aim of I Timothy 2:1-7.

Having examined the historical context of I Timothy, I Timothy 2:3,4 will next be examined within its immediate literary context of I Timothy 2:1-7. In this regard, the objective will be to show that the details of Paul's argument demand the same ethnic universalism which the historical context favors. To facilitate this analysis, Paul's argument in I Timothy 2:1-7 will be broken down into relevant sections with the contested verses italicized for clarity.

(I Timothy 2:1,2: THE COMMAND: PRAYER FOR "ALL" MEN)

I urge, then, first of all, that requests, prayers, intercession and thanksgiving be made for all men (παντων ανθρωπων) — for kings and all those in authority, that we may live peaceful and quiet lives in all godliness and holiness.

(I Timothy 2:3,4: THE BASIS OF THE COMMAND: GOD'S UNIVERSAL BENEVOLENCE)

This is good, and pleases God our Savior,
who wants all men (παντας ανθρωπους)
to be saved and to come to a knowledge of
the truth.

(I Timothy 2:5-7: THE PROOF OF GOD'S BENEVOLENCE: GOD'S PLAN OF SALVATION)

For there is one God and one mediator between God and man, the man Christ Jesus,
who gave himself as a ransom for all
(παντων) — the testimony given in its
proper time. And for this purpose I was appointed a herald and an apostle — I am
telling the truth, I am not lying — a teacher
of the true faith to the Gentiles.

From this break down of Paul's argument, its tightly
reasoned nature clearly emerges. In short, Paul urges
prayer for "all" men on the general basis of God's
benevolence to "all" men as attested by God's plan of
salvation in which Christ died for "all." Thus, in the
first instance, Paul's entire argument is seen to be
unified by the single purpose of advancing a command
to pray for "all" men. Moreover, flowing out of this
unity of purpose, the passage is also characterized by
a unity of content since it is permeated throughout by
a focus on universal benevolence. Consequently, since
the passage is unified in purpose as well as content,
logical considerations demand that the word "all" assume a stable meaning throughout the passage. After
all, since sections 1, 2, and 3 combine to form a tightly
knit argument, the meaning of "all" must remain in-

139

variant to avoid the fallacy of equivocation. Given this fact, the type universalism manifested by sections 1 and 3 necessarily determines the type of universalism observed in section 2. Thus, to establish an ethnic sense for the "all" of I Timothy 2:3,4, it is logically sufficient to establish an ethnic sense for the "all" of sections 1 and 3. To this end, the subsequent discussion will seek to determine an ethnic sense for sections 1 and 3 as a means of "boxing in" and thereby determining the sense of section 2.

With respect to section 1, it is evident that Paul's command to pray for "all" men must be taken in an ethnic sense. In the first place, speaking negatively, an individual sense must be excluded since it is known from elsewhere in Scripture that there are at least some individuals for whom one should not pray, namely those committing a sin unto death.

> If anyone sees his brother commit a sin that does not lead to death, he should pray and God will give him life. I refer to those whose sin does not lead to death. There is a sin that leads to death; I am not saying that he should pray about that. (1 John 5:16, 17)

From this passage, then, it follows that Paul's command to pray for "all" men cannot be made to include every person and thus may not be interpreted in an individual sense. But, while the individual sense is thereby excluded, an ethnic sense is most plausible for several reasons. First, since Paul indicates in Titus 2:11 that "the grace of God that brings salvation has appeared to 'all' men," it is evident that Paul's universalism is here ethnic since the grace of God had clearly not appeared to every individual in Paul's day. Thus, an ethnic "all" is seen to be most consistent with the Pauline vocabulary in the pastoral epistles (*i.e.*, I Timothy, II Timothy, and Titus). Second, since Paul's command to pray for "all" men is likely directed against a Jewish exclusivism which would abominate any prayer for Gentiles and their rulers, the ethnic scope of Paul's command implicitly emerges from the Jewish exclusivism it is intended to oppose. Third, this ethnic interpretation also follows from the fact that Paul's command to pray for "all" men and their rulers exactly matches his apostolic commission to take the Gospel before the Gentiles and their kings (Acts 9:15). In other words, since the scope of Paul's commission is clearly ethnic, and since the language of Paul's command exactly matches the language of his commission, the scope of Paul's command is likely ethnic as well.[4] On the basis of the preceding discussion, then, an ethnic interpretation of Paul's command has been shown to be most plausible while an indi-

---

[4] Since the intimate connection with Paul's commission brings out the ethnic nature of his command, it is interesting to observe the way in which the two elements of this command reinforce one another in the service of an international Gospel ministry. On the one hand, since the rulers are the heads of various ethnic groupings, the reference to prayer for these rulers is clearly ethnic and flows out of Paul's command to pray for "all" men. On the other hand, as heads of state, these rulers wield a considerable amount of power, making such prayer strategic to the international propagation of the Gospel. In other words, the prayer for these rulers is a strategic component in obtaining the goal envisioned in praying for "all" men. Thus, the two elements of Paul's command serve to reinforce one another to the end that the Gospel is propagated among the nations (*i.e.*, "all" men).

vidual interpretation has been excluded. Thus, it follows that the "all" of section 1 is ethnic in scope.

In a similar fashion, the "all" of section 3 may also be shown to assume an ethnic sense. To see this point most clearly, however, it will prove convenient to subdivide section 3 into two separate parts.

(I Timothy 2:5-6a: THE OBJECTIVE VALIDITY OF GOD'S PLAN OF SALVATION)
For there is one God and one mediator between God and man, the man Christ Jesus, who gave himself as a ransom for all (παντων)

(I Timothy 2:6b-7: THE PREACHING OF GOD'S PLAN OF SALVATION)
— the testimony given in its proper time. And for this purpose I was appointed a herald and an apostle — I am telling the truth, I am not lying — a teacher of the true faith to the Gentiles.

As can be seen from this breakdown, parts 1 and 2 of section 3 form parallel blocks of text which serve to clarify one another. Speaking grammatically, part 2 stands in apposition to part 1 and therefore serves to modify it. Speaking theologically, the two sections must manifest certain similarities since they deal with related aspects of the same reality, namely the objective accomplishment of God's salvation and its apostolic proclamation. Consequently, given the grammatical and theological relation of the two parts, the message of part 1 is necessarily clarified by the discussion of part 2 and vice versa. Accordingly, in the subsequent discussion, the scope of the "all" in part 1 will be determined from the combined testimony of parts 1 and 2.

With respect to part 1, Paul refers to God's one plan of salvation as evidenced by the unity of God, the unity of the mediator, and the humanity of the mediator who gave His life as a ransom for "all." To see the ethnic import of this language, it is necessary to consider the cultural background in which Paul was operating. In this regard, it may be said that many of the nations in Paul's day worshipped false gods and thus ascribed to false plans of salvation. The Jews, by contrast, worshipped the true God, yet falsely sought to restrict God's salvation to their nation alone. Thus, while the Jews truly condemned the falsity of the surrounding paganism, they falsely sought to hoard God's truth among themselves. In response to both of these errors, therefore, Paul sets forth the unity of the one true God and the universality of His saving benevolence. Thus, while opposing the various national idolatries, Paul simultaneously holds forth the true salvation to all nations. So understood, Paul's language is clearly ethnic in scope since he is speaking in the realm of people groups (sociology) rather than individual souls (psychology).

Moreover, this conclusion from part 1 is confirmed by the manner in which Paul clarifies the timing and the scope of salvation in part 2. In this regard, Paul refers to the revelation of God's salvation as "the testimony given in its proper time" and then states that he was appointed as an apostle to herald this testimony to the Gentiles. In so doing Paul marks this revelation as something which is both new to his day and ethnic in scope. Confirmation of this interpretation follows from both the content and the mode of Paul's speech.

With respect to content, Paul's ethnic universalism may be confirmed by comparing the substance of Paul's speech with other Pauline passages setting forth a similar timing and scope:

> Now to him who is able to establish you by my gospel and the proclamation of Jesus Christ, according to the revelation of the mystery hidden for long ages past, but now revealed and made known through the prophetic writings by the command of the eternal God, so that all nations (παντα τα εθνη) might believe in him. (Romans 16:25, 26)

> I have become its servant by the commission God gave me to present to you the word of God in its fullness — the mystery that has been kept hidden for ages and generations, but is now disclosed to the saints. To them God has chosen to make known among the Gentiles (εν τοις εθνεσιν) the glorious riches of this mystery, which is Christ in you, the hope of glory. (Colossians 1:25-27)

> Surely you have heard about the administration of God's grace that was given to me for you, that is, the mystery made known to me by revelation, as I have already written briefly. In reading this, then, you will be able to understand my insight into the mystery of

144

Christ, which was not made known to other
men in other generations as it has now been
revealed by the Spirit to God's holy apostles
and prophets. This mystery is that through
the Gospel the Gentiles (τα εθνη) are heirs
together with Israel, members together of one
body, and sharers together in the promise in
Christ Jesus. (Ephesians 3:2-6)

As should be readily apparent, the above passages
agree with I Timothy 2:6b-7 in describing the Gentile
outreach as a function of the apostolic office and as a
distinguishing feature of the new age. Thus, they form a
common universe of discourse with I Timothy 2: 6b-7,
providing a common witness with respect to the timing and scope of God's salvation and the role of the
apostolic office in it. Moreover, since the latter three
passages refer to the Gentile salvation as the mystery
of God revealed in the fullness of time, they set forth
an ethnic universalism both directly and through an
implicit contrast with the ethnic exclusivism of the
old covenant. Consequently, since these latter passages
are obviously ethnic in scope, and since they agree
with I Timothy 2:6b-7 in timing, scope, and apostolic function, it follows that the ethnic scope of
the latter passages is shared by I Timothy 2:6b-7 as
well. Thus, in advancing the Gentile mission as a
radical feature of the new age, Paul sets forth an
ethnic universalism.

However, beyond the content of Paul's speech, an
ethnic universalism is also attested by its mode since
Paul here punctuates his discourse with an apostolic
oath, "I am telling the truth, I am not lying." Now

since Paul would not lie to Timothy, the function of this oath is not to establish Paul's credibility[5] but rather to attest in the most emphatic manner a radical and unexpected feature of the new age, namely the extension of salvation to the Gentiles. Thus, Paul is not using the oath to establish his Gentile calling as an incidental feature of his ministry but rather is attesting a redemptive-historical transition to a new and radical universalism which stands at the base of his particular ministry and which makes the Gentile mission possible. Moreover, when it is remembered that Paul's Judaizing opponents at Ephesus are resisting these new covenant realities, the proximate function of this oath becomes immediately clear. Essentially, Paul's oath functions as an apostolic "trump card" to advance the Gentile mission and the universalism it entails against the Jewish exclusivism of the old age. Accordingly, as an instrument of theological warfare, Paul's oath accentuates the contrast between the new universalism and old exclusivism, thereby revealing the ethnic character of the former. Thus, in addition to his content, the mode of Paul's speech also reveals his ethnic universalism.

On the basis of the preceding discussion, therefore, the ethnic nature of Paul's universalism has been established by the content and the mode of Paul's speech. Accordingly, having established an ethnic universalism for part 2, it remains to apply this result to part 1. In this regard, it must be recalled that since I Timothy 2:5-6a and I Timothy 2:6b-7 form parallel parts dealing with

---

[5] Indeed, if Paul had a credibility problem, his oath would also be suspect and thus powerless to vouch for his own credibility.

the same plan of salvation, they necessarily manifest a related sense. Thus, while Paul in part 2 refers to himself as an apostle of the Gentiles called to herald the testimony given in the proper time, the substance of this testimony is clearly defined in part 1, namely, that the one God has sent a single mediator to die as a ransom for "all." Moreover, since the apostolic mission also seems to grow out of this reality, the fact that Christ died for "all" would seem to be the basis of the apostolic commission in addition to being the substance of the apostolic testimony. Given this fact, the "all" for whom Christ died and the Gentiles to whom Paul was sent are necessarily linked in a substantive manner so that the ethnic nature of the latter carries over to the former as well. In other words, since the character of the "all" is necessarily determined by the character of Paul's mission, it follows that the "all" of I Timothy 2:6a is ethnic in scope. Thus, the evidence of part 2 combines with that of part 1 to demand an ethnic "all" in I Timothy 2:6a.

On the basis of the preceding discussion, an ethnic sense has been established both for Paul's command to pray for "all" men (I Timothy 2:1) and for the "all" for whom Christ died (I Timothy 2:6a). Consequently, since Paul's argument in I Timothy 2:1-7 manifests a unity of purpose and content, and since it is tightly reasoned, the "all" of I Timothy 2:3,4 must manifest an identical ethnic sense to avoid the fallacy of equivocation. After all, since this passage forms the logical connecting link between Paul's command to pray for "all" men and his statement that Christ died for "all," God's desire for "all" to be saved cannot be individual if the other two uses are ethnic. In other words, if Jesus

Christ died for "all" peoples, meaning Gentiles as well as Jews, and if Paul commands us to pray for "all" peoples, Gentiles as well as Jews, it must be because God wants "all" peoples, Gentiles as well as Jews, to be saved. Consequently, when Paul says that God "wants 'all' men to be saved and to come to a knowledge of the truth," his language must be ethnically construed. Accordingly, since I Timothy 2:3,4 does not imply a divine desire to save every individual, these verses are most consistent with the doctrine of reprobation.

In a similar fashion, II Peter 3:9 may be shown to assume an ethnic sense and thus to cohere with the doctrine of reprobation. In this regard, it will be shown below that the "all" of this verse is to be ethnically, and not individually construed. However, since II Peter 3:9 is part of Peter's broader argument (II Peter 3:1-10), it will be necessary to view this verse within the context of the surrounding argument to properly set forth this ethnic sense. To this end, Peter's argument has been reproduced below with the contested verse italicized for clarity:

> Dear friends, this is now my second letter to you. I have written both of them as reminders to stimulate you to wholesome thinking. I want you to recall the words spoken in the past by the holy prophets and the command given by our Lord and Savior through your apostles.
>
> First of all, you must understand that in the last days scoffers will come, scoffing and following their own evil desires. They will

say, "Where is this 'coming' he promised?
Ever since our fathers died, everything goes
on as it has since the beginning of creation."
But they deliberately forget that long ago by
God's word the heavens existed and the earth
was formed out of water and by water. By
these waters also the world of that time was
deluged and destroyed. By the same word
the present heavens and earth are reserved
for fire, being kept for the day of judgment
and destruction of ungodly men.

But do not forget this one thing, dear friends:
With the Lord a day is like a thousand years,
and a thousand years are like a day. *The Lord
is not slow in keeping his promise, as some
understand slowness. He is patient with you,
not wanting any* (τινας) *to perish, but all*
(παντας) *to come to repentance.*[6]

But the day of the Lord will come like a thief.
The heavens will disappear with a roar; the
elements will be destroyed by fire, and the
earth and everything in it will be laid bare.
(II Peter 3:1-10)

As should be evident from the above text, II Peter 3:9
falls within a discussion dealing with the timing of

---

[6] Once again, it should be noted that an antipredestinarian bias
has influenced the NIV translation of II Peter 3:9. Since the
Greek words τινας and παντας are plural, they should be translated simply and indefinitely as "any" and "all" as done above,
and not as "anyone" and "everyone" as done in the NIV.

149

the final judgment and which is therefore redemptive-historical in nature. Given this fact, Peter's use of "all" in II Peter 3:9 is likely ethnic in scope. After all, since redemptive-historical discussions by their very nature deal with the "broad brush strokes" of history, they are primarily concerned with major events and trends within God's economy of salvation, and not with individuals as such. Accordingly, there is every reason to believe that Peter's language is ethnic in character and not individual. Consequently, when Peter speaks of God wanting "all" to come to repentance, the redemptive-historical nature of his discourse would indicate that he is referring to the salvation of all peoples and not every individual. Thus, Peter's language is ethnic in character, and this fact may be confirmed by specific factors in the near and intermediate context of the passage.

In the first place, speaking negatively, an individual interpretation of the "all" in II Peter 3:9 is excluded by explicit references to reprobation within I and II Peter. First, in the immediate context of II Peter 3:9, it is evident that God's desire for "all" to come to repentance does not include the ungodly men of II Peter 3:7 for whom " the present heavens and earth are reserved for fire by His very word, being kept for the day of judgment and destruction of ungodly men." Moreover, it is also evident that God's desire to save does not encompass the false teachers of Chapter 2 since Peter says that "their condemnation has long been hanging over them, and their destruction has not been sleeping," (II Peter 2:3) that "they are like brute beasts, creatures of instinct, born only to be caught and destroyed," (II Peter 2:12) and that "blackest darkness

is reserved for them" (II Peter 2:17). And finally, it is
clear that the "all" of II Peter 3:9 does not include
those who Peter says, "stumble because they disobey
the message — which is also what they were destined
for" (I Peter 2:8). In other words, given the explicit
references to reprobation and reserved judgment by
Peter himself, it is evident that God does not intend the
salvation of every person. Thus, the "all" in II Peter 3:9
cannot be taken in an individual sense.

On the other hand, while an individual sense is excluded on the basis of the preceding considerations, there
is much positive evidence to support an ethnic interpretation. To see this point, the structure of II Peter 3:9 must
first be considered:

> The Lord is not slow in keeping his promise
> as some understand slowness. He is patient
> with you, not wanting any to perish, but all
> to come to repentance.

In regard to this text, the grammatical structure of second half of the verse is of particular importance to the
ethnic nature of Peter's speech. In this regard, it is
most significant that the participial phrase, "not wanting any to perish, but all to come to repentance," serves
to ground God's specific patience to the readers of
the epistle in terms of His more general benevolence.
Given this fact, the meaning of II Peter 3:9b could be
preserved by translating it in a causal sense: "He is
patient with you *because* He does not want any to
perish but all to come to repentance." Now the significance of this grammatical clarification is that it
clearly sets forth the linkage between the readers of

the epistle and the "all" to whom Peter refers. In particular, God's patience to the readers of Peter's epistle is seen to be based on God's general benevolence and thus to stand forth as a specific manifestation of this benevolence. Given this fact, the "you" of II Peter 3:9b to whom God shows patience necessarily forms a subset of the "all" whom God wishes to come to repentance. And since a subset must necessarily share in the generic essence of the set, the "you" is substantively identical to the "all" of which it forms a part. Therefore, to the extent that the "you" is ethnically construed, an ethnic sense will follow for the "all" as well. Thus, to establish the sense of the "all" in II Peter 3:9, it suffices to establish the sense of the "you" to which it is substantively linked.

In seeking to establish the sense of the "you" in II Peter 3:9, it must be observed that Peter addresses his readers as "you" throughout I and II Peter and that both epistles are addressed to the same audience (II Peter 3:1). Accordingly, since both epistles envision an identical audience, the word "you" shares a common referent and should therefore manifest a common sense throughout these two epistles. As a result, passages from either epistle may be used to determine the sense of Peter's "you" in II Peter 3:9. In this regard, the following texts are significant in establishing an ethnic sense:

> Concerning this salvation, the prophets, who spoke of the grace that was to come to you, searched intently and with greatest care, trying to find out the time and circumstances to which the Spirit of Christ in them was

152

pointing when he predicted the sufferings of Christ and the glories that would follow. (I Peter 1:10,11)

As obedient children, do not conform to the evil desires you had when you lived in ignorance. (I Peter 1:14)

For you know that it was not with perishable things such as silver or gold that you were redeemed from the empty way of life handed down to you from your forefathers, but with the precious blood of Christ, a lamb without blemish or defect. (I Peter 1: 18,19)

But you are a chosen people, a royal priesthood, a holy nation, a people belonging to God, that you may declare the praises of him who called you out of darkness into his wonderful light. Once you were not a people, but now you are the people of God; once you had not received mercy, but now you have received mercy. (I Peter 2:9,10)

For you have spent enough time in the past doing what pagans choose to do — living in debauchery, lust, drunkenness, orgies, carousing and detestable idolatry. They think it strange that you do not plunge with them into the same flood of dissipation, and they heap abuse on you. (I Peter 4:3, 4)

From these passages, it is clear that Peter is speaking to a Gentile audience. In the first place, Peter indicates that the grace bestowed upon the readers of his epistle was still future from the perspective of the prophets who spoke of it. Now since this grace was a present possession of Israel in the time of the prophets, the future bestowing of this grace indicates that these future recipients were not Israelites, but rather Gentiles. Consistent with this conclusion is the fact that Peter refers to his audience as formerly not being a people, but now becoming the people of God as a result of a gracious call out of darkness and into God's marvelous light. Once again, this characterization implies a Gentile audience since the Jews of the Old Covenant cannot be regarded as being a non-people devoid of God's light. Finally, the Gentile character of Peter's audience follows from the list of pagan vices attributed to them, including idolatry which would have been detestable to the legalistic Jews of Peter's day and thus inconsistent with a Jewish characterization of Peter's audience. Given these facts, Peter's audience is clearly Gentile. Consequently, when Peter, a Jew, refers to his Gentile audience as "you," an implicit ethnic distinction frequently overlays the explicit grammatical distinction between the first person of the speaker and the second person of the audience. As a result, Peter's "you" frequently carries the meaning of "you Gentiles."

Returning to the point at hand, the significance of the above result is that the "you" and the "all" of II Peter 3:9 are grammatically linked in a manner that makes them materially identical. As a result, the ethnic character of the "you" attaches to the "all" as well. Thus, II Peter 3:9 could be translated:

154

God is not slow in keeping His promise as
some understand slowness. He is patient with
you Gentiles, not wanting *any people* to perish, but *all peoples* to come to repentance.

Though this language seems a bit awkward when the
ethnic undertones are made explicit, such a translation is consistent with the language of the text, the
local context, the Gentile ethnicity of Peter's audience, the redemptive-historical nature of Peter's
discourse, and Peter's explicit references to reprobation. Consequently, while an individual interpretation
of II Peter 3:9 is excluded by Peter's explicit references to reprobation, an ethnic interpretation satisfies
all the remaining constraints. Thus, when Peter says
that God does not want "any" to perish, but "all" to
come to repentance, this language must be ethnically
construed. As a result, II Peter 3:9 harmonizes perfectly with the doctrine of reprobation since it does
not imply a divine desire to save every individual.

On the basis of the preceding discussion, then,
Romans 11:32; I Timothy 2:3,4; and II Peter 3:9 are
seen to harmonize with the doctrine of reprobation.
As seen from the analysis of these texts, an ethnic
sense was supported by the specific word usage and
the various levels of context while an individual interpretation was consistently excluded on the basis of
explicit references to reprobation by the authors themselves. Consequently, since these texts manifest an
ethnic, and not an individual universalism, they in no
way imply a divine intent to save every individual.
Thus, opponents of predestination cannot advance
these texts against the doctrine of reprobation.

Objections to Reprobation; Divine Sorrow for the Wicked

11

In the previous chapter, passages relating to the universal benevolence of God were examined at great length in terms of their compatibility with the doctrine of reprobation. In regard to these passages, it was shown that the word "all" manifests an ethnic and not an individual sense. Accordingly, statements to the effect that God wishes to save "all" men do not implicate a divine desire to save every individual but rather imply a divine intent to extend salvation to all peoples, Gentiles as well as Jews. Given this fact, such passages are most compatible with the reprobation of select individuals.

Having examined such passages in the previous chapter, another set of passages will here be considered, namely, texts expressing a divine sorrow over the destruction of the wicked. With regard to this class of texts, the following passages are frequently brought forward by opponents of predestination:

> But if a wicked man turns away from all the sins he has committed and keeps all my decrees and does what is just and right, he will surely live; he will not die. None of the of-

fenses he has committed will be remembered against him. Because of the righteous things he has done, he will live. Do I take pleasure in the death of the wicked? declares the Sovereign Lord. Rather, am I not pleased when they turn from their ways and live? (Ezekiel 18:21-23)

Therefore, O house of Israel, I will judge you, each one according to his ways, declares the Sovereign Lord. Repent! Turn away from all your offenses; then sin will not be your downfall. Rid yourselves of all the offenses you have committed, and get a new heart and a new spirit. Why will you die, O house of Israel? For I take no pleasure in the death of anyone, declares the Sovereign Lord. Repent and live! (Ezekiel 18:30-32)

O Jerusalem, Jerusalem, you who kill the prophets and stone those sent to you, how often I have longed to gather your children together, as a hen gathers her chicks under her wings, but you were not willing. Look, your house is left to you desolate. For I tell you, you will not see me again until you say, "Blessed is he who comes in the name of the Lord." (Matthew 23:37-39)

On the basis of these passages, a divine sorrow over human destruction is clearly seen. In particular, God laments Israel's destruction, and Jesus weeps over a rebellious Jerusalem which is on the verge of ruin. Given this evident sorrow, opponents attempt to pit such texts against the doctrine of reprobation on the ground that God cannot consistently will the very destruction that grieves Him. As will be shown below, however, such an objection is based on a false opposition and is therefore entirely groundless.

To demonstrate the falsity of this opposition, it will be necessary to juxtapose the above passages with others having a seemingly opposite sense. In this regard, the following passages are most significant:

> The Lord works out everything for his own ends — even the wicked for a day of disaster. (Proverbs 16:4)

> When he was alone, the Twelve and the others around him asked him about the parables. He told them, "The secret of the kingdom of God has been given to you. But to those on the outside, everything is said in parables so that

> "they may be ever seeing but never perceiving, and ever hearing but never understanding; otherwise they might turn and be forgiven!"

> Then Jesus said to them, "Don't you understand this parable? How then will you understand any parable?" (Mark 4:10-13)

> You snakes! You brood of vipers! How will you escape being condemned to hell? Therefore I am sending you prophets and wise men and teachers. Some of them you will kill and crucify; others you will flog in your syna-

gogues and pursue from town to town. And
so upon you will come all the righteous blood
that has been shed on earth, from the blood
of righteous Abel to the blood of Zechariah
son of Berkiah, whom you murdered between the temple and the altar. I tell you the
truth, all this will come upon this generation. (Matthew 23: 33-36)

On the basis of the above passages, God's eternal reprobation is clearly seen. Here, in seeming contrast to
the previous passages, God is represented as working
evil persons to a day of disaster which is expressedly
said to be His intended end. Moreover, in seeming
opposition to His previous weeping over Jerusalem,
Christ here speaks of concealing the saving truth from
those outside the kingdom, and even of setting up the
current Jewish generation for judgment. Consequently,
while the previous passages do indeed attest a divine
sorrow over human destruction, these latter passages
just as clearly set forth God's eternal reprobation.

Given this fact, a dilemma would seem to arise since
the two sets of passages considered above seem to
contradict one another. Yet, since Scripture is inerrant
and infallible, every passage thereof must be true in
its own right and therefore consistent with every other
passage. Thus, due to the requirements of Biblical in-
errancy, the above messages, though seemingly
opposed, must be simultaneously true and internally
consistent. Consequently, to interpret the above passages in a Biblically orthodox fashion, one may neither
jettison a particular set, nor allow a contradiction to
stand. Rather, one must interpret both sets in a man-

ner that preserves the natural sense of each and which also affects a harmony between their respective doctrinal emphases.

To set forth this harmony, however, it is necessary to maintain a difference in the respective senses of the above sets of passages. After all, to avoid a logical contradiction, the sense in which God wills the destruction of the reprobate must differ from the sense in which He wills it not (*i.e.*, in which it grieves Him). Thus, a harmonious interpretation of these passages hinges upon a distinction between two separate wills of God. Consequently, the problem of Chapter 3 has arisen again, namely the distinction and interrelation between the decretive and preceptive wills of God. To properly set the stage for the following discussion, therefore, it will be necessary to review this important distinction.

In this regard, recall that the distinction between God's decretive and preceptive wills arose from a passage concerning the death of Christ:

> Men of Israel, listen to this: Jesus of Nazareth was a man accredited by God to you by miracles, wonders, and signs, which God did among you through him, as you yourselves know. This man was handed over to you by God's set purpose and foreknowledge; and you, with the help of wicked men, put him to death by nailing him to the cross. (Acts 2:22, 23)

In reference to this passage, it is obvious that God willed Christ's death in terms of His eternal decree

161

since Christ is here said to have been handed over "by God's set purpose and foreknowledge." On the other hand, it is also obvious that God willed against Christ's death in terms of His moral law or precept since Christ's murders are referred to as "wicked men." So understood, the above passage attests the concurrent operation of God's decretive and preceptive wills. In terms of this distinction, the decretive will is absolute in nature and concerns historical eventuation (*i.e.*, what God will do). The preceptive will, by contrast, is imperative and therefore conditional in nature and thus refers to moral obligation (*i.e.*, what man should do). Consequently, since the two wills involve distinct agents (God vs. man) and distinct senses of willing (absolute vs. conditional), there is no logical contradiction in God's preceptively willing a particular outcome and decretively willing its opposite. Moreover, since this distinction clearly arises from the passage above, it is seen to be Biblically based and may therefore be legitimately applied to the problem of the present chapter.

In this regard, it was shown above that a distinction of wills was needed to affect a harmony between the doctrine of reprobation and God's sorrow over human destruction. After all, to avoid a logical contradiction, the sense in which God wills human destruction must differ from the sense in which He wills it not (*i.e.*, in which it grieves Him). Applying the distinction between the decretive and preceptive wills, therefore, it may be said that while God decretively wills the destruction of the reprobate, He preceptively wills against it. Consequently, since God's decretive will is absolute and His preceptive will is conditional, God can consistently will these divergent ends in distinct senses without contradiction. Thus, the doctrine of reprobation is ultimately compatible with God's sorrow over human destruction. To see this coherence in a more explicit manner, the relation between these wills has been diagramed in Figure 3.

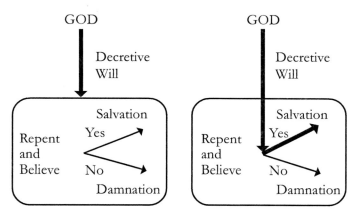

Figure 3a.
Decretive Will Establishes
Preceptive Will Generally

Figure 3b.
Decretive Will Works Through
Preceptive Will Specifically

FIGURE 3: Schematic Illustrating the Coherence
between God's Decretive and Preceptive Wills

As can be seen from Figure 3a, God's decretive will establishes His preceptive will, thereby setting the conditions of salvation for all men. Accordingly, God's preceptive will is seen to be conditional in nature since it suspends various alternatives upon the human response to the requirement of belief and repentance. Moreover, since these conditions are externally announced to all men in the proclamation of the Gospel, God may be said to will everyone's salvation in this preceptive sense. So understood, God's preceptive will is linked to an external call that goes out in the form of a command or precept, announcing the conditions of salvation to all men and commanding them to repent and believe (Mark 1:15; Acts 2:38). Thus, in a conditional and imperatival fashion, God preceptively wishes everyone to be saved and therefore commands all to come. However, since man is dead in trespasses and sins, he is incapable of fulfilling even these minimal conditions of salvation. Accordingly, in addition to the external call which God graciously extends to all men, God even more graciously regenerates His elect, thereby enabling them to respond to the external call. Thus, in harmony with the external call, there is an internal call going to the elect alone in accordance with God's decretive will as shown in Figure 3b. Accordingly, in saving His elect, God works through the conditions of His preceptive offer even as He decretively secures the salvation offered.

On the basis of the preceding discussion, the opposition between the doctrine of reprobation and God's sorrow over human destruction has been shown to be false. After all, since God's decretive will establishes His preceptive will and works through the conditions thereof, there is a necessary harmony between God's preceptive universalism and His decretive exclusivism. In this regard, God's harmonious action is well illustrated by Christ's parable of the soils. On the one hand, God works externally in accordance with His preceptive will, scattering Gospel seed over all types of soil. In accordance with His decretive will, however, God works internally in His elect alone, turning stony and thorny hearts into a fertile soil receptive to His Word. Thus, the external call consists of an objective command addressed to everyone, while the internal call relates to a subjective grace intended for the elect alone.[1] So understood, the external and internal calls work together "hand in glove" in a manner described by the text: "Many are called, but few are chosen" (Matthew 22:14).[2] Thus, there is complete harmony between God's preceptively willing and externally calling everyone, while decretively willing and internally calling His elect

---

[1] Since this internal call is necessarily effective in reaching its end, this internal calling is often referred to as effectual calling.

[2] With regard to the above description, it is possible to be more precise. The decretive and preceptive wills of God relate to the distinct ends which God wills and may thus be said to constitute the formal aspect of the problem. The internal and external calls, on the other hand, relate to the distinct means through which God wills these ends, and may thus be said to constitute the material aspect of the problem. Now, since God's decretive will is absolute and His preceptive will is conditional, the two do not contradict. Rather, considering the formal aspect of the problem, it is precisely God's decretive will that establishes His preceptive will and works through the conditions thereof. Moreover, considering the material aspect of the problem, God's internal call works in the hearts of His elect thereby enabling them to respond to the external call. Thus, while God offers salvation to everyone in general, He enables His elect alone to respond to the offer. Accordingly, in restricting salvation to His elect alone (i.e. excluding the reprobate), God's action is most consistent with the conditions of His universal offer.

165

alone (*i.e.*, excluding the reprobate).[3] Given this fact, passages expressing divine sorrow over human destruction cannot be advanced against the doctrine of reprobation since these two scriptural truths may be harmoniously integrated into an overarching framework in terms of the decretive and preceptive wills of God. Luther's comments corroborate this explanation:

> The words of Matthew 23 come forth in front, the Achilles of the flies: "O Jerusalem,

---

[3] Thus, it is a myth that God's predestination shuts many out of God's kingdom who desperately want to be saved. On the contrary, since the external call goes to everyone, all who wish may come. However, since man is bound by his sinful hatred of God, only those touched by God's electing grace will manifest such a wish. Thus, it is that one who earnestly desires salvation and is troubled over the doctrine of election is not a reprobate who has been shut out of heaven against his wishes. On the contrary, one who is deeply touched by the guilt of his sin shows every sign of electing grace. The reprobate, however, being spiritually dead and blind, generally do not concern themselves with these divine matters and thus do not quibble over the fairness of God's discriminating grace. Luther writes:

If one fears that he is not elected or is otherwise troubled about his election, he should be thankful that he has such fear; for then he should surely know that God cannot lie when in Psalm 51:17 He says: "The sacrifices of God are a broken spirit: a broken and contrite heart, O God, thou wilt not despise." Thus he should cheerfully cast himself on the faithfulness of God who gives this promise, and turn away from the foreknowledge of the threatening God. Then he will be saved as one that is elected. It is not the characteristic of reprobates to tremble at the secret counsel of God; but that is the characteristic of the elect. The reprobates despise it, or at least pay no attention to it, or else they declare in the arrogance of their despair: "Well, if I am damned, all right, then I am damned. (Luther, *Commentary on Romans*, 132)."

Jerusalem, how often would I have gathered
thy children together, and thou wouldst not"
(v. 37). "If all comes to pass by necessity,"
says the Diatribe, "could not Jerusalem have
justly answered the Lord, 'Why dost thou
weary thyself with useless tears? If thou didst
not wish us to hearken to the prophets, why
didst thou send them? Why dost thou lay to
our charge that which came to pass at Thy
will, and so by necessity in us?'" So speaks
the Diatribe...

I say, as I said before, that we may not debate the secret will of Divine Majesty, and
that the recklessness of man, who shows
unabated perversity in leaving necessary
matters for an attempted assault on that will,
should be withheld and restrained from em-
ploying itself in searching out those secrets
of Divine Majesty; for man cannot attain
unto them, seeing that, as Paul tells us (cf.
I Timothy 6:16), they dwell in inaccessible
light. But let man occupy himself with God
Incarnate, that is, with Jesus crucified, in
whom, as Paul says (cf. Colossians 2:3), are
all the treasures of wisdom and knowledge
(though hidden); for by Him man has abundant instruction both in what he should and
in what he should not know.

Here, God Incarnate says: "I would, and thou
wouldst not." God Incarnate, I repeat, was
sent for this purpose, to will, say, do, suffer,
and offer to all men, all that is necessary for

salvation; albeit He offends many who, being abandoned or hardened by God's secret will of Majesty, do not receive Him thus willing, speaking, doing and offering. As John says: "The light shineth in darkness, and the darkness comprehendeth it not" (John 1:5). And again: "He came unto His own, and His own received Him not" (v. 11). It belongs to the same God Incarnate to weep, lament, and groan over the perdition of the ungodly, though that will of Majesty purposely leaves and reprobates some to perish. Nor is it for us to ask why He does so, but to stand in awe of God, Who can do, and wills to do, such things. (Luther, *The Bondage of the Will*, 175,176)[4]

While the explanation offered above provides for a harmonious integration of reprobation and divine compassion, some may reject this explanation as being mechanistic and impersonal. On this objection, it would be held that God's preceptive desire to save all men is a mere formality and not a gracious, well meant offer. As a result, it reduces the Gospel to a divine toying with man and therefore cannot legitimately account for God's genuine sorrow over human destruction. To respond to this objection, therefore, it must

---

[4] Here, Luther refers to God's decretive will as the secret will because unlike His preceptive will which is revealed in Scripture, the decretive will of God is often hidden prior to the occurrence of the events it determines. For this reason, the decretive and preceptive wills are often referred to as the secret and revealed wills of God, respectively.

be shown that the external call is truly a gracious and well-meant offer, the rejection of which is a legitimate cause of divine sorrow.

In this regard, it must first be noted that the non-saving character of an act does not negate its graciousness. For instance, Scripture declares God to be gracious in giving rain and sunshine to all people (Matthew 5:45) even though such gifts are clearly non-saving. Thus, in addition to God's saving grace which goes to the elect alone, there is also a non-saving grace which God extends to men in common. Accordingly, the fact that the external call is non-saving, does not negate its status as a species of common grace and therefore does not impugn its truly gracious character.

Rather, since it announces the conditions of God's preceptive will of salvation, the external call must be regarded as a serious, well meant offer (and for this reason man is rendered more guilty for rejecting it). After all, since fallen man deserves nothing but God's wrath, it is most generous of God to hold forth the conditions of salvation to him at all. Indeed, having forfeited every claim to God's goodness, fallen man cannot despise the grace offered in the external call, nor quibble over its insufficiency. Moreover, since man's inability to respond to God's offer results from the sinfulness of his own heart, this inability is man's own fault, and God is therefore under no obligation to remove man's inability through internal grace. Thus, the graciousness of the external call is not annulled by the surpassing graciousness of the internal call. After all, given the guilt of original sin, the external call is more than anyone deserves.

Consequently, since the external call is a gracious, well meant offer and not a hollow reduction of the Gospel, God's preceptive will of salvation expresses a benevolent intention which fully accounts for God's sorrow over human destruction. Accordingly, in decreeing the destruction of the reprobate, God must therefore be seen as willing the very end that grieves Him. However, since human beings often legitimately will things that cause them anguish (such as a seminary education, for instance), it is not unthinkable that God would do so. After all, in His infinite love and wisdom, God gave His only begotten Son to die a shameful death on the cross, and nothing could be more grievous than that.

On the basis of the preceding discussion, then, God's sorrow over human destruction has been shown compatible with the doctrine of reprobation. By invoking the distinction between God's decretive and preceptive wills, it has been shown that the sense in which God wills the destruction of the reprobate differs from the sense in which He wills against it (*i.e.*, in which it grieves Him). Given this distinction, therefore, God can will the destruction of the reprobate in a decretive sense even as He wills against it in a preceptive sense. After all, since God's decretive will establishes His preceptive will and works through the conditions thereof, there is a necessary harmony between the two. Moreover, such an explanation is not mechanistic and impersonal but rather fully accounts for God's genuine sorrow over human destruction. After all, in decretively willing the death of Christ, God willed the very thing that grieved Him (*i.e.*, that He willed against preceptively). So understood, the above explanation is neither simplistic nor trite but rather robust with respect to the Biblical and theological data. Given this fact, passages expressing a divine sorrow over human destruction cannot be advanced against the doctrine of reprobation since the two Biblical truths can be harmoniously integrated into an overarching framework on the basis of God's decretive and preceptive wills:

> Next: when Christ says in John 6: "No man can come to me, except My Father which hath sent me draw him" (v. 44), what does he leave to "free-will"? He says man needs to hear and learn of the Father Himself, and that all must be taught of God. Here, indeed, he declares, not only that the works and efforts of "free-will" are unavailing, but that even the very word of the gospel (of which He is here speaking) is heard in vain, unless the Father Himself speaks within, and teaches, and draws. "No man, no man can come," he says, and what he is talking about is your "power whereby man can make some endeavour towards Christ." In things that pertain to salvation, He asserts that power to be null.

> "Free-will" is not helped by what the Diatribe quotes from Augustine in an attempt to discredit this plain and powerful Scripture: that is, the statement that "God draws us as we draw sheep, by holding out a branch to them" (cf. Augustine, *Tract. in Joannis ev.,* 26.5). From this simile the Diatribe would

171

have it inferred that there is in us a power to follow the drawing of God. But the simile does not hold in this passage. For God displays, not just one, but all His good gifts, even His own Son, Christ, and yet, unless He inwardly displays something more and draws in another manner, no man follows Him; indeed, the whole world persecutes the Son whom He displays! The simile well fits the experience of the godly, who are already "sheep" and know God as their Shepherd; living in, and moved by, the Spirit, they follow wherever God wills, and whatever He shows them. But the ungodly does not "come," even when he hears the word, unless the Father draws and teaches him inwardly; which He does by shedding abroad His Spirit. When that happens, there follows a "drawing" other than that which is outward; Christ is then displayed by the enlightening of the Spirit, and by it man is rapt to Christ with the sweetest rapture, he being passive while God speaks, teaches and draws, rather than seeking or running himself. (Luther, *The Bondage of the Will*, 310,311)

As to why some are touched by the law and others not, so that some receive and others scorn the offer of grace, that is another question, which Ezekiel does not here discuss. He speaks of the published offer of God's mercy, not of the dreadful hidden will of God, Who according to His own counsel, ordains such persons as He wills to receive and partake of the mercy preached and offered. This will is not to be inquired into, but to be reverently adored, as by far the most awesome secret of the Divine Majesty. He has kept it to Himself and forbidden us to know it: and it is much more worthy of reverence than an infinite number of Corycian caverns!

When, now the Diatribe reasons thus: "Does the righteous Lord deplore the death of His people which He Himself works in them? This seems too ridiculous"—I reply, as I have already said: we must discuss God, or the will of God, preached, revealed, offered to us, and worshipped by us in one way, and God not preached, nor revealed, nor offered to us, nor worshipped by us, in another way. Wherever God hides Himself, and wills to be unknown to us, there we have no concern. Here that sentiment: "what is above us does not concern us," really holds good....

Now, God in His own nature and majesty is to be left alone: in this regard, we have nothing to do with Him, nor does He wish us to deal with Him. We have to do with Him as clothed and displayed in His Word, by which He presents Himself to us. That is His glory and beauty, in which the Psalmist proclaims Him to be clothed (cf. Psalm 21:5). I say that the righteous God does not deplore the death of His people which He Himself works in them, but He deplores the death which He

173

finds in His people and desires to remove from them. God preached works to the end that sin and death may be taken away, and we may be saved. "He sent His word and healed them" (Psalm 107:27). But God hidden in Majesty neither deplores nor takes away death, but works life, and death, and all in all; nor has He set bounds to Himself by His Word, but has kept Himself free over all things.

The Diatribe is deceived by its own ignorance in that it makes no distinction between God preached and God hidden, that is, between the Word of God and God Himself. God does many things which He does not show us in His Word, and He wills many things which He does not in His Word show us that He wills. Thus, He does not will the death of a sinner — that is, in His Word; but He wills it by His inscrutable will....

So it is right to say: "If God does not desire our death, it must be laid to the charge of our own will if we perish"; this, I repeat, is right if you spoke of God preached. For He desires that all men should be saved, in that He comes to all by the word of salvation, and the fault is in the will which does not receive Him; as He says in Matthew 23: "How often would I have gathered thy children together, and thou wouldst not!" (v. 37) But why the Majesty does not remove or change this fault of will in every man (for it is not in the power of man to do it), or why He lays this fault to the charge of the will, when man cannot avoid it, it is not lawful to ask; and though you should ask much, you would never find out; as Paul says in Romans 11: "Who art thou that repliest against God?" (Romans 9:20) (Luther, *The Bondage of the Will*, 169-171)

Objections to Reprobation; Conditional and Imperatival Texts

12

In the previous chapter, passages expressing a divine sorrow over human destruction were examined in terms of their compatibility with the doctrine of reprobation. By invoking the distinction between God's decretive and preceptive wills, it was shown that the sense in which God wills human destruction differs from the sense in which He wills against it (*i.e.*, in which it grieves Him). Given this difference in sense, therefore, it is entirely consistent for God to foreordain human destruction in a decretive sense while willing against it in a preceptive sense. As a result, passages expressing a divine sorrow over human destruction are entirely compatible with the doctrine of reprobation and therefore cannot be advanced against it.

Having considered such objections in the previous chapter, a related class of objections will here be considered, namely those arising from the assumed force of conditional and imperatival texts. With regard to this class of objections, the following passages are frequently brought forward by opponents of predestination:

But if a wicked man turns away from all the sins he has committed and keeps all my decrees and does what is just and right, he will surely live; he will not die. None of the offenses he has committed will be remembered against him. Because of the righteous things he has done, he will live. Do I take pleasure in the death of the wicked? declares the Sovereign Lord. Rather, am I not pleased when they turn from their ways and live? (Ezekiel 18:21-23)

Therefore, O house of Israel, I will judge you, each one according to his ways, declares the Sovereign Lord. Repent! Turn away from all your offenses; then sin will not be your downfall. Rid yourselves of all the offenses you have committed, and get a new heart and a new spirit. Why will you die, O house of Israel? For I take no pleasure in the death of anyone, declares the Sovereign Lord. Repent and live! (Ezekiel 18:30-32)

As should be readily apparent, the above passages set forth God's law through conditional and imperatival modes, respectively. Thus, the two passages are substantively identical and formally distinct. With respect to substance, their common legal nature derives from the fact that both passages make God's blessing contingent upon human obedience. Moreover, it is precisely this legal nature that provides the pretext for the misapplication of these passages. In particular, it is held that a demand to believe and repent cannot be seriously intended apart from an ability to comply. Accordingly, in opposition to the doctrine of reprobation, it is argued that the above passages imply a common ability to believe and repent and thus a common potential for everyone to be saved.[1] In responding to this objection, it will be necessary to consider both the form and the substance of these passages.

With respect to form, the first passage states the law in the conditional manner of an "If, then" type of statement. In so doing, it explicitly suspends a result signified by the word "then" upon a condition signified by the word "If." Thus, reducing the first passage to its bare essentials, it would state: "If you repent and believe, you will be saved." In contrast to this first passage, however, the second passage states the law in the imperatival manner of a command. In so

---

[1] If the above inference is analyzed and broken down into its essentials, it can be more precisely stated in the form of a logical syllogism. In this regard, it would first be stated formally and generally that all conditional and imperatival statements necessarily imply the possibility of their fulfillment in order to be true statements. This would be the major premise. It would then be stated materially and particularly that the above texts constitute specific conditional and imperatival statements requiring belief and repentance for their fulfillment. This would be the minor premise. Finally, it would be concluded on the basis of the two foregoing steps, that the above texts therefore imply the possibility of belief and repentance, thus militating against the doctrine of reprobation.

Given the above premises, of course, this conclusion readily follows since the argument is logically valid. The problem, however, is that it is based on a false major premise and is therefore unsound. It is simply not true that conditional and imperatival texts imply the possibility of their fulfillment, and this fact destroys the entire argument. The key to disposing of the above argument, then, is to demonstrate the falsity of its major premise.

doing, it implicitly suspends a result (blessing) upon the condition of obedience to the command. Thus, reducing the second passage to its bare essentials, it would state: "Repent and believe." On the basis of this discussion, then, the distinct yet related forms of these passages has been set forth.[2] Given this understanding, it remains to determine whether the form of either statement implies a common ability to believe and repent. In answering this question, the conditional statement will first be examined.

With regard to the conditional statement, opponents of predestination argue that a common ability to believe and repent is implied by a statement of the form: "If you repent and believe, you will be saved." In other words, it is asserted that the "If" implies the "can." However, in opposition to this argument, it may be pointed out that such reasoning cannot be consistently maintained for all conditional statements without leading to a patent absurdity. After all, by such reasoning the ability to earn a billion dollars would then be implied by a statement of the form: "If you earn a billion dollars, you will be a billionaire." Clearly, this line of reasoning is fallacious, and the

---

[2] While conditional and imperatival statements are formally distinct, there does seem to be a certain relation between them. After all, since a command makes certain results (reward and punishment) contingent upon obedience or disobedience, a command is an implicit conditional statement. Given this fact, conditional and imperatival statements both involve major uncertainties since each hinges varying results upon the uncertain fulfillment of various conditions. Accordingly, imperatival statements frequently employ the subjunctive verbal mood, the very mood used by conditional statements to express their inherent uncertainty.

reason is that a conditional statement merely suspends a result upon a condition without implying anything as to the possibility of the condition's fulfillment. In fact, it is precisely due to the uncertainty of the condition's fulfillment that conditional statements assume a subjunctive verbal mood and therefore state nothing indicatively. Accordingly, since a conditional statement is therefore incapable of making any indicative assertion with respect to human ability, it is evident that the "If" does not imply the "can." Consequently, arguments against reprobation which seek to infer ability from conditional statements necessarily fall to the ground. Luther writes:

> So when Ecclesiasticus says, "If thou art willing to keep the commandments, and to keep the faith that pleaseth me, they shall preserve thee," I fail to see how 'free-will' can be proved from his words. "If thou art willing" is a verb in the subjunctive mood, which asserts nothing. As the logicians say, a conditional statement asserts nothing indicatively — such statements as, "if the devil be God, he is deservedly worshipped"; or, "if an ass flies, an ass has wings"; or, "if there be 'free-will.' grace is nothing." And if Ecclesiasticus had wished to assert "free-will," he ought to have spoken thus: "man is able to keep God's commandments"; or, "man has power to keep the commandments." (Luther, *The Bondage of the Will*, 151)

With respect to imperatival statements, the situation is similar. Here, opponents of predestination argue that a common ability to believe and repent is implied by a command of the form: "Repent and believe." In other words, it is asserted that the "ought" implies the "can." Once again, however, such reasoning cannot be consistently carried out since the ability to earn a billion dollars would then be implied by a command of the form: "Earn a billion dollars." Clearly, this line of reasoning is fallacious, and the reason is that an imperatival statement merely specifies what should be done without implying anything as to the ability of the person to carry out the action. In fact, it is precisely due to the obligatory nature of such speech that commands assume an imperative verbal mood and therefore state nothing indicatively. Accordingly, since an imperatival statement is therefore incapable of making any indicative assertion with respect to human ability, it is evident that the "ought" does not imply the "can." Consequently, arguments against reprobation which seek to infer ability from imperatival statements necessarily fall to the ground. It is along these lines that Luther responded to some of Erasmus' illogical inferences from assorted imperatival texts:

> Wherefore, my good Erasmus, as often as you confront me with the words of the law, so often shall I confront you with the words of Paul: "By the law is knowledge of sin" — not power of will! Gather together from the big concordances all the imperative words into one chaotic heap (not the words of promise, but the words of the law and its demand) — and I shall at once declare that

they always show, not what men can do, or do do, but what they should do! Even grammarians and schoolboys at street corners know that nothing more is signified by verbs in the imperative. How is it that you theologians are twice as stupid as schoolboys, in that as soon as you get hold of a single imperative verb you infer an indicative meaning, as though the moment a thing is commanded it is done, or can be done? But there's many a slip 'twixt the cup and the lip! — and the things that you commanded and that were possible enough may yet not be done, so great a gulf is there between imperative and indicative statements in the simplest every day matters! (Luther, *The Bondage of the Will*, 159)

As a result of the preceeding discussion, the attempt to infer ability from conditional and imperatival statements has been shown to be groundless on the basis of linguistic form. However, beyond these linguistic concerns, such an approach is also ruled out by the very substance of the above passages. After all, since these passages are both expressions of God's law, a serious theological error is made by those who attempt to infer ability from them. In particular, by inferring ability from such commands, a works salvation is posited which ignores the crippling effects of sin. Consequently, since man's salvation then becomes a function of legal obedience, the Gospel is voided by the law. To see this point more clearly, it will be necessary to consider the distinction between law and Gospel in relation to the problem of sin and salvation.

In this regard, it must first be mentioned that the role of the law is primarily ethical because it shows man his duty. First and foremost, then, the law is a norm or a rule which sets forth the standard of God pleasing, human behavior. (The Lutherans and the Reformed refer to this function as the third use of the law.) Thus, Scripture commands obedience to God's law and love for God with the totality of one's heart, mind, and strength (Deuteronomy 6:5). However, due to the crippling effects of sin, such obedience is impossible for fallen man and so a second function of the law also comes forth. By showing man his duty, first of all, the law secondarily shows man his guilt and inability and thereby reveals his need of saving grace. Thus, in addition to being a norm or a rule, the law is secondarily a mirror which reveals man's sinful condition and thus his need for the Gospel. (The Lutherans and the Reformed refer to this function as the second use of the law.)[3]

So understood, the distinction between law and Gospel would seem to be one of ethics versus salva-

---

[3] Note especially how the second use of the Law, Law as mirror, is logically dependent on the third use, Law as duty or rule. Yet, because this second use of the Law is so essential to evangelism and pastoral care, Lutherans mistakenly view this as the basic use, and therefore treat the third use of the Law as an appendage. This result, however, represents a confusion of pastoral priority with logical priority. In reality, the third use of the Law is not a use at all but is rather the essence of the Law. And since the essence of a thing determines its use, it is the ethical normativity of the Law which establishes its use as mirror. Consequently, the debate in Lutheran circles over the validity of the Law's third use reflects a confusion regarding the very essence of the Law, and this confusion has led to a devaluation of the Law in practice.

tion. By laying out man's ethical duty, the law shows man his guilt, his ethical inability, and thus his need of Gospel salvation. The Gospel, on the other hand, meets man in the depths of his sin, removing his guilt and restoring his ethical ability through a Spirit wrought union with Christ. Thus, far from implying human ability, the imperatives of the law serve to reveal the very inability (and guilt) which makes the Gospel necessary for man's salvation. Accordingly, any attempt to refute predestination by inferring human ability from the imperatives of the law opens the door to a works salvation which opposes the very Gospel of Christ.

Given this fact, a theological approach which infers ability from conditional and imperatival statements, such as those above, is heretical since it makes salvation dependent upon works, whether these be works of law or works of faith. After all, if the implications of such an error are consistently expressed, a full-orbed works righteousness will prevail, and it will be forgotten that man needs God's grace to empower his faith and his law keeping. That such an inference would even be attempted, however, reflects a simplistic approach to Scripture which minimizes the effects of sin, which fails to distinguish between the strains of law and Gospel (command and promise), and which therefore fails to classify the above texts as examples of law. Thus, to show the idiocy of the above inferences and to stop them dead in their tracks, it will be necessary to prove that the demands of the above passages lie beyond the capacities of natural man. To this end, it will be convenient to juxtapose one of the prophetic texts cited above with another prophetic text reflecting the Gospel strain:

Therefore, O house of Israel, I will judge you, each one according to his ways, declares the Sovereign Lord. Repent! Turn away from all your offenses; then sin will not be your downfall. Rid yourselves of all the offenses you have committed, and get a new heart and a new spirit. Why will you die, O house of Israel? For I take no pleasure in the death of anyone, declares the Sovereign Lord. Repent and live! (Ezekiel 18:30-32)

"The time is coming," declares the Lord, "when I will make a new covenant with the house of Israel and with the house of Judah. It will not be like the covenant I made with their forefathers when I took them by the hand to lead them out of Egypt, because they broke my covenant, though I was a husband to them," declares the Lord. "This is the covenant I will make with the house of Israel after that time," declares the Lord. "I will put my law in their minds and write it on their hearts. I will be their God, and they will be my people. No longer will a man teach his neighbor, or a man his brother, saying, 'Know the Lord,' because they will all know me, from the least of them to the greatest," declares the Lord. "For I will forgive their wickedness and will remember their sins no more." (Jeremiah 31:31-34)

As may be clearly seen by this juxtaposition of texts, these prophetic passages center around the themes of command and promise and therefore reflect the differing strains of law and Gospel, respectively. Furthermore, the clarity of this distinction is here heightened by the several literary correspondences between these two passages. Thus, whereas the first passage commands repentance and law keeping with threats of judgment, the second passage envisions a new covenant in which repentance and law keeping spring from grace along with the forgiveness of sins. Moreover, whereas the first passage commands man to get a new heart, the second passage describes God as giving a new heart to man by writing His law there. Thus, due to the literary correspondences between the two texts, their substantive differences are placed in bold relief. In particular, the two texts center around distinct themes of command and promise and may therefore be subsumed under the categories of law and Gospel, respectively. Accordingly, as a Gospel text, the second passage promises the very thing demanded by the first and for the very reason that these demands lie beyond the capacities of natural man. After all, in addition to demanding repentance, the first text requires man to get a new heart and a new spirit, a requirement which basically equates to self regeneration.

Consequently, a most significant proof that demands of the law do not imply human ability is that such an inference applied to the first passage above would imply a human capacity for self regeneration. Clearly, such an inference would entail a severe departure from evangelical faith in which a man could not only merit his salvation but produce it as well. And, of course, if a man could regenerate himself, such a man would have no need of Christ or the Gospel. In contrast to such absurdities, however, the combined message of the above texts is that salvation must come through the Gospel precisely because the effects of sin render man incapable of earning it through the law. Thus, far from exalting a human ability to believe and repent, the above passages show such action to be impossible apart from God's grace.

Therefore, since the attempt to infer ability from demands of the law here reduces to a heretical absurdity, it follows that human ability cannot be deduced from such passages regardless of whether they are conditionally or imperatively expressed. After all, since a single counter example suffices to nullify an opposing universal claim, the above demonstration necessarily refutes the claim that legal demands imply human ability. Thus, beyond the considerations of linguistic form, the very substance of these passages rules out such a pernicious and grace denying approach. Accordingly, such texts imply no common ability to believe and repent, and therefore do not imply a common potential for everyone to be saved. Given this fact, the attempt to advance such passages against the doctrine of reprobation is entirely groundless:

> But what if I prove that the nature of words and use of language, even among men, is not always such as to make it an act of mockery to say to the impotent, "if thou art willing," "if thou shalt do," "if thou shalt hear"? How often do parents thus play with children, bidding them come to them, or do this or that, only in order that it may appear how impotent they are, and that they may be compelled to call for the help of the parent's hand? How often does a faithful physician tell an obstinate patient to do or stop doing things that are impossible or injurious to him, so as to bring him by experience of himself to a knowledge of his

disease or weakness, to which he cannot lead him by any other course? And what is more common and widespread than to use insulting and provoking language when we would show our friends what they can and cannot do?...

If, now, God, as Father, deals with us as with His sons, with a view to showing us the impotence of which we are ignorant; or as a faithful physician, with a view to making known to us our disease; or if, to taunt His enemies, who proudly resist His counsel and the laws He has set forth (by which He achieves this end most effectively), He should say: "do," "hear," "keep," or: "if thou shalt hear," "if thou art willing," "if thou shalt do"; can it be fairly concluded from this that therefore we can do these things freely, or else God is mocking us? Why should not this conclusion follow rather: therefore, God is trying us, that by His law He may bring us to a knowledge of our impotence, if we are His friends? or else, He is really and deservedly taunting and mocking us, if we are His proud enemies? For this Paul teaches, is the intent of divine legislation (cf. Romans 3:20; 5:20; Galations 3:19,24). Human nature is blind, so that it does not know its own strength — or, rather, sickness; moreover, being proud, it thinks it knows and can do everything. God can cure this pride and ignorance by no readier remedy than the publication of His law. (Luther, *The Bondage of the Will*, 152, 153)

189

Objections to Reprobation; Resistible Grace

13

In the previous chapter, objections to predestination arising from conditional and imperatival texts were considered. In response to opponents who claim that such texts imply a universal ability to believe or repent, it was stated that such texts assert nothing indicatively and thus cannot be used to establish human ability. Moreover, beyond these linguistic considerations, it was argued that such an approach when consistently applied to certain imperatival passages would logically imply an ability to perfectly keep the law and thus to earn one's salvation by works. Accordingly, on the basis of both linguistic and theological considerations, it was concluded that such texts establish no universal ability to believe and repent and thus do not imply a common potential for everyone to be saved. Given this fact, such texts cannot be advanced against the doctrine of predestination since they do not militate against a reprobation of select individuals.

Having considered such arguments in the previous chapter, it remains to examine one final objection to the doctrine of predestination, namely, the idea that God's grace may be resisted and that saved Christians therefore do not necessarily persevere in their faith. In this regard, it is argued by some that certain Biblical texts establish the possibility of true Christians falling from grace and thus losing their salvation. However, if true Christians can fall from grace, then the difference between the saved and the lost once again becomes a function of human activity, in this case resistance. As a result, the doctrine of predestination is again undercut as human action rather than divine power becomes the final determinant of human destiny.

Accordingly, in opposition to this objection, it will be the burden of the present chapter to show that God's grace is irresistible and that saved Christians therefore necessarily persevere in their faith. Consequently, in addition to being the sole initiator of saving faith (as seen previously), God will here be shown to sustain it as well. As a result, man's faith and thus his destiny will emerge as a product of divine action from beginning to end. However, before making the case for irresistible grace, it will be necessary to set forth the implications of the resistible grace objection. To this end various soteriological theories prevailing within Christendom will first be examined to provide a panoramic view of the Christian church on the issue of salvation. Once this overview has been provided, the implications of the resistible grace objection will become readily apparent from this broad denominational context.

In considering the competing theories of salvation which prevail within the church, it is helpful to think of salvation as a house having a front entrance and a rear exit, herein called the front and back doors, respectively. With respect to the entrance, one may ask whether it is by human or divine power that one gets through the front door. Moreover, with regard to the exit, it may also be asked whether those inside the house have the power to leave through the back door. Accordingly, based on the various combinations of the two doors being open or closed, four distinct soteriological views have emerged within Christendom. To facilitate the following discussion, these views will here be represented by the points on a clock as shown in Figure 4.

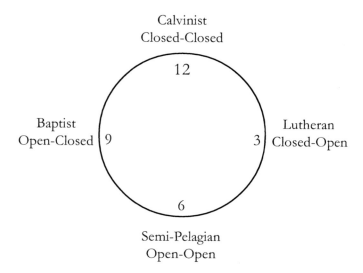

FIGURE 4: Schematic Representation
of Various Soteriological View Points

In terms of this diagram, the Calvinist stands at twelve o'clock. Because the Calvinist believes that the natural man is dead in trespasses and sins, he believes that such a person is incapable of responding to God apart from grace and that a man's salvation is therefore wrought by God's power alone. Moreover, because the Calvinist also believes in irresistible grace, he sees God as the sustainer of man's faith, causing the persons so saved to persevere in their faith. In terms of the house analogy, then, the Calvinist believes both the front and back doors of salvation to be closed to human power since both the initiation and maintenance of man's faith is 100% due to divine action. Thus, the Calvinist believes God, and God alone, to be the ultimate determinant of human destiny, a fact which logically implies a particular election. Historically, this doctrine has been embraced by the Reformed, Presbyterian, and Congregationalist denominations together with a small portion of the Anglicans and Baptists.[1]

---

[1] Historically, the original Baptists believed in a predestination of selected individuals unto life or death but were later out numbered by others who believed that God extends His grace to all men generally and who therefore denied a particular election. Accordingly, due to their belief in a particular election, the former group was later referred to as particular Baptists to distinguish them from the latter group who were called general Baptists. In the present day, particular Baptists commonly refer to themselves as Reformed Baptists to denote their adherence to the Reformed or Calvinistic soteriology (predestination) in distinction from the remainder of the Baptists.

Opposite the Calvinist, the Semi-Pelagian or Arminian[2] stands at six o'clock. This position holds that man's will, though weakened by sin, has sufficient strength to seek God, much as a sick man might seek out a doctor. Accordingly, on this view God is represented as extending His salvation to all men indiscriminately who are then free to accept or reject it at will. Moreover, since the sinner, once saved, is not maintained by God in this state, it is thought that a saved Christian can fall from grace. Consequently, on this view, both the front and back doors of salvation are left open to human power so that man can come

---

[2] Here, the term Semi-Pelagian is derived from the heretic Pelagius who opposed St. Augustine's views on original sin and predestination. In opposition to St. Augustine's view that the natural man was dead in trespasses and sins and thus dependent upon divine grace, Pelagius argued that the human will was totally healthy and thus capable of responding to God and perfectly obeying His will. In contrast to both of these views, Semi-Pelagianism attempts to split the difference between spiritual death and total health, arguing in effect that the natural man, though not spiritually dead, has nevertheless been weakened by original sin. Thus, while the natural man does not possess the strength to obey God's will, he is said to possess sufficient strength seek God's help, much as a sick man seeks a doctor. Accordingly, within the Semi-Pelagian system, salvation is thought to depend upon the human decision to accept God's help. Moreover, because this Semi-Pelagian doctrine was taught for a time by one Jacob Arminius within the Reformed church of Holland, the name "Arminian" is also used as a synonym for "Semi-Pelagian." In fact, it was precisely this teaching by Arminius which precipitated the Synod of Dordt in 1618 at which the five major theses of the Arminian party were rejected. In response the synod drew up and adopted five antitheses to the Arminian position which have became known to posterity as the five points of Calvinism.

and go at will. Thus, in the Semi-Pelagian or Arminian position, human decision, and not divine action, becomes the ultimate determinant of human destiny. The denominations which have traditionally embraced this viewpoint are the Roman Catholics, Greek Orthodox, Methodists, Assemblies of God, Campbellite churches (Christian Churches, Church of Christ, and Disciples of Christ) and the majority of the Anglicans.[3]

Between the previous two positions, the Lutheran stands at three o'clock. Like the Calvinist, the Lutheran believes that the natural man is dead in trespasses and sins so that he is incapable of responding to God apart from grace. Accordingly, since man's salvation must be wrought by God's power alone, the Lutheran, like the Calvinist, believes the front door of salvation to be closed to human power. However, unlike the Calvinist (and in opposition to Martin Luther himself), the Lutheran believes the back door of salvation to be open to human power so that a saved Christian can fall from grace. Indeed, the Lutheran believes that even

---

[3] Here it should be mentioned for completeness that the Augustinian view of predestination which Luther and Calvin both adopted remained as a minority position within the Roman Catholic Church until well past the Protestant Reformation. Moreover, the first generation of leaders in the Anglican Church were also solid Calvinists. Finally, even the early Methodists were divided between the followers of John Wesley who were Arminian in theology and the followers of Whitefield who were Calvinistic. However, because Wesley's followers left the Church of England while Whitefield's remained within it, the Methodist denomination was early dominated by the Arminian position. By contrast, Whitefield Methodism soon vanished by reabsorption into the Anglican Church.

the elect are capable of falling for a time but are eventually brought back into the fold through the power of divine grace. Consequently, while the Lutheran believes that the elect are ultimately saved by God's power alone, he believes that the remainder of humanity fall due to a rejection of God's grace which is universally extended to all. Thus, while the Lutheran believes divine action to determine the destiny of the elect, he believes that human action, in this case rejection, determines the destiny of the non-elect. Consequently, in contrast to the "double predestination" of Calvinism which implies a predestination unto both life and death, the Lutheran holds only to a "single predestination" unto life. Accordingly, in Lutheran theology the doctrine of predestination is weakened as the back door of salvation is left open to human power. Obviously, as the name implies, the denominations which have embraced this view have all been Lutheran.[4]

Finally, opposite the Lutheran stands the most typical of the many varieties of Baptists. This position

---

[4] In this regard, it should be obvious by now that the original Lutheranism stemming from Martin Luther embraced a view that would today be regarded as Calvinistic. Unfortunately, however, within a decade after Luther's publication of *The Bondage of the Will* in 1525, Luther's co-reformer, Philip Melanchthon reverted to the Semi-Pelagian position of the Church of Rome. Thus, two rival parties arose within the ranks of Lutheranism which were later unified by the "single predestination" compromise   adopted in the *Formula of Concord*   in 1580. Nevertheless, while this compromise has so far prevented a robust "double predestination" from returning, the synergistic, Semi-Pelagian strain has continuously reasserted itself as various pietistic groups have exerted both regional and sometimes denomination wide influences.

holds that the human will, though weakened by sin, has sufficient strength to accept the grace which God indiscriminately extends to all men. However, once having accepted the Gospel, the sinner is thought to be transformed by an act of divine grace which maintains him in the state of salvation through divine power. Accordingly, while the Baptist believes the front door of salvation to be open to human power, he believes the back door to be shut in accordance with the phrase, "once saved, always saved." The denominations which have traditionally embraced this position have been a majority of the Baptist groups, the Four Square Church, and many independent community churches influenced by Baptist theology.[5, 6]

---

[5] In regard to the variety among Baptists, it may be stated that Baptist views range from the Reformed Baptist position at twelve o'clock to the Free Will Baptist position at six o'clock. However, in spite of this broad range of views, most Baptists are well characterized by the nine o'clock position above.

[6] With respect to practical matters, it is feared by some that the idea of irresistible grace, perseverance, or eternal security promotes spiritual laxity. To show that such is not the case, it is necessary to distinguish between Baptist and Calvinist understandings of the term. In this regard, it should first be mentioned that there is nothing wrong with the phrase, "once saved, always saved," since it reflects the scriptural truth. The problem is with the Baptist understanding of it. In contrast to the Calvinist who would apply this phrase to the elect alone, the Baptist, leaving the front door of salvation open to all men, believes that any person making a profession of faith at any time in life is saved, no matter how backslidden. In other words, every "decision for Christ" is taken as a valid conversion so that what the Baptist really believes is not "once saved, always saved," but rather "once professed, always possessed!" The Calvinist, on the other hand, argues that many professions of faith are false since there are many tares [continued]

On the basis of the previous discussion, then, the significance of irresistible grace and perseverance may readily be seen. When the various positions of Christendom are arranged and examined within a single framework, it is found that Calvinism alone holds to a particularism in which the specific destiny of each individual is determined by God's discriminating action. By contrast, all other positions hold to some form of universalism in which human destiny is finally determined by a human response (acceptance, rejection, or both) to a universally extended grace. Indeed, even Lutheranism, which is the best of these alternate viewpoints, is seen to waver between these two opinions. Now when the reason for Calvinism's uniqueness is sought, it is readily seen that it is Calvinism, and Calvinism alone, that closes both doors of salvation to human power. All other positions, by contrast, open one or both doors to human power, thereby making human decision the final determinant of human destiny. Thus, as seen from the brief com-

---

(reprobate) among the wheat (elect) (Matthew 13:24-30). And while the Calvinist believes in the certain perseverance of the elect, he sees this as both requirement and gift. Perseverance in faith and morals, then, is not only a gift, but an obligation and a mark of the elect. And while it comes by grace, it must necessarily manifest itself in life. Perseverance, then, is the criterion of election without which one is not elect. Consequently, within a Calvinist framework, the doctrine of eternal security does not produce spiritual laxity since it not only promises, but also demands, the perseverance of the saints. In the Baptist case, of course, spiritual laxity follows easily since the promise is given apart from the obligation to persevere. Rightly understood, however, this doctrine does not produce spiritual laxity but rather a strict scrutiny. After all, it has never been a charge that Calvinists are too lax!

parison of viewpoints discussed above, the doctrine of predestination is undercut whenever either door of the house of salvation is left open to human power. Given this fact, the implications of the resistible grace argument are readily apparent. Through this objection, opponents of predestination seek to attack this doctrine through the back door.

Consequently, given the implications of the resistible grace argument, a thorough defense of predestination must respond to this objection. To this end, the following discussion will proceed in two major steps. First, positive scriptural evidence supporting the doctrine of perseverance will be assessed to show that God's grace is irresistible. Then, having set forth the positive evidence, the passages thought to establish the opposite view will be thoroughly examined. From this analysis, it will be shown that "problem passages" notwithstanding, the Biblical data consistently and uniformly militate against the concept of resistible grace and therefore support the doctrine of predestination.

With respect to the positive Biblical support, the following Scriptures are decisive in establishing the irresistibility of God's grace and thus the resulting perseverance of God's elect:

And we know that in all things God works for the good of those who love him and who have been called according to his purpose. For those God foreknew, he also predestined to be conformed to the likeness of his Son, that he might be the firstborn among many brothers. And those he predestined, he also called; those he called, he also justified; those he justified, he also glorified.

What, then, shall we say in response to this? If God is for us, who can be against us? He who did not spare his own Son, but gave him up for us all — how will he not also, along with him, graciously give us all things? Who will bring any charge against those whom God has chosen? It is God who justifies. Who is he that condemns? Christ Jesus, who died — more than that, who was raised to life — is at the right hand of God and is also interceding for us. Who shall separate us from the love of Christ? Shall trouble or hardship or persecution or famine or nakedness or danger or sword? As it is written: "For your sake we face death all day long; we are considered as sheep to be slaughtered." No, in all these things we are more than conquerors through him who loved us. For I am convinced that neither death nor life, neither angels nor demons, neither the present nor the future, nor any powers, neither height nor depth, nor anything else in all creation, will be able to separate us from the love of God that is in Christ Jesus our Lord. (Romans 8:28-39)

Praise be to the God and Father of our Lord Jesus Christ, who has blessed us in the heavenly realms with every spiritual blessing in Christ. For he chose us in him before the creation of the world to be holy and blameless in his sight. In love he predestined us to be adopted as his sons through Jesus Christ, in accordance with his pleasure and will.... In him we were also chosen, having been predestined according to the plan of him who works out everything in conformity with the purpose of his will, in order that we, who were the first to hope in Christ, might be for the praise of his glory. And you also were included in Christ when you heard the word of truth, the gospel of your salvation. Having believed, you were marked in him with a seal, the promised Holy Spirit, who is a deposit guaranteeing our inheritance until the redemption of those who are God's possession — to the praise of his glory. (Ephesians 1:3-5, 11-14)

Peter, an apostle of Jesus Christ,

To God's elect, strangers in the world, scattered throughout Pontus, Galatia, Cappadocia, Asia and Bithynia, who have been chosen according to the foreknowledge of God the Father, through the sanctifying work of the Spirit, for obedience to Jesus Christ and sprinkling by his blood:

Grace and Peace be yours in abundance.

Praise be to the God and Father of our Lord Jesus Christ! In his great mercy he has given us new birth into a living hope through the resurrection of Jesus Christ from the dead, and into an inheritance that can never perish, spoil or fade — kept in heaven for you, who through faith are shielded by God's power until the coming of salvation that is ready to be revealed in the last time. (I Peter 1:1-5)

Then Jesus declared, "I am the bread of life. He who comes to me will never go hungry, and he who believes in me will never be thirsty. But as I told you, you have seen me and still you do not believe. All that the Father gives me will come to me, and whoever comes to me I will never drive away. For I have come down from heaven not to do my will but to do the will of him who sent me. And this is the will of him who sent me, that I shall lose none of all that he has given me, but raise them up at the last day. For my Father's will is that everyone who looks up to the Son and believes in him shall have eternal life, and I will raise him up at the last day."

At this the Jews began to grumble about him because he said," I am the bread that came down from heaven." They said, "Is this not Jesus, the son of Joseph, whose father and mother we know? How can he now say, 'I came down from heaven?'"

"Stop grumbling among yourselves, " Jesus answered. "No one can come to me unless the Father who sent me draws him and I will raise him up at the last day..." (John 6:35-43).

On the basis of the above texts, the salvation of the elect is seen to be certain. Consequently, since even redeemed sinners naturally resist God's grace, the doctrines of irresistible grace and perseverance are necessarily implied as the respective means and end of God's predestination.

Beyond these general considerations, however, these doctrines are also attested directly by specific content of the passages themselves. For instance, in the Romans passage, those who are foreknown and predestined by God are seen to be necessarily glorified since nothing in creation can separate them from God's eternal love. Thus, since the emphasis in the passage is upon divine and not human action, the irresistible nature of God's grace together with the resulting perseverance of the elect is clearly seen. Moreover, in the Ephesians passage, Christians are said to be predestined in conformity to the plan of the one who works everything according to His will, and also to be sealed with the promised Holy Spirit Who is a guarantee of their eternal inheritance. Thus, unless the Spirit testifies falsely when He seals, the sealed ones necessarily persevere. Furthermore, in the Petrine passage, the elect of the Father are seen to be shielded by God's power until the coming of salvation that is ready to be revealed in the last time. Finally, in John's Gospel, it is seen that Christ will raise up all whom the Father has given Him on the last day. On the basis of the above texts, therefore, the doctrines of perseverance and irresistible grace are seen to be scripturally attested.

Moreover, beyond the specific content of these passages is a consideration springing from the meaning of predestination itself. Since predestination implies the predetermination of an end in view, the doctrines of perseverance and irresistible grace are necessarily implied as the respective end and means of God's predestination. After all, predestination without perseverance would be oxymoronic and would therefore make as little sense as dry water. Thus, in addition to the evidence noted above, the doctrines of perseverance and irresistible grace follow from the very meaning of predestination itself.

Having presented evidence in support of perseverance and irresistible grace, it remains to consider some of the objections against these doctrines. In this regard, it is thought by some that the above considerations are too general and therefore cannot succeed in establishing these doctrines against specific texts to the contrary. Consequently, to advance these doctrines in a persuasive manner, it will also be necessary to consider the texts which are thought by some to oppose them. In this regard, it will be shown below that despite initial appearances, such texts do not oppose these doctrines and therefore cannot be used as the basis for objections against them.

In this respect, the first objection to be considered is based on a passage in the book of Hebrews:

> It is impossible for those who have once been enlightened, who have tasted the heavenly gift, who have shared in the Holy Spirit, who have tasted the goodness of the word of God and the powers of the coming age, if they fall away, to be brought back to repentance, because to their loss they are crucifying the Son of God all over again and subjecting him to public disgrace. (Hebrews 6:4-6)

At first glance, the above passage seems to indicate the possibility of a true Christian falling away. Accordingly, the passage would appear to undermine predestination by contradicting the doctrines of perseverance and irresistible grace. In spite of these first impressions, however, the force of the passage is open to serious question since it nowhere indicates that those falling away are in fact saved. All it says is that these people have in some sense shared in the Holy Spirit and tasted the powers of the coming age. Accordingly, to assess the doctrinal significance of the above passage, it is necessary to determine whether or not its language implies regeneration.

To make this determination, the scope of the passage must first be considered. With respect to this scope, it should be understood that the book of Hebrews was written to a congregation of Christians who were on the verge relapsing into Judaism due to persecution. Thus, it is important to note, in the first instance, that the epistle was written to a congregation. Given this fact, the experience of the Holy Spirit mentioned in this passage need indicate nothing more than the power that anyone entering a first century church would have felt. After all, miracles were so common in the first century churches that even the unconverted could feel their power, and the manifest power of these miracles was so great that Jesus rebuked Capernaum for not repenting in the face of them (Matthew 11:20-26). Thus, within the passage above, tasting the powers of the coming age does not necessarily imply conversion.

But the issue goes deeper still. Since Jesus spoke of an enemy sowing tares among the wheat and of the wheat and tares growing together until the final harvest (Matthew 13:24-30), there are evidently many persons within the church who have an external profession of faith and who have tasted the powers of the Spirit externally, but who nevertheless have never been regenerated internally. Indeed, the existence of such people is explicitly confirmed elsewhere in Christ's description of the final judgment:

> Not everyone who says to me, "Lord, Lord," will enter the kingdom of heaven, but only he who does the will of my Father who is in heaven. Many will say to me on that day, "Lord, Lord, did we not prophesy in your name, and in your name drive out demons and perform many miracles?" Then I will tell them plainly, "I never knew you. Away from me, you evildoers!" (Matthew 7: 21-23)

Clearly, this passage attests the existence of a group of people who have tasted the powers of the coming age to the extent of prophesying, driving out demons, and working miracles, and yet because they are eternally unknown by Christ (*i.e.*, eternally non-elect)[7],

---

[7] Note that in saying, " I never knew you," Christ attests that the perishing ones are eternally reprobate. After all, by using the word "never," Jesus makes a universal statement which denies relational (not cognitive) knowledge at even one point in the past. Thus, it is not as though they had an intimate relationship with Christ and then slipped away, for in that event he would not have said, " I never knew you," but rather, "Once we knew each other, but drifted apart." Through his very choice of words, then, Jesus attributes their perishing to a lack of election, and not their lack of perseverance in a grace once obtained.

they remain unregenerate and thus unconverted. Along similar lines is the example of Judas who as a disciple of Christ was intimately involved in Christ's miraculous ministry and yet was declared to be eternally reprobate by Christ himself:

> After Jesus said this, he looked toward heaven and prayed:
>
> "Father, the time has come. Glorify your Son, that your Son may glorify you. For you granted him authority over all people that he might give eternal life to all those you have given him....
>
> I have revealed you to those whom you gave me out of the world. They were yours; you gave them to me and they have obeyed your word. Now they know that everything you have given me comes from you. For I gave them the words you gave me and they accepted them. They knew with certainty that I came from you, and they believed that you sent me. I pray for them. I am not praying for the world, but for those you have given me, for they are yours.... Holy Father, protect them by the power of your name — the name you gave me — so that they may be one as we are one. While I was with them, I protected them and kept them safe by that name you gave me. None has been lost *except the one doomed to destruction*. (John 17:1-12)

On the basis of the above texts, it clearly follows that even a dramatic spiritual experience within a Christian setting does not imply conversion.

Additional evidence for this conclusion arises from a statement in the parable of the soils which is significantly quite germane to the situation addressed in Hebrews. In the parable of the soils, Jesus spoke of certain seed falling on rocky ground and sprouting up quickly but then wilting under persecution due to its shallow rootage in the soil (Mark 4: 16,17). Now since the seed in the parable represents God's Word and since the soil represents the condition of the human heart, the parable attests a condition of shallow Christian experience which lacks penetration precisely because the heart remains stony and unregenerate. Thus, the parable attests the possibility of an unregenerate person tasting the powers of the coming age and then falling away. Consequently, since the church addressed in Hebrews was also in danger of wilting under persecution, it may well be that many in the church were like the seed sown on rocky ground, having a shallow Christian experience without adequate rootage (*i.e.*, regeneration) and thus liable to wilt under persecution. As a result, it is not certain that those referred to in Hebrews 6:4-6 were in fact converted Christians.

Consequently, from an analysis of parallel passages, it has been shown that an experience of the Holy Spirit such as that described in Hebrews 6:4-6 does not necessarily imply conversion. Thus, Hebrews 6:4-6 cannot be used against the doctrines of perseverance and irresistible grace since it is unclear whether those falling away are in fact converted (regenerate) Christians. Yet, while the experience described in Hebrews 6:4-6 remains unclear, the fact that the elect cannot fall away is the clear statement of Christ Himself:

For then there will be great distress, un-
equaled from the beginning of the world until
now — and never to be equaled again. If
those days had not been cut short, no one
would survive, but for the sake of the elect
those days will be shortened. At that time if
anyone says to you, "Look, here is the
Christ!" or, "There he is!" do not believe it.
For false Christs and false prophets will appear and perform great signs and miracles
to deceive even the elect — if that were possible. See, I have told you ahead of time.
(Matthew 24:21-25)

Consequently, since it is a rule (hermeneutic) of Biblical interpretation (exegesis) that clear passages
should interpret those less clear, it follows that doctrine should be based on the clear passages of Scripture
since it is precisely these passages which illumine the
more obscure ones. Given this fact, the clear statement of the Lord that the elect cannot fall away
together with the positive evidence introduced above
must be allowed to settle the matter of perseverance
and irresistible grace, not the ambiguous passage from
Hebrews. After all, since the Hebrews passage has an
uncertain meaning, it cannot overturn the clear, con-
vincing, and cumulative evidence adduced above in
support of perseverance and irresistible grace. Given
this fact, the Hebrews passage provides no solid basis
for objections to these doctrines and is therefore irrelevant to the doctrinal discussion.

Having answered the objection based on Hebrews 6:4-6,
it remains to consider another. In this regard, two pas-

sages in II Peter 2 dealing with false teachers will next be considered:

> But there were also false prophets among the people, just as there will be false teachers among you. They will secretly introduce destructive heresies, even denying the sovereign Lord who bought them — bringing swift destruction on themselves. (II Peter 2:1)

> For they mouth empty, boastful words and, by appealing to the lustful desires of sinful human nature, they entice people who are just escaping from those who live in error. They promise freedom, while they themselves are slaves of depravity — for a man is a slave to whatever has mastered him. If they have escaped the corruption of the world by knowing our Lord and Savior Jesus Christ and are again entangled in it and overcome, they are worse off at the end than they were at the beginning. It would have been better for them not to have known the way of righteousness, than to have known it and then to turn their backs on the sacred command that was passed on to them. Of them the proverbs are true: "A dog returns to its vomit," and, "A sow that is washed goes back to her wallowing in the mud." (II Peter 2:18-22)

As with Hebrews 6:4-6, opponents of predestination use these passages to attack the doctrines of perseverance and irresistible grace since they seem to indicate the possibility of true Christians falling away. In particular, the false teachers are referred to as "denying the sovereign Lord who bought them" and as becoming entangled and overcome by the world again after having escaped corruption through the knowledge of Christ. However, while it seems clear from the passage that the false teachers can fall away, this fact in no way contradicts the doctrines of perseverance and irresistible grace unless it is established that these false teachers are in fact true Christians. Thus, just as with Hebrews 6:4-6, the argument hinges upon whether or not the falling ones are regenerate.

In seeking to make this determination, it should first be noted that the entire context in II Peter 2 is loaded with statements of reprobation pertaining to these same false teachers:

> In their greed these teachers will exploit you
> with stories they have made up. Their con-
> demnation has long been hanging over them,
> and their destruction has not been sleeping.
> (II Peter 2:3)

> But these men blaspheme in matters they do
> not understand. They are like brute beasts,
> creatures of instinct, born only to be caught
> and destroyed, and like beasts they too will
> perish. (II Peter 2:12)

> These men are springs without water and
> mists driven by a storm. Blackest darkness
> is reserved for them. (II Peter 2:17)

From these explicit statements of reprobation, it is clear that the preponderance of false teachers (*i.e.*, those who actually fall) are not Christian. After all, one for whom destruction is reserved (vv. 3, 17) and who is born to be caught and destroyed like a beast (v. 12), is eternally non-elect and thus not the object of God's saving (regenerating) grace. Given this fact, the falling away of these teachers does not contradict the doctrines of perseverance and irresistible grace since those who actually fall are not elect and therefore not regenerate. After all, since perseverance and irresistible grace have reference to the elect alone, the falling away of the non-elect is of no consequence to these doctrines.

However, if the false teachers are not regenerate, it is still necessary to explain how Peter's language — relating to their escape from corruption through the knowledge of Christ and to their denial of "the sovereign Lord who bought them" — is compatible with their unregenerate status. With regard to the first point, the context of II Peter 2 makes it clear that these people are merely externally washed and not internally regenerate since according to Peter they remain dogs and sows: "A dog returns to its vomit," and, "A sow that is washed goes back to her wallowing in the mud" (v. 22). Thus, just as it was previously seen that those who tasted the powers of the coming age in Hebrews 6:4-6 were not necessarily regenerate, so a merely external faith is seen here, but the reason seems to be different. Whereas the group in Hebrews is like the seed sown on rocky ground that wilts under persecution, the present group is like the seed sown among thorns that is choked out by the concerns of the world (Mark 4:16-19). In both cases, however, the resulting spiritual state implies a lack of regeneration. After all, God's regeneration does not merely wash sows nor leave the weeds in place, but rather changes goats into sheep and tills the thorny soil of the human heart. Given this fact, the language in II Peter 2 implies a merely external faith on the part of the false teachers and thus a lack of regeneration.

However, if these false teachers are truly reprobate and unregenerate, then how can Peter speak of "the sovereign Lord who bought them," for surely Christ did not die to purchase the reprobate? In this regard, the answer would seem to be that Peter's language reflects a judgment of charity in view of the distinction between the visible (external) and invisible (elect) church. After all, while not everyone who professes the Faith is a true Christian (*i.e.*, elect), in Christian charity all professors of Christ are to be regarded as Christians while they remain in good standing with the church (*i.e.*, church members). The reason for extending such favorable judgments is that since man has no knowledge of whom God has elected, he must assume the best of all professing Christians. However, just as not all professing Christians are elect, so not all heretics are reprobate. After all, while many heretics depart from the Faith and fall completely, some repent and return to the fold as did Peter himself after his triple denial of Christ. Given Peter's repentance and restoration, then, his language naturally allows for the possibility that some of these heretics may be elect. Nevertheless, since Peter has no specific knowledge of whom God has elected, he is forced by the rule of charity to accept the totality of these false teachers as true Christians while they remain in good standing with the church. So understood, Peter's language reflects a simple judgment of charity and is therefore most compatible with his references to reprobation and reserved destruction in the same passage. After all, while the judgment of charity has reference to the temporal standing of the whole group as church members, the reprobation statements refer to the eternal standing of a particular subset, namely those who actually fall. Given this distinction, Peter's charitable judgment in no way implies that the false teachers are elect or regenerate and therefore does not support the notion that a true Christian can fall away. With respect to the matter of charitable judgments, Luther's comments are most enlightening:

> I call them saints, and so regard them; I call them the church, and so judge them — but by the rule of charity, not by the rule of faith. By which I mean that charity, which always thinks the best of everyone, and is not suspicious, but believes and assumes all good of its neighbour, calls every baptized person a saint. There is no danger involved if she is wrong; it is the way of charity to be deceived, for she is open to all the uses and abuses of every man, as being handmaid of all, good and bad, believing and unbelieving, true and false. Faith, however, calls none a saint but him who is proclaimed such by divine sentence; for the way of faith is not to be deceived. Therefore, though we should all look on each other as saints as a matter of charity, none should be declared a saint as a matter of faith, as if it were an article of faith that so and so were a saint. (Luther, *The Bondage of the Will*, 122, 123)

On the basis of the previous discussion, the significance of II Peter 2:1, 18-22 for the doctrines of perseverance and irresistible grace may be readily assessed. Given the clear references to reprobation in the context of II Peter 2, the evidence that those falling away are only externally washed, and the fact that the statement in verse 1 is a simple judgment of charity, it is clear that these passages are not referring to elect, regenerate Christians. Thus, they do not imply that a true Christian can fall away and therefore do not contradict the doctrines of perseverance and irresistible grace.

On the other hand, these doctrines are strongly supported by a passage in I John:

> Dear children, this is the last hour; and as you have heard that the antichrist is coming, even now many antichrists have come. This is how we know it is the last hour. They went out from us, but they did not really belong to us. For if they had belonged to us, they would have remained with us; but their going showed that none of them belonged to us.

> But you have an anointing from the Holy One, and all of you know the truth. I do not write to you because you do not know the truth, but because you do know it and because no lie comes from the truth. Who is the liar? It is the man who denies that Jesus is the Christ. Such a man is the antichrist — he denies the Father and the Son. No one who denies the Son has the Father: whoever

> acknowledges the Son has the Father also.
> (I John. 2:18-23)

In this passage, John differentiates between two opposing groups and makes an unambiguous case for perseverance through the combination of both a positive and a negative argument. To begin with, John refers to those who have denied Christ and left the church as antichrists and further states that they never really belonged to the church in the first place. Then, to support this latter assertion, John sets forth a two-pronged argument relating perseverance to one's Christian status. First, John argues positively, stating that if they had truly belonged to the church in the first place, they would have remained in it. Then, arguing negatively, John states that their failure to remain within the church showed that they did not truly belong to it in the first place. Thus, in two logically equivalent ways, John makes the case for the perseverance of the elect, first by affirming the antecedent (A→B) and then by denying the consequent (-B →-A). In other words, John is boldly stating that if one is elect, he will persevere and that if he doesn't persevere, then he is not elect. Consequently, when this passage is combined with previous passages having a similar import, the accumulation of positive evidence for the doctrines of perseverance and irresistible grace becomes overwhelming, and this evidence is in no way challenged by Peter's discussion of the false teachers since the falling teachers are not true Christians. Given this fact, the passages from II Peter 2 provide no basis for objections against these doctrines.

Finally, having considered the passages from II Peter 2, one further objection to the doctrines of perseverance and irresistible grace must now be addressed. In this regard, the implications of a passage concerning Christian liberty will be examined below:

> If your brother is distressed because of what you eat, you are no longer acting in love. Do not by your eating destroy your brother for whom Christ died. (Romans 14:15)

As with the objections previously considered, the above passage is seized by opponents of perseverance and irresistible grace since it seems to indicate the possibility of a true Christian falling away. In this regard, it is argued that Paul's command not to destroy a brother implies the possibility of destroying a true Christian through one's conduct. However, since a command never implies the ability to fulfill it,[8] it follows that the above method of inferring indicative realities from imperative commands is illogical. After all, as a command, Paul's language utilizes the imperative verbal mood and therefore implies nothing indicatively. Given this fact, the above passage may not be used to imply the possibility of a true Christian falling away, and therefore may not be advanced against the doctrines of perseverance and irresistible grace.

To be fully persuasive, however, it does not suffice to eliminate this text on linguistic grounds alone. Rather, it must also be shown that its practical import is not diminished by the doctrine of perseverance.

---

[8] For instance, the command to jump over The Empire State Building does not imply the ability to do so.

However, in seeking to demonstrate this point, it is necessary to consider two factors which impinge upon the interpretation of this passage and which therefore determine the nature of the constraint which this passage places on the doctrine of perseverance. First, since Paul elsewhere states that those foreknown and predestined by God are also called, justified, and glorified (Romans 8:28), Paul is in no way implying that a true brother can fall from the faith. Second, given the weak brother's genuine (though obviously misplaced) concern over dietary practices, his tender conscience attests the fact that he is not a church member only but rather a true brother who is therefore destined to persevere. Given this fact, a judgment of charity cannot be invoked to harmonize the above passage with perseverance in general. Rather, it is necessary to determine how the practical import of Paul's command to guard one's brother coheres with the specific perseverance of this very same brother.

In this regard, the context of Romans 14 shows that Paul's specific concern is that one's conduct not cause his brother to stumble by indulging against the dictates of conscience in otherwise lawful behavior. After all, since whatever is not of faith is sin, and since the wages of sin is death, causing one's brother to violate his conscience in these matters would put him on path of death. Now obviously, since the weak brother is elect, he will not follow this path to its bitter end. However, if he follows it at all, he may well be injured in the mean time, and thus it is imperative that he never start down this path to begin with. Consequently, from both the immediate context and other Pauline passages, it seems that Paul is commanding the strong brother to abstain from practices that might place the weak brother on the path of death, but is in no way implying that the weak brother, once on this path, would follow it to the bitter end.

Consequently, since the passage concerns the duty of the strong brother and not the issue of perseverance *per se*, the language used by Paul pursuant to his main purpose may be taken as hyperbolic and thus compatible with the eternal security of the weak brother. After all, in saying, "Do not by your eating destroy your brother for whom Christ died," Paul is not implying that the strong brother can undo the work of Christ, for he elsewhere speaks of the elect as being eternally united with Christ (Ephesians 1:4). Rather, Paul is using hyperbolic language to shame the strong brother into a wholesome conformity by contrasting his selfish lack of concern with Christ's ultimate sacrifice for this weak brother's life. In other words, Paul is commanding the strong brother not to engage in practices whose natural tendency if unchecked would be to overturn the work of Christ, and is in no way implying that the work of Christ may be overturned. So understood, the practical import of Paul's command is a prudent concern for one's brother which is neither mitigated nor diminished by this brother's assumed perseverance. Given this fact, Paul's command conflicts in no material way with the doctrines of perseverance and irresistible grace and therefore constitutes no basis for objections against them.

On the basis of the preceding discussion, then, it has been shown that the doctrines of perseverance and irresistible grace are fully Biblical and are demanded by the very concept of predestination itself. Additionally, three objections to these doctrines have been considered on the basis of the following texts: Hebrews 6:4-6, II Peter 2:1; 18-22, and Romans 14:15. In all three cases, the objections were seen to be groundless and thus of no consequence against the clarity and preponderance of evidence to the contrary. Given these facts, the doctrines of perseverance and irresistible grace must be affirmed as orthodox, Biblical doctrines. Consequently, in addition to the impossibility of entering salvation apart from God's power, it now follows that those so drawn cannot leave. Accordingly, since both the front and back doors of salvation are therefore closed to human power, God emerges as the sole determinant of human destiny and thus the predestinator of both the elect and the reprobate. Given this fact, a double predestination is necessarily implied:

> Even should we grant that some of the elect are held in error throughout their whole life, yet they must of necessity return into the way before they die; for Christ says in John 8: "None shall pluck them out of my hand" (John 10:28). But what is hard and problematical is just this: ascertaining whether those whom you call the church were the church — or, rather, whether after their lifetime of error they were at last brought back to the truth before they died. (Luther, *The Bondage of the Will*, 120)

So, too, I say that man, before he is renewed into the new creation of the Spirit's kingdom, does and endeavors nothing to prepare himself for that new creation and kingdom, and when he is recreated he does and endeavors nothing towards his perseverance in that kingdom; but the Spirit alone works both blessings in us, regenerating us, and preserving us when regenerate, without ourselves; as James says: "Of His own will begat He us with the word of His power, that we should be the first fruits of His creation" (James 1:18). (James is speaking of the renewed creation.) But He does not work in us without us for He recreated and preserves us for this very purpose, that He might work in us and we might co-operate with Him. Thus he preaches, shows mercy to the poor, and comforts the afflicted by means of us. But what is hereby attributed to "free-will"? What, indeed, is left it but — nothing! In truth, nothing! (Luther, *The Bondage of the Will*, 268)

This passage is the foundation on which rests everything that the Apostle says to the end of the chapter; for he means to show that to the elect who are loved of God and who love God, the Holy Spirit makes all things work for good even though they are evil. He here takes up the doctrine of predestination or election. This doctrine is not so incomprehensible as many think, but it is rather full of sweet comfort for the elect and for all who have the Holy Spirit. But it is most bitter and hard for the wisdom of the flesh. There is no other reason why the many tribulations and evils cannot separate the saints from the love of God than that they are the called "according to his purpose." Hence God makes all things work together for good to them, and to them only. If there would not be this divine purpose, but our salvation would rest upon our will or work, it would be based upon chance. How easily in that case could one single evil hinder or destroy it! But the Apostle says: "Who shall lay anything to the charge of God's elect?" "Who is he that condemneth?" "Who shall separate us from the love of Christ?" (8:33, 34, 35), he shows that the elect are not saved by chance, but by God's purpose and will. Indeed for this reason, God allows the elect to encounter so many evil things as are here named, namely, to point out that they are saved not by their merit, but by His election, His unchangeable and firm purpose. They are saved despite their many rapacious and fierce foes and the vain efforts.

What then is there to our own righteousness? to our good works? to the freedom of the will? to chance in the things that occur? That (the denial of these things) is what we must preach, for that means to preach rightly. That means to destroy the wisdom of the flesh. So far the Apostle has destroyed merely the hands, feet, and tongue of the wisdom of the flesh: now he wipes it out utterly. Now he makes us see that it amounts to nothing, and that our salvation altogether lies in His hands. God absolutely recognizes no chance: it is only men who speak of chance. Not a single leaf falls from the tree without the will of the Father. All things are essentially in His hands, and so are also our times. (Luther, *Commentary of Romans*, 128, 129)

I frankly confess that, for myself, even if it could be, I should not want "free-will" to be given me, nor anything to be left in my own hands to enable me to endeavor after salvation; not merely because in face of so many dangers, and adversities, and assaults of devils, I could not stand my ground and hold fast my "free-will" (for one devil is stronger than all men, and on these terms no man could be saved): but because, even were there no dangers, adversities, or devils, I should still be forced to labour with no guarantee of success, and to beat my fists at the air. If I lived and worked to all eternity, my conscience would never reach comfortable certainty as to how much it must do to satisfy God. Whatever work I had done, there would still be a nagging doubt as to whether it pleased God, or whether He required something more. The experience of all who seek righteousness by works proves that; and I learned it well enough myself over a period of many years, to my own great hurt. But now that God has taken my salvation out of the control of my own will, and put it under the control of His, and promised to save me, not according to my working or running, but according to His own grace and mercy, I have the comfortable certainty that He is faithful and will not lie to me, and that He is also great and powerful, so that no devils or opposition can break Him or pluck me from Him. "No one," He says, "shall pluck them out of my hand, because my Father which gave them me is greater than all" (John 10:28-29). Thus it is that, if not all, yet some, indeed many, are saved; whereas, by the power of "free-will" none at all could be saved, but every one of us would perish. (Luther, *The Bondage of the Will*, 313, 314)

Predestination and
Pastoral Counseling

14

Having discussed various objections to the doctrine of predestination, its relation to Christian practice will now be addressed. In this regard, a particular area of concern is the relation of predestination to pastoral counseling in the event of an extreme tragedy. To begin this discussion, suppose that a middle aged, Christian man who is both a husband and a father is suddenly murdered. For this particular situation, the question becomes one of determining how the doctrine of predestination will impact the pastor's ministry to the grieving family. After all, since the pastor believes in predestination, he must necessarily hold the murder to have been foreordained by God. Given this fact, it is reasonable to ask whether this doctrine places God on the side of the murderer, thereby destroying any basis for hope, anger, or grief. In other words, does the doctrine of predestination unduly magnify or trivialize the event in such a way as to prevent the extension of comfort to the grieving family and thereby short circuit the pastoral counseling process? To answer this question, it will be necessary to consider predestination in relation to its philosophical competitors in terms of its implications for pastoral counseling.

In this regard, it was mentioned in Chapter 2 that chance and fate form the basic building blocks of all non-Christian systems. Thus, in turning from a Biblical view of predestination, one necessarily embraces some combination of chance and fate. Accordingly, when all hybrid positions are reduced to their bare essentials, there would seem to be three basic options available, namely predestination, chance, and fate. Given these three basic options, therefore, it would seem prudent to test each with respect to its suitability in a pastoral counseling context. In particular, it would be necessary to determine whether any viewpoint provided a solid basis for hope, anger, and grief. Now to the extent that predestination alone was shown to provide such a basis, its practicality would clearly emerge, even as the impracticality of the remaining alternatives was laid bare. To this end, each of the three positions mentioned above will be examined with respect to its implications for both an ultimate benevolent purpose and for human responsibility. After all, since these entities are essential to hope, anger, and grief, the affinity of any viewpoint with these entities will determine its conduciveness toward pastoral counseling. To facilitate this discussion, the basic metaphysics of each viewpoint has been diagramed in Figure 5.

In examining these basic positions, it is most convenient to begin the discussion by considering the option of chance. With respect to this option, it may generally be said that a chance universe is characterized by a complete lack of connection and interrelation among its parts and is therefore devoid of any possible order. Consequently, in such a universe, a radical individuality prevails in which all quantities behave as brute atoms, moving in complete independence of one another. Thus, to the extent that God is even thought to exist, He becomes at best another atom in a meaningless void, having no relation or influence on any of the remaining parts. For this reason the option of chance has been diagramed as separate circles in Figure 5c.

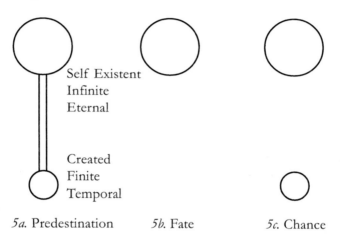

5a. Predestination   5b. Fate   5c. Chance

FIGURE 5: Schematic of Metaphysical Options

That such a universe would destroy any basis for pastoral counseling may be readily seen by considering its implications. First, because such a universe would be random and meaningless, it would be directionless and thus devoid of any ultimate purpose. Accordingly, in such a universe there could be no basis for hope since there would be no benevolent purpose behind the events. Moreover, since man himself would become the product of an impersonal chaos, the human personality would be lost as man dissolved into the void. Finally, since chance itself is the very negation of order, any basis for a binding moral law would also be destroyed. Consequently, there could remain no ground for anger and grief since human responsibility cannot be maintained apart from a human personality and a binding moral law. As a result, it must be concluded that a chance universe would not be conducive to pastoral counseling since such a universe could provide no basis for hope, anger, or grief. After all, in a universe of impersonal chance such personal quantities could have no proper ground.

In a system of fate, on the other hand, the results are identical but for slightly different reasons. With respect to this option, it may generally be said that a fatalistic universe is characterized by a radical connection and interrelation to the exclusion of all distinction or difference. Accordingly, in such a universe a suffocating unity prevails which destroys the uniqueness of every part and locks the whole into a single system of rigid, mechanical law. Thus, to the extent that God is even thought to exist, He reduces to the level of a mindless force which penetrates and quickens the whole. For this reason, the option of fate has been diagramed as a single circle in Figure 5b.

That such a universe would destroy any basis for pastoral counseling may be readily seen by considering its implications. First, since such a universe would reduce to the product of impersonal law, it would be driven by mechanism rather than a conscious personality. Accordingly, even though a certain order could still be retained, all sense of purpose would vanish since the events would occur apart from a conscious future aim. Consequently, in such a universe there would be no basis for hope since there could be no benevolent purpose behind the events. Moreover, since man himself would become the product of impersonal law, the human personality would also be lost as man reduced to a cog in an impersonal machine. Finally, since a personal "ought" could find no basis in a system of impersonal law, moral law, as a personal concept, would vanish. Accordingly, in such a universe there could be no basis for anger or grief since human responsibility cannot be maintained apart from a human personality and a binding moral law. As a result, it must be concluded that a universe of fate would not be conducive to pastoral counseling since such a universe could provide no basis for hope, anger, or grief. After all, in a universe of impersonal mechanism, such personal quantities could have no proper ground.

In contrast to the preceding views, however, predestination sets forth a personal universe in which a benevolent purpose and human responsibility are each maintained. Accordingly, predestination provides a solid basis for hope, anger, and grief, and is therefore most conducive to pastoral counseling. The reason for this result is that the unique combination of God's transcendence and immanence allows for both a connection and a distinction between God and the universe as shown in Figure 5a. In this regard, the distinction prevents God from becoming confused with the creation so that His being is not derived from an impersonal chance or fate. As a result, God remains irreducibly personal and thus infused with an ultimate purpose. However, while this distinction prevents the personality of God from being compromised, the connection between God and creation ensures that the world is established by His transcendent personality

and thus governed in accordance with His good purpose. Moreover, since man and the universe are
therefore exhaustively determined by a personal God,
the connection also ensures the integrity of the human personality and a system of moral order, the very
criteria of human responsibility. Thus, counter to one's
natural intuition, human responsibility is established
precisely because of, and not in spite of, God's predestination. However, while this connection ensures
that God is the ultimate cause of all human action, the
distinction between God and creation prevents the
respective acts of God and man from being ethically
confused. Consequently, just as the crucifixion of
Christ was simultaneously the most gracious act of
God and the most wicked act of man, so the daily acts
of human evil are simultaneously, yet mysteriously,
the good acts of a gracious God. In other words, due
to the combination of God's immanence and transcendence, God is able to work everything for good without
Himself becoming the author of evil. Accordingly, in
contrast to the competing options of chance or fate,
Biblical predestination is most conducive to pastoral
counseling since it provides for an ultimate benevolent purpose in conjunction with human responsibility.

Consequently, in counseling the Christian family of a
murder victim, the pastor believing in predestination has
a basis for extending hope while yet acknowledging
anger and grief. On the one hand, because the evil
acts of man are simultaneously the good acts of God,
they are ultimately infused with His benevolent purpose and thus intended for the family's good.
Accordingly, the pastor believing in predestination can
comfort the surviving family with these words of Paul:

> And we know that in all things God works
> for the good of those who love him and who
> have been called according to his purpose.
> For those God foreknew, he also predestined
> to be conformed to the likeness of his Son, that
> he might be the firstborn among many broth-
> ers. And those he predestined, he also called;
> those he called, he also justified; those he
> justified, he also glorified. (Romans 8:28-30)

At the same time, however, because the acts of God
and man remain ethically distinct, the evil of the human action is in no way mitigated by God's benevolent
intention. Thus, in providing hope to this grieving family, the pastor can also acknowledge the terrible evil
of the situation and appeal with the family for justice:

> For rulers hold no terror for those who do
> right, but for those who do wrong. Do you
> want to be free from fear of the one in au-
> thority? Then do what is right and he will
> commend you. For he is God's servant to do
> you good. But if you do wrong, be afraid, for
> he does not bear the sword for nothing. He is
> God's servant, an agent of wrath to bring pun-
> ishment on the wrongdoer. (Romans 13:3, 4)

On the basis of the preceding discussion, therefore,
the doctrine of predestination is seen to be most conducive to pastoral counseling when its implications
are properly considered. After all, by maintaining
God's good purpose alongside human responsibility,
predestination provides a basis for hope without
trivializing an evil situation.

Nevertheless, while asserting God's ultimate control makes good sense in theory, affirming God to be the ultimate cause of a tragedy is difficult in practice. After all, to the extent that God is seen as causing such an event, God is necessarily connected with the event and therefore properly identified as the source of trauma. However, as hard as it may be to accept this reality, the alternative is even harder, for on the alternative a tragedy would become a meaningless act of chance or fate, or worse, an act of raw evil subject to no good purpose. Consequently, for the pastor to minister a message of hope and justice, it is essential that the doctrine of predestination inform his approach. Of course, it is not intended by this statement that the minister should drag a grieving family through an abstruse discussion of predestination. Rather, all that is intended is that these concepts be part of his broad theological training so that in a grave crisis he has a solid metaphysical basis upon which to minister God's comfort.

After all, in light of the cross, God's predestination is seen to maintain a benevolent purpose, even in its determination of human evil. Moreover, since Jesus Christ is the only begotten Son of God, the cross reveals the additional fact that God is often grieved by the very ends He determines. Thus, God's predestination is not that of an impersonal force devoid of ethics and pathos but rather expresses the benevolent purpose and personal concern of a fully engaged participant. Accordingly, the doctrine of predestination does not demand a stoic resignation to the course of events but rather provides a true foundation for hope, justice, and compassionate care in ministry. After all, when viewed from the cross, the Biblical God is seen to be both all-powerful and big hearted. As such, He is large enough to be the predestinator of every event and the God of all consolation:

> If, then, we are taught and believe that we ought to be ignorant of the necessary fore-knowledge of God and the necessity of events, Christian faith is utterly destroyed, and the promises of God and the whole gospel fall to the ground completely; for the Christian's chief and only comfort in every adversity lies in knowing that God does not lie, but brings all things to pass immutably, and that His will cannot be resisted, altered or impeded. (Luther, *The Bondage of the Will*, 84).

Predestination
and Missions

15

I n relating predestination to Christian practice,
another area of concern is its impact on evangelism and Christian missions. In this regard, it
is often objected by opponents of predestination that this doctrine will dampen the zeal for missions by rendering evangelism superfluous. After all,
it is asked, if one's eternal destiny has been determined
in advance, then what is the point of evangelism? In
response to this objection, however, it will be shown
below that it is precisely predestination that makes evangelism possible. Thus, far from impeding Christian
missions, predestination will be seen to form their very
ground. To facilitate this discussion, evangelism will be
viewed as a threefold interaction as shown in Figure 6.

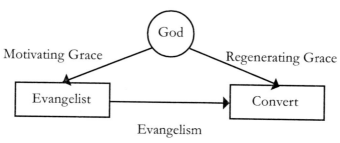

FIGURE 6: Schematic Illustrating the
Threefold Interaction of Evangelism

As can be seen from Figure 6, evangelism is a complex process involving a simultaneous three-fold interaction between the evangelist, the convert, and God. Accordingly, in examining evangelism it will be necessary to account for the relationships between God and the evangelist, between the evangelist and the convert, and between the convert and God. Moreover, since all three relationships operate simultaneously and are integral to the evangelism process, the deterioration of any single relationship will undermine the process as a whole. Consequently, for predestination to positively impact evangelism, it is necessary that predestination undergird the three relationships considered above.

With respect to the first relationship, the impact is most positive. After all, since God's predestination determines both the conversion and the preparation of the evangelist, it is this same predestined grace which motivates him to preach the Gospel. Thus, predestination is essential to evangelism since it is precisely God's predestination that establishes the evangelist and sustains him in his calling. In agreement with this conclusion, it is the scriptural witness that all good works have been eternally prepared for the saints in accordance with God's predestinating activity:

> For we are God's workmanship, created in Christ Jesus to do good works, which God prepared in advance for us to do. (Ephesians 2:10)

With respect to the second relationship, the impact is again positive since God's predestination extends to means as well as ends. Given this fact, there can be no ultimate tension between predestination and evangelism. Rather, just as God has predestined the building of bridges through the means of engineers, so God has predestined the conversion of the nations through the means of evangelism. Thus, rather than an ultimate tension, there is a complete harmony between predestination and evangelism since evangelism is itself the predestined means of salvation. In agreement with this conclusion, it is the scriptural witness that the elect are to be gathered through the means of evangelism, a means which has been predestined to achieve an ultimately successful end:

> One night the Lord spoke to Paul in a vision: "Do not be afraid; keep on speaking, do not be silent. For I am with you, and no one is going to attack and harm you, because I have many people in this city." (Acts 18:9, 10)

> Then Paul and Barnabas answered them boldly; "We had to speak the word of God to you first. Since you reject it and do not consider yourselves worthy of eternal life, we now turn to the Gentiles. For this is what the Lord has commanded us: 'I have made you a light for the Gentiles, that you may bring salvation to the ends of the earth.'"

> When the Gentiles heard this, they were glad and honored the word of the Lord; and all who were appointed for eternal life believed. (Acts 13:46-48)

With respect to the final relationship, a positive impact is again observed. After all, while God works externally through the means of evangelism, the blindness of sin will prevent the convert from heeding the message apart from God's direct intervention. Therefore, in addition to working externally through the means of the evangelist, God also works directly and internally to regenerate the convert, thereby enabling him to respond. Moreover, because the convert is dead in trespasses and sins and is therefore incapable of cooperating in his salvation, this regeneration is 100% God's activity, a fact which makes salvation dependent upon God's work alone. However, since one's salvation therefore hinges upon exclusive divine action, it follows that salvation results from God's choice, not man's. Thus, predestination is necessarily implied since one's reception of Gospel light hinges upon God's decision to remove his blindness. Accordingly, predestination is essential to the success of evangelism since the salvation of sinners would be impossible apart from the direct and exclusive intervention of God. In agreement with this conclusion, it is the Biblical witness that evangelism is made effectual through divine action alone:

> While Peter was still speaking these words, the Holy Spirit came on all who heard the message. (Acts 10:44)

> What, after all, is Apollos? And what is Paul? Only servants, through whom you came to believe — as the Lord has assigned to each his task. I planted the seed, Apollos watered it, but God made it grow. So neither he who

plants nor he who waters is anything, but only God, who makes things grow. The man who plants and the man who waters have one purpose, and each will be rewarded according to his own labor. For we are God's fellow workers; you are God's field, God's building. (I Corinthians 3:5-9)

On the basis of the preceding discussion, predestination has been shown to drive every aspect of the evangelism process. Thus, far from impeding evangelism, predestination constitutes its very ground. Indeed, this relationship between predestination and evangelism is reflected in the fact that the conversion of the nations follows a divinely orchestrated timing and geography. Thus, in accordance with the divine plan, the major evangelistic outreach to the Gentile nations awaited Calvary and Pentecost, and it was for this reason that the Old Testament prophets spoke of an extension of salvation to the Gentiles which would come in the last days (*i.e.*, the inter advent period). Moreover, even when these last days had begun to dawn, and the missionary outreach was in full swing, Paul himself was restrained by the Holy Spirit from preaching in Asia and from entering Bithynia, but was instead called to Macedonia (Acts 16:6-10). Thus, in both its major and its minor movements, the timing and geography of missions proceeds according to a divine plan.

But if missions proceed according to a divine plan, then God's predestination is necessarily implicated as the very cause and ground thereof. Thus, predestination and missions relate as cause and effect, and for this reason missionary minded Christians should receive this doctrine with thanksgiving. After all, since the Gentile outreach was divinely orchestrated to follow Christ's passion, it follows that evangelistic success is itself the predestined outworking of the cross. Thus, far from undermining the Gospel, predestination ensures its success by securing the salvation of those for whom Christ died. Accordingly, predestination does not void the cross but rather secures its saving effect. As a result, missionaries can go forth in confidence, knowing that the Gospel of Christ will ultimately triumph in accordance with God's timing:

> So, too, I say that man, before he is renewed into the new creation of the Spirit's kingdom, does and endeavors nothing to prepare himself for that new creation and kingdom, and when he is recreated he does and endeavors nothing towards his perseverance in that kingdom; but the Spirit alone works both blessings in us, regenerating us, and preserving us when regenerate, without ourselves; as James says: "Of His own will begat He us with the word of His power, that we should be the first fruits of His creation" (James 1:18). (James is speaking of the renewed creation.) But He does not work in us without us for He recreated and preserves us for this very purpose, that He might work in us and we might co-operate with Him. Thus he preaches, shows mercy to the poor, and comforts the afflicted by means of us. But what is hereby attributed to "free-will"?

What, indeed, is left it but — nothing! In truth, nothing! (Luther, *The Bondage of the Will*, 268)

If Reason should here wrinkle up her nose and say: "Why does God will that these things be done by His words, when nothing is achieved by such words, and the will cannot turn itself in either direction? Why does He not do what He does without speaking a word, when He can do all things without a word? For a will that has heard His Word can do and does no more than before, if the inner moving of the Spirit is wanting; nor could it avail or do any less without the Word being spoken, if the Spirit was with it; for all depends on the power and operation of the Spirit" to this I shall say: It has pleased God not to give the Spirit without the Word, but through the Word; that He might have us as workers together with Him, we sounding forth without what He alone breathes within wheresoever He will. This He could do without the Word; but He will not. And who are we to inquire into the cause of the Divine will? It is enough for us to know that God so wills, and it becomes us to worship, love and adorn His will, bridling the presumption of reason. Thus, He might feed us without bread; He has, indeed, given us power to feed without bread, as Matthew 4 tells us: "Man is not fed by bread alone, but by the word of God" (v. 4); yet it has pleased Him to feed us by means of bread, by the provision of bread without, and by His Word within. (Luther, *The Bondage of the Will*, 184)

Predestination
and World View[1]

16

A s argued in the preceding chapter, the doctrine of predestination does not undercut, but rather establishes, an aggressive Christian outreach. In harmony with this aggressive outreach, the doctrine is also foundational to the development of a Christian worldview. After all, it is only when God is viewed as the creator and controller of all things that every area of life is seen to be exhaustively defined by God and thus demanding a specifically God-centered approach. In other words, it is only when God's absolute predestination is maintained that a Christian philosophy of science, literature, history, and all else becomes possible. Thus, the doctrine of predestination is essential to

---

[1] The following two sections concern applications of predestination (world view and political liberty) which are peculiar to Calvinism and therefore do not follow from a narrow consideration of Luther's views. However, since these applications are significant to the practical import of the doctrine, it is largely these applications that have provided the motivation for writing the present manuscript. Given this fact, these topics are here included alongside other applications (pastoral counseling and evangelism) of the doctrine. In this regard, it is hoped that these applications will highlight the usefulness of predestination and thus cause the church to see the broader implications of Luther's theology.

the comprehensive, life embracing philosophy known as a Christian world view.

However, when God's control is denied at even one point of creation, such as the eternal destiny of men, His control is soon denied at other points as well. Eventually, this denial spreads to all of life, just as a single rotten apple eventually ruins an entire bushel. As a result, entire areas of culture are then viewed as outside of God's control and thus beyond His definition. Accordingly, the basis for an explicitly God-centered approach is shattered, and the Christian worldview falls to the ground. As a result, God's Word becomes restricted to the sphere of the church, and Christians therefore retreat from culture. In the final analysis, then, a Christian worldview hinges upon the doctrine of predestination which alone affirms a divine control of life. To illustrate this point, the significance of predestination for a Biblical view of science, language, and history will now be set forth.

With respect to science, a crucial theological issue is the explanation of the scientific enterprise itself. In particular, it is necessary to account for the amazing correspondence between the mathematical models of the human mind and external reality. Needless to say, scientists denying God's control and opting instead for a chance universe have trouble accounting for any order in the physical realm, let alone any connection between this order and the human mind. As a result, scientists operating on secular premises are driven to an ultimate agnosticism and therefore have trouble accounting for science itself. In harmony with this agnosticism, the Nobel Prize winning physicist, Eugene Wigner, wrote an article entitled "The Unreasonable Effectiveness of

Mathematics in the Natural Sciences" in which he stated that "it is not at all natural that 'laws of nature' exist, much less that man is able to discern them" (Nickel, *Mathematics: Is God Silent?*, 68). In a similar fashion Princeton Physicist, Remo J. Ruffini, reacted to the successful lunar landing as follows:

> How a mathematical structure can correspond to nature is a mystery. One way out is just to say that the language in which nature speaks is the language of mathematics. This begs the question. Often we are both shocked and surprised by the correspondence between mathematics and nature, especially when the experiment confirms that our mathematical model describes nature perfectly. (Nickel, *Mathematics: Is God Silent?*, 69)

As these examples clearly demonstrate, scientists operating on secular premises have trouble accounting for the very operation of science itself.

On the other hand, when divine predestination is maintained, accounting for the scientific enterprise becomes relatively straightforward. After all, since God's predestination implies an absolute control over creation, the entire creation is viewed as exhaustively God-defined and thus infused with a personal, rational order. Moreover, since man is part of this created order, it follows that the human mind has been divinely preadapted to comprehend the very order which God Himself has placed in creation. So understood, God's predestination grounds the scientific enterprise through the provision of both a rational order and a receptive human mind.

Given this fact, it is most significant that The Royal Society of London, one of the more prestigious scientific associations of the present day, was founded in 1661 by English Puritans (Nickel, *Mathematics: Is God Silent?*, 38).

Beyond the field of science, predestination has significant implications for human language as well. To demonstrate this point, a most convenient issue to consider is the development within language of a definite future tense. In this regard, it should be obvious that predestination aids such development by supplying a definite future. After all, to the extent that predestination is maintained, the future has already been decided by an omnipotent God and is therefore certain in advance. So understood, predestination undergirds the development of a future tense by supplying a view of time and history within which such a tense is meaningful. However, to the extent that history is viewed as an unconscious (and thus an unplanned) process, the future becomes murky at best and uncertain at worst. As a result, the future tense becomes a problematic aspect of grammar since it loses all connection to objective reality. Accordingly, while predestination is most conducive to the development of a future tense, its denial is equally detrimental. After all, since the viability of a future tense hinges upon a definite future, predestination is essential to its objective validity. In this regard, the observations of R.J. Rushdoony are most significant:

> Let us illustrate this time-difference by citing two very similar statements with very different meanings. According to Plutarch, the Temple of Isis as Sais had this inscription: "I am all that has come into being, and that which

is, and that which shall be; and no man hath lifted my veil." Contrast this with the declaration of our Lord: "I am the Alpha and the Omega, the beginning and the ending, saith the Lord, which is, and which was, and which is to come, the Almighty" (Revelation 1:8). Isis declares herself to be process, the procession of time and being. Everything has come into being out of her and is identical with her, a pantheistic concept. She herself is past and present and all that was and is. There is, however, no knowledge of the future: it is veiled and beyond knowing. Isis (of tomorrow) neither sees nor is seen. Thus, we have here a world of chance, not of predestination.

By contrast, Jesus Christ, the Almighty God, declares Himself to be the Eternal One who is the creator of all things and the only source of the meaning of all things, their Alpha and Omega. Moreover, He is the absolute predestinator of all things and shall appear or come as their judge.

The two "similar" statements are thus a world apart. Christ's statement has reshaped Western languages and grammars, and, through Bible translation, is reshaping the languages of peoples all over the world. Bible translating is an exacting task, because it involves in effect the reworking of a language in order to make it carry the meaning of the Bible. This means a new view of the world, of God, time, and language. I was told once by a missionary that a native convert, having now a Wycliffe

Bible translation of portions of Scripture, declared, "We speak a new tongue now."

All our Western languages manifest clearly the marks of Biblical faith and translation. They have been made more and more relative to Biblical categories of thought and meaning. Our ideas of grammar, of tense, syntax, and structure, of thought and meaning, bear a Christian imprint. Very clearly, our language and grammar are relative, but relative to a heritage of Biblical faith. The new grammar is hostile to this faith and tradition: its motivation is an existential humanism. Any compromise with it involves a radical surrender of much more than language forms. (Rushdoony, *The Philosophy of the Christian Curriculum*, 49, 50)

As noted above, predestination establishes a certain view of time and history within which the future is definite and meaningful. Thus, related to the issue of the future tense is the deeper consideration of history itself. In this regard, a central issue from a theological standpoint is to account for historical meaning. Moreover, since it is precisely the whole of history that provides the meaningful context for each of its component events (parts), the meaning of each event necessarily hinges upon an overall meaning for history as a whole. Thus, to establish the historical meaning of particular events, it is necessary to account for an overall historical process which provides a meaningful framework for the events in question. To this end, it will be shown below that only a Biblical view of history, springing from the doctrine of predestination, renders history meaningful. To facilitate this discussion the Biblical view will be contrasted with three competing viewpoints, all of which are diagramed in Figure 7.

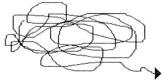

7a. Existentialism:
Existence Without Essence Leads to Chaos

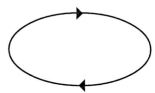

7b. Cyclical View:
Cyclical Fate Produces a Meaningless Eternal Treadmill

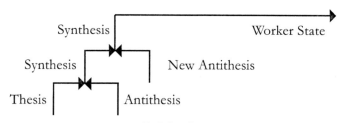

7c. Marxism:
Dialectical Materialism Predestines the Worker State

7d. Biblical View:
History is the Outworking of God's Plan

FIGURE 7: Schematic Illustrating
the Differing Views of History

As can be seen from Figure 7, existentialism posits a view of history which is chaotic and aimless. The reason for this trend is that existentialist philosophy holds to a meaningless, bare existence (a that) apart from any defining essence (a what). Accordingly, since each fact of existence (including every instant of time) is therefore viewed as brute and unconnected, the existentialist world reduces to a meaningless collection of atoms moving aimlessly in a void. So understood, existentialism posits a random view of history within which there is no direction or purpose. As a result, history and its component events reduce to a loose collection of chance occurrences devoid of any possible meaning.

In the cyclical view, by contrast, the universe moves by fate (blind law) rather than chance (blind whim). Accordingly, in contrast to existentialism, the universe is here driven by an underlying order which produces a precise and repeating sequence of events. However, since this cyclical motion also lacks an overall development, history again loses all sense of direction or purpose. As a result, history and its component events reduce to a series of meaningless steps on an eternal treadmill. Thus, despite certain metaphysical differences, the cyclical view is also meaningless.

In contrast to existentialism and the cyclical view, Marxism holds to an ultimate direction and development. In this regard, history is thought to be driven by a series of material dialectics (*i.e.*, nonspiritual, naturalistic conflicts) to the end that a human paradise is finally established in the worker state. However, since the historical development is driven by mechanism (material dialectics) rather than personality (such as a predestinating God), history as a whole becomes impersonal and thus devoid of any conscious aim or purpose. Consequently, in spite of its overall direction, history reduces to the meaninglessness of a bland mechanism and its events to a series of meaningless cogs in a giant machine. Thus, like existentialism and the cyclical view, Marxism reduces to a meaningless abstraction because it lacks both the personal universe and the eternal purpose of a predestinating God.

In contrast to the preceding alternatives, however, the Biblical view of history is laden with meaning due the controlling hand of a personal God. After all, because God is all knowing and all powerful, His predestination of history is both exhaustive and purposeful. As a result, history develops from creation to consummation in accordance with His foreordained purpose, namely the manifestation of His kingdom and glory. Consequently, history and its component events are inherently meaningful because they occur in accordance with the intelligent, purposeful, and flawlessly executed blueprint of a personal God. Thus, in contrast to the other approaches, the Biblical view of history is alone meaningful, and it is meaningful precisely because of God's predestination.

On the basis of the preceding discussion, then, predestination has been shown essential to a Biblical view of science, language, and history. After all, by maintaining God's total control, predestination necessarily implies that every subject has been predefined in terms of an exhaustive divine blueprint. Given this fact, the above results may be generalized to say that predestination is essential to a proper view of every subject and thus to the comprehensive, life embracing philosophy known as a Christian worldview. In agreement with this assertion, it is most significant historically that such radically Biblical thinking has been unique to Calvinism, the only theological system in which the doctrine of predestination has been vigorously maintained. Thus, in addition to the logical considerations adduced above, the historical evidence also attests the inseparable connection between predestination and worldview. To further illustrate this connection, it will be shown in the next chapter that predestination lies at the basis of the Calvinist devotion to liberty.

Predestination and
Political Liberty

17

As mentioned in the preceding chapter, the doctrine of predestination is essential to a Biblical worldview. Accordingly, since the consistent exposition of this doctrine is unique to Calvinism, Calvinism is the only theological system capable of taking distinctly Christian stands at all points of culture. Given this fact, it should come as no surprise that the Calvinists have surpassed all other Christians in their zealous devotion to political liberty. As will be shown below, such behavior is but the logical consequence of their underlying theology.

With regard to this theology, the Calvinist posits an ethical warfare at every point of culture as a result of his belief in both predestination and total depravity. On the one hand, believing in God's absolute predestination, he holds to God's exhaustive control and definition of creation. Accordingly, he maintains a Biblical worldview and therefore believes that a divine order governs every area of life, including the state. Consequently, the Calvinist conducts his political affairs subject to the conviction that the civil portion of God's law, when properly interpreted, forms the normative standard for civil justice. However,

believing also in total depravity, he holds that fallen
man will seek to overturn God's created order in his
attempt to be as God. Thus, due to these twin emphases in his theology, the Calvinist believes that a war
of definition permeates every point of culture with
fallen man trying to usurp God's role as judge, law-
giver, and king.[1] In the realm of the state, therefore,
tyrannical rulers will attempt to assert their own sovereignty by evading the constraints of God's law and
thereby oppressing their fellow man.

In terms of this battle, the Calvinist champions the
divine blueprint over the philosophies of fallen man,
and in so doing his approach consists of a simultaneous affirmation and denial. On the one hand,
believing in predestination, the Calvinist sees the created order as God given and therefore good. Accordingly,
he affirms human culture metaphysically. Yet, believing
also in human depravity, he sees fallen man as rebelling
against God's order at every point of culture and so is
forced to challenge fallen culture ethically. In other words,
(to make good use of a pious platitude), the Calvinist
loves the sinful culture and hates the cultural sin. Given
this fact, the uniquely Calvinist approach to culture consists of both metaphysical affirmation and ethical
confrontation. Thus, in a poetic sense, the Calvinist chal-
lenges the world for the sake of the world.

In contrast to this approach, however, other theological traditions tend to affirm the fallen culture both
ethically and metaphysically or else to deny the culture

---

[1] In other words, throughout the realm of culture, there is a battle
over sovereignty and thus over the prerogative to set law.

ture in both ways simultaneously. As a result, such churches tend to accommodate the evil of fallen culture or else flee the battle altogether. After all, since such groups do not hold to a consistent doctrine of predestination, they necessarily regard the creation as being partially independent of God and thus devoid of an exhaustive divine blueprint. Consequently, lacking a God centered view, they are forced to regard the creation as natural or evil.

Now when the creation is viewed as natural, Christians and non Christians are thought to operate on an equal footing in terms of "natural law" and thus apart from a necessary commitment to Scripture. Consequently, since human cultural activity is then seen to occur apart from a specific divine blueprint, it is viewed as a "neutral" realm of "Christian freedom" subject only to the rules of "common sense." As a result, except for extreme and obvious abuses like abortion, much cultural activity that is truly sinful is never challenged. Thus, in Lutheran and Roman Catholic churches where the creation is rightly affirmed in a metaphysical sense, cultural evil is ethically accommodated through natural law theories.

However, whereas Lutherans and Roman Catholics tend to view creation as natural, many evangelicals view it as evil. Thus, whereas the Lutherans and Roman Catholics affirm the culture both ethically and metaphysically, certain evangelicals tend to deny culture in both ways simultaneously. In this mindset, a Gnostic dualism is posited in which a benevolent "spiritual" world is opposed to an evil "material" world. Consequently, since human culture is necessarily identified with the material world, cultural warfare is then viewed in metaphysical rather than ethical categories. Thus, the battle with fallen culture becomes a battle between various types of substance (spirit vs. matter) rather than an ethical conflict between grace and sin. Accordingly, since the culture itself is now identified with an evil material world, the church either flees the battle altogether or wars against culture *per se*. As a consequence, fallen culture is again accommodated, or else the evil is compounded by a violent church. At the time of the Reformation, the Anabaptists wavered between these divergent extremes precisely because they saw the conflict as metaphysical, rather than ethical. Sadly, as American culture continues to decline, many evangelicals are repeating these errors today.

On the basis of the preceding discussion, therefore, it is evident that a denial of predestination undercuts the basis for a uniquely Christian approach to culture. After all, apart from predestination, creation lacks a specific divine blueprint and is therefore viewed as natural or evil. Consequently, since the culture is part of the created order, Christians then tend to affirm the culture both ethically and metaphysically or else to deny the culture in both ways simultaneously. On either extreme, however, whether through active accommodation or aloof hostility, cultural evil is allowed to flourish.

However, when predestination is boldly maintained, every area of culture is seen to be infused with a divinely created order which provides the normative standard for cultural activity. Moreover, since fallen man is held to oppose this order in every cultural sphere, the reconstruction of culture in terms of a divine blueprint becomes an integral aspect of the church's prophetic mission. Accordingly, in the realm of the state, it becomes necessary to assert God's sovereignty and the binding authority of His law against the pompous pretensions and evil laws of petty tyrants. Given these implications, it should come as no surprise that the Calvinists, who alone held to an absolute predestination, were the foremost champions of human liberty:

> When in the great toil and roar of the conflict the fiery nature of Luther began to chill, and he began to temporize with civil rulers, it was this same uncompromising theology of the Genevan school which heroically and triumphantly waged the conflict to the end. I but repeat the testimony of history, friendly and unfriendly to Calvinism, when I say that had it not been for the strong, unflinching, systematic spirit and character of the theology of Calvin, the Reformation would have been lost to the world. That is one thing which Calvinism has done. That is one of the fruits which have grown on this vigorous old tree. (McFetridge, *Calvinism in History*, 15)

> Charles I of England gave as the reason why his father James I, had subverted the republican form of government of the Scottish Church, that the presbyterial and monarchical forms of government do not harmonize.

And De Tocqueville, admitting the same, calls Calvinism "a democratic and republican religion." This is the historical fact, that, while Calvinism can live and do its divine work under any form of civil government, its natural affinities are not with a monarchy, but with a republic.

This is the reason that it has made so splendid a record in the history of human freedom. Where it flourishes despotism cannot abide. This, says the historian D'Aubigne, "chiefly distinguishes the Reformation of Calvin from that of Luther, that wherever it was established it brought with it not only truth, but liberty, and all the great developments which these two fertile principles carry with them." (McFetridge, *Calvinism in History*, 19, 20)."

It would be almost impossible to give the merest outline of the influence of the Calvinists on the civil and religious liberties of this continent without seeming to be a mere Calvinistic eulogist; for the contestants in the great Revolutionary conflict were, so far as religious opinions prevailed, so generally Calvinistic on the one side and Arminian on the other as to leave the glory of the result almost entirely with the Calvinists. They who are best acquainted with the history will agree most readily with the historian, Merle D'Aubigne, when he says: "Calvin was the founder of the greatest of republics. The pilgrims who left their country in the reign of James I, and, landing on the barren soil of New England, founded populous and mighty colonies, were his sons, his direct and legitimate sons; and that American nation which we have seen growing so rapidly boasts as its father the humble Reformer on the shores of Lake Leman." (McFetridge, *Calvinism in History*, 39, 40)

Amongst the Calvinistic churches the Congregationalists and Dutch Reformed and Presbyterians were the leaders, and none of them took a more decided and active part in favor of independence than the Scotch-Irish Presbyterians. They threw into the movement all the fearlessness of the Scotch and all the fire and wit of the Irish character. Hence their speeches and sermons and papers and bulletins were at once irritating and amusing to their opponents. Bancroft accredits to them the glory of making the first bold move toward independence, and of lifting the first public voice in its favor. To the Synod of the Presbyterian Church, convened in Philadelphia in 1775, belongs the responsibility — and may we not say the glory? — of being the first religious body to declare openly and publicly for a separation from England, and to counsel and encourage the people, who were then about taking up arms. It enjoined upon its people to leave nothing undone that could promote the end in view, and called upon them to pray for the Congress then assembled. (McFetridge, *Calvinism in History*, 51)

So also Bancroft: "He that will not honor the memory and respect the influence of Calvin knows but little of the origin of American independence."... "The light of his genius shattered the mask of darkness which Superstition had held for centuries before the brow of Religion." (McFetridge, *Calvinism in History*, 69)

As should be evident from these citations, the Calvinists were unique in their vigorous promotion of liberty, and this uniqueness flowed from their basic theology. After all, holding simultaneously to the doctrines of predestination and total depravity, Calvinism posited the highest view of God and the lowest view of man. Accordingly, believing that God, and not the king, was the ultimate sovereign, and that God had therefore established His own order for the state, the Calvinists naturally championed God's law against the evil laws of tyrants. Thus, the battle for liberty was first and foremost a battle over sovereignty and therefore secondarily a battle over law. In terms of this battle, the Calvinist holding to God's ultimate sovereignty, held that God's law was totally binding, even for kings. Thus, there were limits to human rule both because the kings themselves were limited by the higher law of God and because men had to be free in order to fulfill their various divine callings. So understood, the Calvinist notion of liberty was not anarchistic but rather one of an ordered and limited liberty, namely a liberty under law. After all, in his pursuit of liberty, the Calvinist did not oppose sovereignty or law but rather championed the sovereign law of God.

Given this evident activism, it is clear that the doctrine of predestination did not dampen human initiative by producing a fatalistic resignation. On the contrary, through the provision of a cultural blue print, predestination set the stage for an ethical confrontation. Moreover, beyond these intellectual factors, the doctrines of depravity and predestination established a psychology of humble boldness which provided the impulsion to battle. On the one hand, believing in total depravity, the Calvinist harbored no pretensions as to his own goodness. Rather, believing himself to be as sinful as others, he had a profound humility which prevented him from dominating others as his inferiors. On the other hand, since he believed that God had chosen him to fulfill His plans, he was both humbled and energized by a sense of calling which bid him to enter the battle. After all, as a result of his conversion, he was now fighting on the side of the sovereign and predestinating God who could remove any obstacle from his path. Accordingly, while the Calvinist was humble before God and men, the sense of his calling and his greater humility before God often forced him to be bold in personal confrontation. Consequently, he stepped forth into battle, believing that God had predestined both an eternal and a temporal victory for His elect. Motivated by this confidence, therefore, he asserted the "crown rights of King Jesus" against the usurpations of every tyrant. In this regard, the following citations give insight into the Calvinistic boldness:

Another reason why Calvinism is favorable to liberty lies in its theology. "The sense of the exaltation of the Almighty Ruler," says Dr. Fisher, "and of his intimate connection with the minutest incidents and obligations of human life, which is fostered by this theology, dwarfs all earthly potentates. An intense spirituality, a consciousness that this life is but an infinitesimal fraction of human existence, dissipates the feeling of personal homage for men, however high their station, and dulls the lustre of all earthly grandeur."... "The Calvinist, unlike the Romanist, dispenses with a human priesthood, which has not only often proved a powerful direct auxiliary to temporal rulers, but has educated the sentiments to a habit of subjection, which renders submission to such rulers more facile and less easy to shake off."

Its doctrine of predestination also is calculated to have a tremendous influence on the political character of its adherents. This has not escaped the notice of historians. Bancroft, who, while adopting another religious creed, has awarded to Calvinism the palm for its influence in favor of religious and civil liberty, remarks that "the political character of Calvinism, which, with one consent and with instinctive judgment, the monarchs of that day feared as republicanism, is expressed in a single word — predestination. Did a proud aristocracy trace its lineage through generations of highborn ancestry, the republican Reformers, with a loftier pride, invaded the invisible world, and from the book of life brought down the record of the noblest enfranchisement, decreed from eternity by the King of kings.... They went forth in confidence...and standing surely amidst the crumbling fabric of centuries of superstition, they had faith in one another and the martyrdoms of Cambray, the fires of Smithfield, the surrender of benefices by two thousand nonconforming Presbyterians, attests their perseverance."

This doctrine "inspires a resolute, almost defiant freedom in those who deem themselves the subjects of God's electing grace; in all things they are more than conquerors through the confidence that nothing shall be able to separate them from the love of God. No doctrine of the dignity of human nature, of the rights of man, of national liberty, of social equality, can create such a resolve for the freedom of the soul as this personal conviction of God's favoring and protecting sovereignty. He who has this faith feels that he is compassed about with everlasting love, guided with everlasting strength; his will is the tempered steel that no fire can melt, no force can break. Such faith is freedom; and this spiritual freedom is the source and strength of all other freedom." (McFetridge, *Calvinism in History*, 11-13)

So also the Reverend Henry Ward Beecher: "It has ever been a mystery to the so-called liberals that the Calvinists, with what they have considered their harshly despotic and rigid views and doctrines, should always have been the staunchest and bravest defenders of freedom. The working for liberty of these severe principles in the minds of those that adopted them has been a puzzle. But the truth lies here: Calvinism has done what no other religion has ever been able to do. It presents the highest human ideal to the world, and sweeps the whole road to destruction with the most appalling battery that can be imagined.

"It intensifies, beyond all example, the individuality of man, and shows in a clear and overpowering light his responsibility to God and his relations to eternity. It points out man as entering life under the weight of a tremendous responsibility, having, on his march toward the grave, this one sole solace — of securing heaven and of escaping hell." (McFetridge, *Calvinism in History*, 69, 70)

As these citations amply demonstrate, the Calvinists were driven by a psychology of humble boldness to champion God's law against tyrants. In so doing, however, they made an additional contribution to human liberty in the establishment of the idea of checks and balances. Once again, this development flowed from their basic theology. After all, holding to the twin doctrines of predestination and total depravity, Calvinism set forth the highest view of God and the lowest view of man. Accordingly, in structuring their institutions they attempted to limit human power so that God's rule could more visibly shine forth. To this end, they sought to structure human institutions in terms of a Biblically revealed, divine blueprint having a system of checks and balances. Thus, by dividing power against power, they sought to design institutions that would check the pretensions of human depravity, and with them the vain ambitions of tyrants.

Of course, such a bold program did not develop all at once. Initially the Calvinists sought to reform the church alone and had no intention to change the form of the state. However, as civil rulers began to interfere with their church reforms, it became obvious that civil and religious liberty were inextricably linked and that the state too would have to be limited. Accordingly, a full scale battle for civil liberty developed in which the initial program of church reform came to be applied to the state. Given this fact, the Calvinist views of civil and religious liberty are linked historically as well as theologically. As a result, it will be necessary to trace the historical development somewhat in order to illustrate the principles involved.

In terms of this development, it was mentioned above that the Calvinist reform concentrated initially on the church. Believing the top down rule of bishops to be unscriptural, they opposed the episcopal system of church government common to both the Anglican and Roman Catholic churches. In its place, they supported either congregationalism, (government by direct congregational vote), or presbyterianism, (government by elected elders.) Thus, to draw a civil analogy, they sought to replace ecclesiastical monarchy (episcopalianism) with ecclesiastical democracy (congregationalism) or republicanism (presbyterianism). Accordingly, as these analogies amply demonstrate, their system of church government had latent, yet profound civil implications. Thus, quite apart from any overt attempt to restructure the state, the seed of civil liberty already lay within the Calvinist principles of church government.

However, the civil rulers of the day also recognized this fact and reacted to guard their power. Fearing that such republican principles would eventually spread to the state, they attempted to squelch these ecclesiastical reforms. In this regard, their fears were well founded since people accustomed to electing their church officials would be all the more apt to demand civil liberty. And conversely, (as Roman Catholic Latin America currently bears witness), people subjected to the top down rule of bishops would all the more readily acquiesce to tyrants. Given this fact, the civil rulers favored the Anglican, Roman Catholic, and pliant Lutheran Churches while vigorously opposing the Calvinists. In short, they waged war against Calvinism out of fear that Calvinistic church government would eventually undermine their civil power.

Beyond their form of church government, however, there were additional aspects of Calvinist theology which spurred the conflict on. First, believing in a strong theological connection between church and state, they believed that human rule was limited by the higher law of God. Thus, while they did not initially try to change the form of the state, they nevertheless attempted to impose material limits on the monarch by binding him to the law of God. Moreover, while maintaining this strong theological connection, they simultaneously held to an institutional separation between church and state as part of a system of checks and balances among the various institutions of society. Consequently, as civil rulers began to interfere in the government of their churches, they held such actions to be null and void because exercised outside the realm of legitimate civil authority. Thus, by maintaining both a strong theological connection and an absolute institutional separation between church and state, the Calvinists sought to limit the scope of civil authority and to impose strict material limits within that scope. Accordingly, even apart from any attempt to alter the form of the state, Calvinist theology demanded strict limits on both the quantity and quality of civil government. Consequently, when the monarchs began to interfere with the government of their churches, they resisted these impositions as being both contrary to the law of God and outside the Biblically defined sphere of civil jurisdiction. As a result, the struggle for religious liberty turned into a full scale battle for civil liberty as well. In terms of this development, several comments by McFetridge illustrate the connection between civil and religious liberty:

> On this point I will quote a few sentences from the late Dr. Charles Hodge. "The theory," he observes, "that all church power vests in a divinely-constituted hierarchy begets the theory that all civil power vests, of divine right, in kings and nobles. And the theory that church power vests in the Church

itself, and all church officers are servants of the Church, of necessity begets the theory that civil power vests in the people, and that civil magistrates are servants of the people. These theories God has joined together, and no man can put them asunder. It was therefore by an infallible instinct that the unfortunate Charles of England said, 'No bishop, no king;' by which he meant that if there is no despotic power in the Church, there can be no despotic power in the State, or if there be liberty in the Church there will be liberty in the State." (McFetridge, *Calvinism in History*, 9, 10)

Now, consider, for a moment, some of the reasons which lie in the system of Calvinism for its strong hostility to all despotism and its powerful influence in favor of civil liberty.

One reason for this may be found in the boundary line which it draws between Church and State. It gives to each its distinct sphere, and demands that the one shall not assume the prerogatives of the other. In this it differs from Lutheranism, "which soon settled down at peace with princes, while Calvinism was ever advancing and ever contending with rulers of the world; and from the Anglican system, which began with Henry VIII as its head in place of the pope. This distinction between Church and State is, as the eminent Yale professor, Dr. Fisher, remarks, "the first step, the necessary condition, in the development of religious liberty, without which civil liberty is an impossibility."

Another reason is found in the republican character of its polity. Its clergy are on a perfect equality. No one of them stands higher in authority than another. They are all alike bishops. Its laymen share equally with its clergymen in all official acts — in the discussion and decision of all matters of doctrine and practice. They have a most important part given them in the right of choosing and calling their own pastor. By being thus rulers in the Church they are taught to claim and exercise the liberty in the State. It is this feature of the Calvinistic system which has, from the first, exalted the layman. It constitutes, not the clergy, but the Christian people, the interpreter of the divine will. (McFetridge, *Calvinism in History*, 10, 11)

This was the Calvinism which flashed forth in the great Reforming days — the spirit which, when Romanists and despots claimed the right to burn all who differed from them, inspired men and women and youth to go forth, Bible and sword in hand, to the greatest daring, appealing for the justice of their cause and the victory of their arms to the Lord of hosts. This was the spirit which acted in those men 'who attracted to their ranks almost every man in Western Europe who hated a lie;" who when they were crushed down rose again; who "abhorred all conscious mendacity, all impurity, all moral wrong of every kind, so far as they could recognize it;" who, though they did not utterly destroy Romanism, "drew its fangs, and forced it to abandon that detestable principle that it was entitled to murder those who dissented from it." This was the spirit out of which came, and by which was nourished, the religious and civil liberties of Christendom; of which Bancroft says, "More truly benevolent to the human race than Solon, more self-denying than Lycurgus, the genius of Calvin infused enduring elements into the institutions of Geneva, and made it for the modern world the impregnable fortress of popular liberty, the fertile seed plot of democracy." (McFetridge, *Calvinism in History*, 18)

The spirit in which they carried on the conflict is well illustrated in the case of Jennie Geddes. Charles I had determined to carry out his father's policy of compelling the Scotch Church to adopt Prelacy. The city of Edinburgh and the church of St. Giles was the place where the public use of the Liturgy was to be commenced. The church was crowded, and "a deep, melancholy calm brooded over the congregation," presaging the fierce tempest which was about to sweep away every barrier. At length the dean, attired in his surplice, began to read the Liturgy, but his voice was speedily drowned in tumultuous clamor. An old woman, Jennie

272

Geddes, was the heroine of the occasion. "Villain!" she cried, "doest thou say mass at my lug?" and with that she hurled the stool on which she had been sitting at the dean's head. Others quickly followed her example, and compelled the dean to fly, leaving his surplice behind him. This was really the death-blow to the Liturgy in Scotland, and it exhibits the earnest, fearless spirit of even the aged and humble. (McFetridge, *Calvinism in History*, 23, 24)

As should be evident from the citations above, Calvinism is conducive to civil liberty as a result of its republican structure, its independence of the state, and the extreme boldness of its adherents. However, since the rulers of Europe also recognized this fact, they logically saw it as a threat to their power and therefore attempted to crush it. As a result, a conflict developed in various regions of Europe with the Calvinists resisting the state suppression their churches.

In regard to this conflict, the struggle became acute in France, England, and Scotland, and eventually drove many Calvinists to America. Moreover, beyond this demographic effect, the very existence of the struggle served to clarify the connection between civil and religious liberty and therefore to focus attention on the Biblical principles of civil and ecclesiastical government. Consequently, as a result of this battle, America received a disproportionately large number of Calvinist settlers who were well versed in these Biblical principles. Moreover, since their opinions had been forged through conflict, they came to America battle tested and thus committed to the principles for which they had fought. Accordingly, in a continent where they would be given a free hand in the structuring of their institutions, the Calvinist settlers, beginning with the Pilgrims and the Puritans, sought to apply their Calvinistic principles to the government of both church and state.

With respect to these groups, the Pilgrims were Separatists from the church of England who had adopted a direct congregational form of church government. Moreover, while still aboard the Mayflower in 1620, these Pilgrims drafted a civil covenant, known as The Mayflower Compact, for the better ordering of their civil affairs. In so doing, they structured their civil government along the lines of their congregational church polity, producing a democratic form of government at the township level (Slater, *T&L*, 179, 196). Furthermore, since many others immigrated to New England for religious reasons, they also came and settled near one another as entire congregational units. Accordingly, they too structured their respective townships along the lines of their church polity with the result that New England became populated by the formation of tight knit townships. Consequently, the basic unit of civil government in New England became the township whose structure was patterned after that of the various churches (Hall, *CHOC*, 271). In this regard, the vigorous debate of township meetings would eventually prove invaluable to the later training of mature statesmen (Hall, CHOC, 274, 275).

However, it was soon realized that these several townships would need a higher and broader government to secure the harmony between them. Consequently, in Connecticut the various townships federated together to form a colony. For the first time in history, a government would be created by the people from the ground up and not imposed upon them from the top down. In this endeavor, the central problem would be to give the federal government sufficient power to fulfill its necessary functions while leaving the balance of power, and thus the maximum possible liberty, with the townships.

In striking this balance, the Calvinists had the example of the Presbyterian churches where a cluster of local churches would send elected elders (*i.e.*, presbyters) to their common presbytery meetings for the better ordering of their common affairs. Accordingly, the principle of the Connecticut federation became that of representative government through elected delegates together with the limitation of central power through a written constitution. In this regard, all powers not specifically granted to the federal government by the several townships, remained as by original right in the townships themselves (Hall, *CHOC*, 252). Thus, unlike the government of the New England townships which had been founded on the democratic congregational model, the federal government of Connecticut was based upon a republican presbyterianism. In this regard, the resulting structure was finalized and encapsulated in a written constitution known as The Fundamental Orders of Connecticut, "a document far in advance of anything the world had ever seen, in its recognition of the origin of all civil authority as derived, under God, from the agreement and covenant of the whole body of the governed" (Hall, *CHOC*, 249).

As mentioned above, the form of this federal government was presbyterian and not congregational since it involved representative government under law (republicanism) and not rule by direct vote (democracy). In this regard, it is most significant that this particular form of government was self consciously based on a Biblical pattern as a result of the advocacy of a Puritan pastor, Reverend Thomas Hooker of the First Church in Hartford, Connecticut. In preaching to the opening session of the general Court at which The Fundamental Orders of Connecticut were being drafted, he presented the Biblical basis for representative government in a three point, sermonic exposition of Deuteronomy 1:13 (Hall, *CHOC*, 250-252):

TEXT

Deuteronomy 1:13. "Take you wise men, and understanding, and known among your tribes, and I will make them rulers over you." Captains over thousands, and captains over hundreds — over fifties — over tens, etc.

DOCTRINE

I. That the choice of public magistrates belongs unto the people by God's own allowance.

II. The privilege of election which belongs unto the people, therefore, must not be exercised according to their humors, but according to the blessed will and law of God.

276

III. They who have power to appoint officers and magistrates, it is their power, also,
to set the bounds of the power and place unto
which they call them.

As can be seen from this citation, the three points of
Hooker's sermon correspond to the Calvinist principles of representative government, Biblical
government, and limited government, respectively.
Accordingly, since these principles were self consciously incorporated into The Fundamental Orders
of Connecticut, the governmental structure of Connecticut was therefore self consciously Biblical and
Calvinist. Moreover, since The Fundamental Orders
of Connecticut would become the model for the U.S.
Constitution, these Calvinistic principles, so encapsulated, would eventually diffuse outward to shape
the government of an entire nation (Hall, *CHOC*, 252).

However, before these principles could reach their
complete ascendancy, an intense struggle would en-
sue since the developments on the American continent
were being resisted by the English monarchs. View-
ing American liberty as a threat to their power, they
resisted its civil progress and also sought to eradicate
the movement at the level of its religious roots. Accordingly, as they and others had done in Europe, the
British kings now sought to suppress civil and religious liberty in America. However, since the American
colonists had previously fled Europe to avoid such
persecution in the first place, the resurgence of the
struggle on American soil underscored the fact that
America was no longer a safe haven from persecution
and that barring America, there was no place left to

run. Consequently, having their backs against a wall, the colonists decided to fight since the only other alternative was to surrender their civil and religious liberties. Accordingly, the American Revolution grew out of a principled resistance to an attempted British suppression of American civil and religious liberty. In this battle, it was British oppression which provided the spark and Calvinist theology which provided the fuel:

> The king and the bishop stood side by side in the popular conception of the times; hence when war broke forth the dissenting churches were on the side of independence, and the Episcopal churches were as unanimously on the side of the Crown. This is not, however, so much to the discredit of the Episcopal clergy as it might now appear under the present order of things; for we are not to forget that they all, at that time, belonged to the Church of England, whose supreme authority on earth was vested in the reigning sovereign, to whom every clergyman of that Church had sworn allegiance. (McFetridge, *Calvinism in History*, 46)

> Thus the liberties of the Church were suspended on the will of the reigning monarch, and her clergy were but the vicars for the Crown, which might, and sometimes did, suspend them from the exercise of their functions. Henry VIII by one stroke of his pen at one time suspended every prelate in England, and restored them only on their individual petition. And Elizabeth more than once

threatened, with her usual vulgarity and profanity, to "unfrock" the clergy who manifested any opposition to her will.

It is not, therefore, surprising that the dissenting spirit of independence rebelled against such an Act of Uniformity, or that, their Church and living being at the mercy of the Crown, the clergy of the Establishment were unwilling to take up arms against the king. This was the very thing, however, to which the Calvinistic non-conformists would not submit. They believed, and maintained with their blood, that the sphere of the Church is distinct from that of the State, and that no king or Parliament has the right to bind the human conscience.

Hence, in the war for American independence, the dissenting churches arrayed themselves on the side of the colonies, and the Anglican Church arrayed itself on the side of the Crown. The independent and democratic spirit of Calvinism, cherished in the hearts of its adherents and nourished by their mixed assemblies and free discussions, rose up in rebellion against all despotic measures, whether of Church or State, and girded itself again for the great conflict on this Western continent. (McFetridge, *Calvinism in History*, 48, 49)

On the basis of the preceding discussion, the Calvinist devotion to liberty should be clearly evident. In comparison to other Christian systems, Calvinism favors republican principles in church and state, and this preference stems from its basic theology. After all, believing in both predestination and human depravity, Calvinism simultaneously asserts the highest view of God and the lowest view of man. Thus, in every realm the sovereignty, law, and salvation of God are exalted, even as the idolatrous human substitutes are pulverized. On the basis of predestination, of course, the Calvinist holds to an exhaustively ordered creation and thus to a transcendent divine blueprint which is normative for the state. However, believing also in total depravity, he knows that fallen man will seek to oppose God's order. Accordingly, in the realm of the state, the Calvinist champions God's law over man's law, and seeks to restrain human depravity through a system of checks and balances. Moreover, in fighting this battle the Calvinist is both humbled by the knowledge of his own depravity and emboldened by a predestination which secures his ultimate victory. Accordingly, in the battle for liberty, the Calvinist is driven by a psychology of humble boldness and does not succumb to a fatalistic resignation. Finally, because God is the predestinating savior, not the state, the state is viewed as a ministry of justice under God's law and not a divine institution subject to its own authority. Thus, rather than rushing into every zone of human activity as the lord and savior thereof, the state is restrained and limited to the more narrow matters of Biblical justice under God's law. In other words, because man is saved by grace through faith and not by the works (programs) of the state, Calvinist society is characterized by a sociology of justification by faith in which limited institutions prevail (Rushdoony,

The Politics of Guilt and Pity, 263). After all, resting in the security of the predestinating God, Calvinism has no motive to establish a predestinating, expansionist state.

However, whereas Calvinism promotes republicanism and liberty, Arminianism promotes monarchy and tyranny as the logical outgrowth of its basic theology. After all, in Arminianism predestination and total depravity are both denied with the result that human ability eclipses the sovereignty of God. Thus, of all Christian systems, Arminianism holds to the lowest view of God and the highest view of man. Accordingly, the sovereignty, law, and salvation of man are exalted, even as God's sovereignty is denied. On the one hand, having denied predestination, the Arminian cannot hold to an exhaustively ordered creation or to any divine blueprint which is normative for the state. Thus, the transcendent limits (divine law) to tyranny are destroyed with the result that human law rushes in to fill a legal void. Moreover, having also denied total depravity, the Arminian views original sin as merely a spiritual sickness (not spiritual death) and therefore opts for a view of salvation in which man cooperates with God, perhaps pulling 10% of the load. However, since some people work better than others, an allowance must then be made for the exceptional people who can pull 15%, 25%, or even 50% of the load in salvation. Thus, works necessarily enter the realm of salvation, producing a ground for boasting which caters to the smug superiority of civil rulers. Accordingly, in addition to elevating man's law over God's, Arminianism produces an arrogant psychology which further compounds the problem of tyranny. Finally,

since salvation is thought to occur by a combination
of grace and works, the state, as a realm of works (programs), is then seen as a saving institution.
Consequently, rather than being limited to the ministry of justice under God's law, the state expands into
every realm of human activity as the lord and savior
thereof. In other words, since salvation is thought to
occur by a combination of grace and works, Arminian
society is characterized by a sociology of works righteousness in which centralized institutions prevail.
After all, lacking the security of a predestinating God,
Arminian theology embraces a predestinating state.
With respect to the influence of Arminian theology,
consider the following quotes:

> Buckle, who, himself a fatalist, cannot be
> charged with partiality toward any Church,
> says: "It is an interesting fact that the doc-
> trines which in England are called
> Calvinistic have always been connected with
> a democratic spirit, while those of
> Arminianism have found most favor among
> the aristocratic, or protective, party. In the
> republics of Switzerland, of North America
> and of Holland, Calvinism was always the
> popular creed. On the other hand, in those
> evil days immediately after the death of
> Elizabeth, when our liberties were in immi-
> nent peril, when the Church of England,
> aided by the Crown, attempted to subjugate
> the consciences of men, and when the mon-
> strous claim of the divine right of Episcopacy
> was first put forward, — then it was that
> Arminianism became the cherished doctrine

of the ablest and most ambitious of the ecclesiastical party. And in that sharp retribution which followed, the Puritans and Independents, by whom the punishment was inflicted, were, with scarcely an exception, Calvinists; nor should we forget that the first open movement against Charles proceeded from Scotland, where the principles of Calvin had long been in the ascendant."

Thus we see how Arminianism, taking to an aristocratic form of church government, tends toward a monarchy in civil affairs, while Calvinism, taking to a republican form of church government, tends toward democracy in civil affairs.

Allow me to quote again from this eminent English author. He says: "the first circumstance by which we must be struck is that . Calvinism is a doctrine for the poor and Arminianism for the rich. A creed which insists upon the necessity of faith must be less costly than one which insists upon the necessity of works. In the former case the sinner seeks salvation by the strength of his belief; in the latter case he seeks it by the fullness of his contributions." (McFetridge, *Calvinism in History*, 7,8)

That religious and civil liberty have an organic connection and a natural affinity is quite obvious. They hold together as root and branch. "By the side of every religion is to be found a political opinion connected with it by affinity. If the human mind be left to follow its own bent, it will regulate the temporal and spiritual institutions of society in a uniform manner, and man will endeavor, if I may so speak, to harmonize earth with heaven," but other influences may be powerful enough to interfere with this natural connection of the religious and political belief. The Romanist may choose to be a republican rather than a monarchist, because of the greater advantages which a republic confers, or because he finds himself in the midst of republican institutions which he cannot hope to alter; but when a man is free to follow his own inclinations, he will body forth his religion in his political beliefs. Hence it comes that the influence on our republican institutions of a rigid Arminianism, which has always been wedded to an aristocratic form of church government, is unfavorable to their perpetuity. Its whole tendency, politically, is to educate the sentiments of the people to a spirit of subjection to the rich and powerful, and thus to prepare them for the monarchic form of civil government. (McFetridge, *Calvinism in History*, 18, 19)

Having considered Calvinism and Arminianism, it is necessary to say a few words about the political tendencies of Lutheranism. With respect to the state, Lutheranism generally acquiesces to political tyranny because its basic theology produces both a radical cowardice and a total indifference to political affairs. After all, in maintaining total depravity apart from an absolute predestination, it has no high view of God to counterbalance its low view of man. Consequently, it partakes of all the Calvinist guilt but lacks its predestinarian boldness. On the positive side, of course, its doctrine of total depravity serves to check the tyrannical ambitions of its adherents. However, apart from an absolute predestination, it lacks both the transcendent divine blueprint and the aggressive posture needed to resist tyrants. Thus, it is spineless and indifferent in the face of evil, and therefore tends to accommodate tyranny through "natural law" theories. After all, being theologically weakened, it lacks both the program and the spirit to engage the cultural battle, much less prevail. Consequently, while the state is not considered a saving institution in Lutheran theology, it is nevertheless given a free hand to do essentially as it pleases. Thus, the Lutheran approach to politics derives from a psychology of powerless guilt and leads to a sociology of slavish submission. Essentially, it is a "worm theology" and as such has produced a cultural vacuum.

However, in contrast to Lutheranism and Arminianism which are conducive to tyranny, Calvinism has been shown to promote human liberty. In this regard, the uniqueness of Calvinism stems from its dogged adherence to predestination. After all, by securing an exhaustively ordered creation, predestination provides for a divine blueprint which is normative for the state. Moreover, by guaranteeing the ultimate victory of God's elect, it provides for a confident posture in battle. Finally, by delimiting God as the one and only Savior, it exalts the Kingdom of God over the kingdom of man, thereby dashing the salvific pretensions of the expansionist state. Thus, from a theological stand point, predestination provides the standard, the motive, and the goal needed to wage cultural warfare against oppressive tyrants. Moreover, from an historical stand point, it is most significant that only in Calvinism where this doctrine has been uniquely maintained has civil liberty been vigorously championed. Accordingly, from both a theoretical (theological) and an empirical (historical) stand point, predestination has been shown essential to maintenance of civil liberty. Given this fact, this doctrine is vitally needed to prevent the continued floundering of modern evangelicalism in its opposition to a wicked culture and a power state.

Predestination and the Protestant Reformation

18

In the previous chapter, it was shown that the predestinarian theology of John Calvin had a broad cultural impact, eventually resulting in the formation of the United States of America. However, with respect to the issue of predestination, Calvin was by no means an innovator. On the contrary, Calvin along with the other Protestant Reformers took this theology straight from Martin Luther with little or no modification.[1] Thus,

---

[1] Of course, in the areas of church polity and civil relations, Calvin's formulations were more systematic than those of Luther, but here it is to be remembered that Calvin walked in the path that Luther had cleared. Calvin thus had a two-fold advantage. First, since he was spared the task of original thinking, he was able take Luther's doctrines and refine, or correct them as needed. In this regard, Luther had to develop the theology step by step and so could often not "see the forest for the trees." Calvin, by contrast, had the luxury of a panoramic view, and it is on the basis of such a view that systems are made. Second, while having his own problems with the Geneva city council, Calvin was relatively free from the threat of bodily harm. Luther, on the other hand, being more in the thick of the battle and therefore having a more tenuous existence, was often forced to "shoot from the hip." Nevertheless, in the area of predestination, Luther's thinking as reflected in his master work, *The Bondage of the Will*, was lucid and systematic, and therefore taken by Calvin with little modification.

despite some sharp sacramental differences, the doctrine of predestination was embraced by the entire first generation of Protestant Reformers and therefore by such diverse persons as Luther and Melanchthon[2] in Wittenberg, Zwingli and Oecolampadius in Zurich, Calvin and Beza in Geneva, and Bucer and Capito in Strasbourg.

Consequently, when due regard is taken of the differing opinions expressed by these Reformers, their unanimous agreement on the doctrine of predestination argues strongly for the centrality of this doctrine to the Reformation itself. In fact, as will be shown below, this doctrine was of such importance that in virtually every major confrontation between the Reformers and Rome, the underlying theological issue could be reduced to a battle over predestination vs. free will. To illustrate this point, the major battle over indulgences will be examined below in terms of its theological underpinnings. To the extent that predestination is seen to drive the indulgence issue, its centrality to the Reformation will clearly emerge.

With regard to the battle over indulgences, the most obvious theological differences dividing the two parties were their respective views of salvation. In terms of this division, the Roman Catholics believed that a

---

[2] Unfortunately, in 1535 Melanchthon rejected the doctrine of predestination and eventually pulled many of the Lutherans with him. Luther, however, never changed his view of the matter, and when asked in 1537 about making a collection of his writings, he said that he would scrap them all except the small Catechism and *The Bondage of the Will* because they alone were right.

man was saved by a combination of grace and works and thus supported the sale of indulgences as a substitute work of penance. On the other hand, the Protestants believed that a man was saved by grace alone and therefore consistently opposed the sale of indulgences. Of course, in the initial stages of the Reformation, the theological issues were not that clear to Martin Luther. As a pastor charged with the care of souls, Luther's initial opposition was motivated by the harmful effect these indulgences were having on his parishioners and was therefore more pragmatic than theological. However, as Luther began to delve more deeply into the matter, it became apparent to him that the errors in practice were driven by bad theology. The basic problem, as Luther came to understand it, was that the Roman church held to an admixture of grace and works in salvation rather than a salvation by grace alone. Moreover, as Luther considered the implications of this distinction, he was driven to the underlying issue of predestination vs. free will. Thus, predestination entered the indulgence debate in connection with the issue of salvation. Accordingly, to set forth the relation between predestination and the sale of indulgences, it will be necessary to consider the competing views of salvation.

With respect to salvation, the Reformation theologians took their point of departure in their view of sin. Believing that the cure of salvation was adequate to the disease of sin, their radical view of sin and its effects led quite naturally to a radical view of God's grace in salvation. Thus, their emphasis on the total depravity of man lent itself to a correlative emphasis on the exclusivity of God's grace in salvation. With respect to depravity, they viewed man as being spiritually dead and bound in sin so that his will was not free. Consequently, because man was spiritually dead, he could not move toward God until quickened by grace. Thus, if a man were to be saved, God's work of regeneration had to causally precede the human response. (In other words, one had to be born again in order to come to Christ, not the reverse.) Moreover, since a spiritually dead man could not even cooperate with God in his conversion, salvation involved an exclusivity or monergism (a working alone) of God's grace in addition to its causal priority. Accordingly, man was seen to be 100% dependent upon God's grace for salvation, a fact which made salvation dependent upon God's decision, not man's. Thus, the Reformers' view of total depravity necessarily implied a correlative doctrine of predestination since a spiritually dead man had to be saved by grace alone. Consequently, the Reformers were driven to reject the sale of indulgences precisely because their view of original sin and predestination implied an exclusivity of God's grace in salvation which negated any contribution of human works.

To the Protestant position, of course, the Roman Catholics were opposed since they believed in salvation by a combination of grace and works. Moreover, as with the Protestant view, the Roman Catholic view of salvation was also rooted in a particular view of sin and its effects. However, in contrast to the Protestants who believed in total depravity, the Roman Catholics believed in what might be called "partial depravity" and thus conceived of original sin as a spiritual sickness rather than a spiritual death. Consequently, while they believed man's will to be weakened by sin, man's will was not considered spiritually dead and was therefore thought to possess a small measure of freedom. As a result, they naturally held that man was both able and required to use this freedom to cooperate with God's grace in salvation. Accordingly, in contrast to the Protestants who held to an exclusivity of God's grace and thus a divine monergism (a working alone) in salvation, the Roman Catholics held to a divine-human synergism (a working with), believing salvation to result from a combination of grace and works. Consequently, in placing the burden of salvation partially upon man's shoulders, they necessarily denied the exclusivity of God's action in salvation. Moreover, as a logical consequence, they were also led to reject the doctrine of predestination since they held salvation to depend upon the human response and not upon God's action alone. Thus, the Catholic rejection of predestination was but the logical counter part of a view of free will which exalted man's contribution to salvation and which therefore denied the exclusivity of God's grace. Consequently, it was precisely this denial of predestination together with the exaltation of free will which led to the system of works salvation of which indulgences were an integral part. Thus, when the theological underpinnings of indulgences are laid bare, they are seen to flow from a weak view of original sin which exalted the cooperation of free will in salvation and which therefore denied the exclusivity of God's predestined grace. To see this point more clearly, the Roman Catholic system of indulgences will now be examined in some detail.

In this regard, it may be stated that the system of indulgences arose from the unique combination of two elements in the Catholic view of salvation. First, as mentioned above, salvation was thought to result from a combination of grace and works and was therefore considered to be a cooperative venture between God and man. In the second place, however, salvation was thought to be mediated through the sacraments by the hierarchy of the church rather than directly through Christ to man. Thus, in contrast to the view of the Protestant Reformers, the Roman Catholic view of salvation was distinct both in terms of its underlying theology and in its peculiar mode of application. Accordingly, the particular view distinguishing Roman Catholicism was not merely that of a works salvation but more particularly that of a works salvation mediated through the church. Thus, beyond the inherent problems in any system of works salvation, error was compounded as the church took latitude in mediating this salvation to men. In particular, the penitential system based on a mediated works salvation arose within the sacramental system of the church and in turn gave birth to the system of indulgences as substitute works of penance. Accordingly, as will be shown below, indulgences arose from the dovetailing of bad theology with ecclesiastical presumption.

With respect to theology, the Roman Catholics believed that although man is born spiritually dead, all men are initially touched by a small measure of God's grace, called prevenient grace, which partially renews the will. As a result, men are supposedly transformed from a state of total depravity into one of partial depravity and thereby enabled to begin a slight motion toward God. Thus, men were represented as having been delivered from a state of spiritual death into one of spiritual weakness and of having to work out their salvation from this point. Now, if a man made good use of this prevenient grace, he consented to the doctrines of the church and was baptized. As a result of this baptism, he was infused by God with additional grace which made him capable of doing good works. Moreover, since God would reward these subsequent works with ever more infusions of sacramental grace, man could then earn his salvation through works in a cooperative venture with God. Thus, while the Roman Catholics formally affirmed the priority of God's grace, they denied its monergism, believing salvation to occur by a combination of grace and works.

However, because salvation thereby became contingent upon human works, the process described above could work backwards as well. For instance, if man a sinned mortally, he would lose all of this infused grace which then had to be restored through the sacraments of the church, and particularly through works of penance. In other words, because man's salvation was dependent upon works, he was continually gaining and losing ground in accordance with his latest behavior. As a result, he had no basis for spiritual peace and was therefore continuously subject to the terror and dread of the penitential system. No matter how hard he worked, his works were continually stained by sin, a fact which slowed or even prevented his forward progress, making a long stay in purgatory inevitable.

Since salvation was mediated by the church, however, a transfer mechanism known as an indulgence was devised to solve this problem. Through the purchase of an indulgence, the merits of the saints could be appropriated by penitent laymen and used to offset their own demerits. That is to say, an indulgence allowed a person without sufficiently good works to be saved through the substitute works of the saints as mediated through the church. Thus, the system of indulgences was a natural outgrowth of the Catholic theory of salvation.

After all, since the Catholic theory honored the contribution of human works, it necessarily honored human potential in the area of salvation. Thus, there seemed to be no limit to what man could achieve working in cooperation with God, and it was therefore believed that some hard working people could bypass purgatory and enter heaven directly. Moreover, certain extraordinary saints could enter heaven with room to spare through what were called works of supererogation (super works). In other words, it was thought that these saints could build up a surplus of merit as a result of their extraordinary works. However, since this surplus merit was supposedly stored up and pooled by the church, it could be dispensed by priests through the sacramental system in general and indulgences in particular. Thus, through the mechanism of indulgences, the surplus merit of the saints could be appropriated by the average layman, enabling him to reduce his time in purgatory or even bypass it altogether. In other words, one could be saved by the works of the saints instead of his own. Through the sale of indulgences, then, the Catholic theory of works salvation was pushed to great extremes in an attempt to bridge

the gap between sinful men and the holy requirements of God.[3]

Within the context of the Reformation, therefore,
the theological significance of indulgences was clear-
cut. As expressions of a mediated works salvation,
indulgences grew from a weak view of original sin
which championed the freedom of the human will and
which therefore upheld man's ability to contribute to
his own salvation. Accordingly, the free will theology
of which indulgences were the expression denied a
salvation based exclusively on God's predestined

---

[3] In this regard, the Roman Catholic view of salvation may be
likened to a bank account where salvation depends upon attain-
ing a $1 balance, and God contributes the matching funds.
Initially, God places 10 cents of prevenient grace into man's
account because original sin has eliminated his balance. Moreover, if he invests this money wisely by being baptized and
consenting to the doctrines of the church, God will infuse another 15 cents into his account, bringing the total to 25 cents.
Now with 25 cents in his account, man has enough capital to
increase his balance by investing in a program of good works.
Moreover, as these investments yield their dividends and begin
to increase the balance in the account, this process is acceler-
ated by matching infusions from God. Accordingly, the account
balance begins to grow toward the required sum of $1 both as a
result of wise investments in works and the gracious infusion
matching funds. However, because man can also make bad investments in sinful deeds, the account balance is always in jeopardy
and in the event of a mortal sin could be completely lost at any
time. In such an event, man would have to start over again, increas-
ing his balance through good investments (works) and through
cash infusions from the sacramental system of the church. Fortunately for man, however, the sacramental system is flush with
cash since many extraordinary saints have retired with balances
in excess of $1 and have given the surplus back to the church.

grace. That is to say, indulgences were an expression of a theology which down played original sin, exalted free will, and therefore denied predestination. By contrast, the Reformers held to the total depravity of the human will, the spiritual death of fallen man, and thus man's complete inability to contribute to his own salvation, let alone anyone else's. Accordingly, the Reformers held to the exclusivity of God's grace in salvation and thus to predestination, a view which struck at the theological root of both the works salvation and the priestly mediation inherent in the system of indulgences.

Initially, however, Luther's opposition was more pragmatic than theological since he was more immediately concerned with the harmful effect these indulgences were having on his parishioners. Thus, he initially opposed indulgences as external and moral abuses of the sacramental system without questioning the theological integrity of the system itself. However, as Luther began to examine the problem in greater depth, he was driven to its theological root. It soon became apparent to Luther that radical theological surgery was needed to correct the errors in practice. Such surgery, moreover, required an acknowledgment of the total bondage of the human will into the slavery of sin and its consequent dependence upon God's predestinated grace. Furthermore, as Luther's understanding deepened, he came to see this issue as the theological bedrock of the entire Reformation, underlying such surface issues as the dispute over indulgences, the sacramental system, the papacy, and purgatory. Thus, when attacked by Erasmus over the issue of free will, Luther identified the bondage of the will as the hinge and vital spot of the Reformation:

Now, my good Erasmus, I entreat you for Christ's sake to keep your promise at last. You promised that you would yield to him who taught better than yourself. Lay aside respect of persons! I acknowledge that you are a great man, adorned with many of God's noblest gifts — wit, learning and an almost miraculous eloquence, to say nothing of the rest; whereas I have and am nothing, save that I would glory in being a Christian. Moreover, I give you hearty praise and commendation on this further account — that you alone, in contrast with all others, have attacked the real thing, that is, the essential issue. You have not wearied me with those extraneous issues about the Papacy, purgatory, indulgences and such like — trifles, rather than issues — in respect of which almost all to date have sought my blood (though without success); you, and you alone, have seen the hinge on which all turns, and aimed for the vital spot. For that I heartily thank you; for it is more gratifying to me to deal with this issue, insofar as time and leisure permit me to do so. If those who have attacked me in the past had done as you have done, and if those who now boast of new spirits and revelations would do the same also, we should have less sedition and sects and more peace and concord. But thus it is that God, through Satan, has punished our unthankfulness. (Luther, *The Bondage of the Will*, 319)

According to Luther, therefore, the doctrine of pre-destination was of central importance to the Protestant Reformation, and clearly he was in a position to know! Moreover, this centrality is attested by the fact that the entire first generation of Protestant Reformers, despite their sacramental differences, were in agreement on the issue of predestination. Finally, beyond the Reformation itself, predestination had previously been affirmed by St. Augustine[4] and St. Thomas Aquinas, arguably the two most significant theologians of the pre-Reformation church. Thus, the doctrine of predestination was no theological innovation of the Reformers but rather marked a return to an established doctrine of the church.

---

[4] In fact, as an Augustinian monk, Luther drew his doctrine of predestination directly from Augustine who had first formulated the doctrines of predestination and original sin in his controversy with Pelagius, a British monk who had denied original sin and therefore endorsed the total ability (no original sin = total spiritual health) of the will. Due to this direct Augustinian influence, therefore, Lutherans and Calvinists may be referred to as Augustinian Protestants since their theology marked a revival of Augustinianism in the life of the church. By contrast, the Roman Catholics may be referred to as Semi-Pelagians since they tried to defend a position intermediate between Augustine and Pelagius by arguing for the partial ability of the fallen will. Thus, in terms of this characterization, the Reformation may be represented as a battle between the Augustinians, who believed in the total inability (original sin = spiritual death) of the fallen will, and the Semi-Pelagians, who believed in the partial ability (original sin= spiritual sickness) of the will. In terms of this division, the centrality of predestination to the Reformation becomes quite clear. The Protestant Reformers embraced this doctrine due to their robust Augustinianism while the Semi-Pelagian Roman Catholics abhorred it.

Now, of course, it is not being argued that one should embrace a doctrine simply on the testimony of the church Fathers or the Reformers. However, when the doctrine is supported by all the major Reformers and is moreover seen to be central to the theology of the Reformation itself, it is wrong for "doctrinally challenged," modern Christians to flippantly dismiss predestination on the basis of their emotional whims. Clearly, such attitudes, especially on the part of confessional Protestants, reflect a profound ignorance of Scripture, doctrine, and history. Contrary to their superficial objections, however, the doctrine of predestination is firmly rooted in Scripture, necessitated by the doctrine of grace, and central to the historical tradition of the various Reformation churches. Thus, when the doctrine is rightly understood and viewed within its various contexts, the error is seen to lie with its modern detractors and not the Protestant Reformers.

After all, in the area of salvation (soteriology), only two positions present themselves to the modern church. Either a man is saved by grace alone, or there is an admixture of works involved. Now, if man is saved by grace alone, then predestination is necessarily implied since salvation is exclusively God's work. On the other hand, if predestination is denied, then the exclusivity of God's grace in salvation cannot be maintained, and a works salvation results. Given this fact, the choice is clear. Either one is committed to the thorough going predestination of Luther and Calvin, or to the works salvation of Wesley and Rome. After all, since predestination is central to a salvation by grace alone, those who deny predestination must therefore deny the Reformation as well. For all practical purposes, such people are on the road to Rome.

BIBLIOGRAPHY

1. Loraine Boettner, *The Reformed Doctrine of Predestination* (Phillipsburg: Presbyterian and Reformed, 1932).

2. Verna M. Hall, *The Christian History of the Constitution of the United States of America (CHOC)* (San Francisco: The Foundation for American Christian Education, 1966).

3. Martin Luther, *Commentary on Romans* (Grand Rapids: Kregel, 1976).

4. Martin Luther, *The Bondage of the Will* (Grand Rapids: Revell, 1957).

5. N.S. McFetridge, *Calvinism in History* (Edmonton: Still Waters Revival Books, 1989).

6. Richard E. Muller, "A Lutheran Professor Educated at Westminster Theological Seminary Looks for Similarities and Dissimilarities," *Concordia Theological Quarterly*, Vol. 61, No. 1-2 (1997).

7. James Nickel, *Mathematics: Is God Silent?* (Vallecito: Ross House Books, 1990).

8. J. I. Packer, *Evangelism & the Sovereignty of God* (Downers Grove: Inter-Varsity Press, 1961).

9. Rousas John Rushdoony, *Politics of Guilt and Pity* (Fairfax: Thoburn Press, 1978).

10. Rousas John Rushdoony, *The Philosophy of the Christian Curriculum* (Vallecito: Ross House Books, 1985).

11. Rosalie J. Slater, *Teaching and Learning America's Christian History (T&L)* (San Francisco: The Foundation for American Christian Education, 1965).

About the Author

John B. King, Jr. was raised in Stockton, California by his paternal grandparents, John and Aletha King. As a result of declining educational standards, his grandmother removed him from the local public school and sent him to Trinity Lutheran School for his fifth through eighth grade years. At that time he became a member of the Lutheran Church, Missouri Synod (LCMS) and has remained a member ever since.

After graduating from St. Mary's Catholic High School in 1981, he moved to Corvallis, Oregon to study nuclear engineering at Oregon State University (OSU), completing his Ph.D. in Mechanical and Nuclear Engineering in 1991. He has had research fellowships at several national laboratories and is currently an instructor of mechanical and nuclear engineering at OSU. John and his wife Donna make their home in Corvallis, Oregon with their two cats Sophie and Tasha.

In the late 1980s and early 1990s, John became politically involved as a Christian activist and through his contacts was introduced to Christian Reconstruction by a gentleman named Paul Carlson. As a result of this exposure, John began to see the cultural relevance of Reformed Theology generally and Christian Reconstruction in particular. Accordingly, to assist Chalcedon in the task of cultural reconstruction, he took a three year break from teaching to attend Westminster Theological Seminary in Escondido, California, completing his M.Div. in 1997.

Realizing that the cultural relevance of Reformed Theology flows out of its doctrine of predestination and motivated by R.J. Rushdoony's comment that Luther was a stronger predestinarian than John Calvin, the author wrote the present book in the hope that Christians generally and Lutherans in particular would return to this culturally significant, Reformation doctrine. After all, since the doctrine of predestination was the hinge of the Protestant Reformation, the cultural impact of Protestant Christianity necessarily depends upon a theology that revolves about this hinge.